HOW TO HELP

PRACTICAL SUGGESTIONS
FOR INSTILLING
SPIRITUAL VALUES

YOUR CHILD really LOVE JESUS

DONNA J. HABENICHT, ED.D.

REVIEW AND HERALD® PUBLISHING ASSOCIATION
HAGERSTOWN, MD 21740

The author assumes full responsibility for the accuracy of all facts and quotations as cited in this book.

Scriptures credited to ICB are quoted from the *International Children's Bible, New Century Version*, copyright © 1983, 1986, 1988 by Word Publishing, Dallas, Texas 75039. Used by permission.

Texts credited to NIV are from the *Holy Bible, New International Version*. Copyright © 1973, 1978, 1984, International Bible Society. Used by permission of Zondervan Bible Publishers.

Verses marked TLB are taken from *The Living Bible*, copyright © 1971 by Tyndale House Publishers, Wheaton, Ill. Used by permission.

This book was
Edited by Gerald Wheeler
Designed by Patricia Wegh
Typeset: 10.5/13 Times Roman

PRINTED IN U.S.A.

99 98 97 96 95 94   10 9 8 7 6 5 4 3 2 1

Library of Congress Cataloging in Publication Data
    How to help your child really love Jesus / Donna J. Habenicht.
        p.   cm.
    1. Christian education of children. 2. Children—Conversion
to Christianity. 3. Children—Religious life. 4. Seventh-day
Adventists—Membership. 5. Adventists—Membership.
6. Sabbatarians—Membership.   I. Title.
BX6154.H23   1994
248.8'45—dc20   93-39937
                                                        CIP

ISBN 0-8280-0792-6

Contents

Acknowledgments

When I was 11 years old I began teaching a kindergarten Sabbath school class in Monterrey, Mexico. From then until now nurturing the spiritual growth of children has been a central focus of my professional and personal life. This book is the culmination of a lifetime of study into how to help children develop spiritually.

Many people have contributed to this book. It could not have been written without the support of the School of Education at Andrews University. My special thanks go to Warren Minder, the dean, and to Elsie Jackson, Marion Merchant, and my other colleagues in the Department of Educational and Counseling Psychology. Their support was essential.

Aileen Sox provided me with the opportunity to write for *Our Little Friend*, my first chance to write "whatever I wanted" for parents. Parts of this book first appeared in "Parents' Place" in that magazine. Without Aileen's encouragement to keep writing, I might have given up.

Because Penny Wheeler enthusiastically endorsed the idea of this book, I was brave enough to write. Gerald Wheeler's expert editing made my manuscript into a "real book."

I want to thank the parents and teachers who have attended my workshops over the years. They have contributed more than they know to this book. For many years I have taught children, young people, and adults in school and in church. They too have contributed significantly by challenging my thinking and sharing their experiences. While the stories in this book are about real people, I have changed names and identifying details to protect their privacy.

Most important, I want to thank my family for their help. First, my parents, Edward and Cora Lugenbeal, who nurtured my own spiritual growth during childhood and adolescence. While they have both gone to sleep in Jesus, their influence lives on in these pages. My husband, to whom I have dedicated this book, was my staunchest supporter during the difficult process of producing it. He built me a place to write, tolerated my "impossible schedule," cooked, cleaned, paid the bills, and ran errands. In short, he did "everything else" so I could write. Our children and grandchildren deserve a big thank-you too. Over the years they have taught me many things about how children grow spiritually. Larry and Debbie graciously provided me with a beautiful room overlooking the Caribbean where I wrote a major portion of the book. Nancy and Bruce read part of the manuscript and gave encouragement and friendship along the way. Liza, Jeff, Jonathan, and David—our grandchildren—are the heroes of some of the stories. They are the real reason I wanted to write this book. I want to see them—and all the children of the world— jumping up and down and shouting excitedly at the sight of their Best Friend, Jesus, when His glory fills the sky and He comes to take them home!

Dedication

This book is dedicated to
Herald
who loved me through each page.

A Word to the Reader

Dear Parents (grandparents, teachers, and anyone else who loves children):

When my children were young I read *Child Guidance* again and again. I wanted so much to help my children grow spiritually. But often I felt discouraged. The standard seemed so high and I didn't know just what to do about all the everyday problems. As a result I wanted someone to give me ideas, to make it practical.

This book is my attempt to make it practical for you. No family could ever do all the things suggested in these pages. It is a sourcebook of ideas, as well as an explanation of how children develop spiritually. When you understand how spiritual growth occurs during childhood, the everyday problems will not seem so overwhelming. Pick and choose from the many ideas presented the ones that best fit your family and the children you love.

As I look back, I wish many things had been different. But despite my youthful inadequacies, God blessed. I now realize He loves our children even more than we do. His Spirit follows them wherever they go. He yearns to cradle them in His arms, to bless them, and to offer them eternal life. And He never gives up. His Spirit is with them every minute, His promises sure.

May His Spirit be with you as you read,

Donna J. Habenicht

First Steps: Love

"I love you people with a love that will last forever.
I became your friend because of my love and kindness."
—Jeremiah 31:3, ICB

When you proudly brought your baby home from the hospital, wrapped in a gift blanket from Grandma and with instructions from the nurses on how to feed, burp, bathe, and change him or her, probably the farthest thing from your mind just then was your cherub's spiritual growth. Oh, yes, you did have some questions about character development, and while waiting for baby to arrive you'd read quite a bit in *Child Guidance*. But what you found seemed so overwhelming—a standard of parenting perfection that only angels could reach! And right then the most pressing concerns were feeding, burping, bathing, changing, and—don't forget—*sleeping*. Spiritual growth—surely that would come later.

Actually, when you fed, burped, bathed, and changed your baby, you *were* teaching his first spiritual lessons—lessons of love and trust. Long ago Ellen White, divinely inspired by God, wrote: "As the mother teaches her children to obey her because they love her, she is teaching them the first lessons in the Christian life. The mother's [or father's] love represents to the child the love of Christ, and the little ones who trust and obey their mother [or father] are learning to trust and obey the Saviour" (*The Desire of Ages*, p. 515).

In this one brief statement God has clarified the mystery of spiritual growth during early childhood. Love, trust, and obedience are the most important spiritual lessons for the beginning years, and children learn them through earthly relationships.

As usual, God goes right to the heart of the matter, to the real foundation of our relationship with Him—love, trust, and obedience. "This is what your children need to learn," He declares. "They need to know I love them always—more than they can even imagine. I love them when they're good *or* bad. I love them whether they return my love or not. I long to enjoy their friendship. My love sent a Saviour to rescue them from Satan's deception so we could enjoy each other's company eternally. My love reaches out to them, tenderly calling them to love Me in return and in turn to reach out to others with My love.

"They also need to know I can be trusted. Because I love them so much, I will always do what is best for them. Just as they can depend on Me to provide for their needs, so they also can trust Me with their life—all of it—their joys, sorrows, ambitions. Their character development, salvation, and eternal life. Even their doubts. I will never let them down because I want the best for them.

"When they love and trust Me, they will find it easier to obey Me. They will know that even when obeying is difficult, it is best for them, and that I will always be there to help. When obeying Me, they are simply trusting Me to develop in them a likeness to Me.

"For, you see, while learning childhood spiritual lessons of love, trust, and obedience, your children will also be discovering what I am like. They will come to know, somewhere deep inside, that God can be trusted and that Satan's lies about Me are just that—attempts to undermine their trust in Me."

These fundamental lessons of love, trust, and obedience form the basic structure for all later spiritual experiences. They are absolutely essential to an understanding of God because He is the perfect, balanced blend of each attribute. The integrated combination of mercy and justice, He is neither one nor the other, but both. Because He is the same yesterday, today, and tomorrow, He can be counted on, He can be trusted.

But children can learn lessons of love, trust, and obedience in only one way—through experience. Since these are not "book lessons," children can acquire them only through a loving, trusting relationship with the people most important to a child—his or her parents (and other caregivers). And they are learned early.

Learning to trust is a primary stage in personality development. All later personality growth rests on the foundation of trust. A normally developing baby learns trust during the first year of life as loving adults meet her needs and convince her that the world is a good place where she can trust others. Naturally, a child can unlearn trust later on if life hands her cruel experiences in which she has to be suspicious and distrust in order to survive.

This is where feeding, burping, bathing, and changing baby come in. Learning the spiritual lessons of love and trust involves much more than hugs and kisses, although they are important. To an infant, love is having food when she's hungry, comfort when she's distressed, and warmth when she's cold. Love is having a smiling person talk to her. It is security, feeling warm and cozy, close to Mom or Dad, especially if something good to eat comes with the cuddling.

All through early childhood, learning about love means having parents who are "tuned in" to their child's needs. They listen to the child's emotional broadcasting station so that its needs come in loud and clear, and they respond appropriately.

They sense when Mr. Two-Year-Old is afraid and offer comfort and the security of their arms, never belittling his fear. Recognizing that some things frighten little children, they also know that comfort—not shame— alone will help him outgrow his fears and will teach the spiritual lessons of love and trust.

"Tuned-in" parents perceive when Miss Three-Year-Old is cross because she's hungry—not merely contrary—and thus provide some distraction to help until mealtime instead of scolding. They also try to keep meals on a regular schedule.

Such parents recognize when Mr. Four-Year-Old is challenging their authority and asking to be reminded who is in control—and they remind him! Sensing when Miss Five-Year-Old is bored and needs a new challenge before she picks a fight with her younger brother to relieve that boredom, they suggest an interesting activity.

"Tuned-in" parents understand how difficult it is to start in a new school, and thus they provide plenty of family togetherness to help offset the loneliness of a move. Detecting when their teenager's self-concept needs a boost, they provide an encouraging look and words that say, "You're OK!"

Listening for and anticipating a child's needs is a real test of personal maturity for parents. Many times it means setting aside your own feelings of tiredness or irritation to respond to your child's needs. But it has an enormous payoff.

Thus, "tuned-in" parents give their children an overwhelming message of love. Their children *know* Mom and Dad are on their side. And that is the fundamental message of God's love: He's on our side all the time, walking beside us, encouraging us, even carrying us in moments of extreme despair. Your children discover the nature and reality of spiritual love by experiencing your love.

Imagine your child holding up a mug with the word "Love" written all over it. Instead of asking for a drink, your child requests love. Will you fill her cup? She has an almost insatiable need for love. It is as important for her emotional and spiritual growth as liquid is for her physical growth. Will you deny your child her need? Or, worse yet, roughly knock the cup out of her hands, spilling the contents, and leaving it empty? No, you may not do it purposefully, because most parents say they love their children. But maybe without realizing what is happening, you might be failing to fulfill her needs for love. If your child emerges from early childhood with her love needs only half met, she will likely spend the rest of her life trying to satisfy those deep, unfilled thirsts and hungers. But if her "love cup," as Kay Kuzma puts it, is running over with love experienced during early childhood, she will feel satisfied the rest of her life. She will not have to spend her emotional energy trying to fill the emptiness. Instead, she will understand God's love and will have love in abundance to give to others.

Communicating God's love to our children is an every-moment-of-every-day process. One of the most powerful ways of displaying love is through really listening to our children. We grow accustomed to their endless chatter and often don't really listen to what they are saying. Many children have rarely had the experience of having an adult pay close attention to them. When I see a child in therapy for emotional difficulties, one of the most powerful tools I have to help that child get well is my undivided attention. I listen in ways the child has probably never experienced before, and in so doing I communicate a powerful love and caring. You can communicate that same message.

Tommy was 9 years old. He had two older sisters, and his mother was a single parent. She had asked me to have a few counseling sessions with her son to see if we could figure out why he was acting so belligerently.

During one of our sessions I asked Tommy a question I often raise when counseling children. "Tommy, let's pretend I can change anything you don't like. Now, we both know I can't really do that, but we can pretend. In this make-believe game, what would you like me to change about your family?"

"Well, you could make my sisters stop teasing me so much," he quickly responded. After a pause, he continued, "But what I really wish most is that you could make my mother listen to me! She doesn't even hear what I say."

"What makes you think she doesn't listen to you?" I queried.

"Well, about the only time we get to talk is after supper while we're washing dishes. When we get home from school, she's too busy getting supper and stuff. And my sisters talk while we're eating. So the only time to tell her anything is while we're doing dishes. But when I talk, she just keeps right on washing dishes. She doesn't even look at me! I know she doesn't hear anything I say."

The boy's mother, of course, thought she was hearing him. But a vast difference exists between the physiological process of hearing and the emotional one of listening. She was hearing, but to Tommy she wasn't listening. And as a result he thought she didn't care.

I found an excellent clue to what listening really means in *The Living Bible* version of Psalm 116:1, 2. "I love the Lord because he hears my prayers and answers them. Because he bends down and listens, I will pray as long as I breathe!"

In the hurry-scurry of everyday home life, how can you communicate real listening to your children?

First, stop what you are doing. Mumbling "uh-huh" while you continue to read the newspaper isn't listening. But pausing in your activity means "you are more important to me than anything else."

Second, bend down to the child's level and look her in the eye and smile. Eye contact and smiling say "I care about you."

Third, make appropriate comments. Responding to what the child is saying communicates "your ideas are worthwhile and important."

If Tommy's mother had momentarily stopped washing dishes, looked at him, and responded to his ideas briefly, she could have then continued with the dishes while the conversation developed. Her son would have felt that she was really listening. She would have communicated caring.

Actually, listening doesn't take much time—usually only a moment or two. It takes less time, in the end, than dealing with an insistent child who feels slighted. Imagine God bending down to listen, then imagine yourself a channel through which His love flows to your child. It takes only a moment to listen, but the message of love lasts a lifetime.

What happens when a child doesn't experience love during childhood? Ann's little girl, Carole, had been one of my husband's patients since infancy. When Carole was 4 years old her parents decided to send her to the nursery school on the Andrews University campus. There Carole heard many children talking about Sabbath school and wanted to go too. So Ann asked my husband what they had to do to get to attend the children's Sabbath school at the campus church. My husband, of course, eagerly invited them to attend the following Sabbath. I met them at the door and introduced them to the kindergarten division leaders.

As I became acquainted with Ann over the next several weeks, I learned that she was waiting in the student lounge all morning while Carole attended nursery school because she didn't want to make the long drive from home twice each morning. Since the student lounge is not where I would choose to spend all morning, I invited her to come to our home where she could be more comfortable. Offering her the house key, I told her she could make herself at home while I was on campus teaching. She nodded and looked at me rather blankly, but wouldn't accept the key. So I didn't push the idea but simply said that I'd be happy to share our home with her.

Months went by, and I gradually became better acquainted with Ann. She began attending the pastor's Bible class, and our friendship grew. When H.M.S. Richards, Jr., came to our campus for the spring Week of Prayer I invited her to attend with me, since she was still waiting all morning in the student lounge. Accepting my invitation, she attended the morning meetings with me.

Thursday morning Elder Richards spoke on John 17 and God's unconditional love. As we were leaving the church Ann turned abruptly to me and said, "Now I know what you're all about!" Puzzled, I wondered what she was talking about.

"Do you remember when you offered me the key to your house so I could stay there while waiting for Carole?" I nodded. "Well, I couldn't understand how you could offer me the key to your house when you had known me for only a couple months. It didn't make sense. Now I understand. Love—that's what you're all about! Love is what makes you tick. I see it now—God's love in you!"

As I became better acquainted with Ann over the ensuing years, I discovered that she had grown up in a home where love was extremely scarce. In fact, she had been so severely abused as a child that she had only vague memories about many years of her childhood. The only way she could cope with the hurt of those years was by largely blanking them out. And so when I, a relative stranger, offered her love and trust, it was simply beyond her comprehension.

I'm sure you know children or adults like Ann who grew up with empty "love cups." They're members of your Sabbath school class, neighbors, or coworkers. Maybe you have just come to the sudden realization that, although you meant well, you haven't really communicated love to your own children. What can you do now? **Love them!** Remember, we learn love only through experiencing it. You can always begin today by sharing your love.

But what if you just realized that your own "love cup" was never filled during childhood and so you have had little to give to your own children? What can you do now? Start immersing yourself in God's love. Read His Word, find Bible texts about God's love and meditate on them, write them on cards and tape them where you will see them frequently, and pray for a special outpouring of His love to fill your life. If you have endured deep childhood hurts, such as abuse and abandonment, I would encourage you to find a Christian counselor who can help you sort through those experiences and come into the fullness of God's love. Only then will you be able to communicate that love to your family.

Begin today with one or two of the ideas on the Communicating God's Love chart, then add others as you become more comfortable showing love. Communication skills can be learned. You can help your child make up for the years when love was rare. One of my favorite sayings is "Today is the first day of the rest of your life." With God it is never too late to fill your own or your child's "love cup." His supply is inexhaustible!

COMMUNICATING GOD'S LOVE

- Be generous with hugs and kisses.
- Be aware of your child's physical needs. Is he hungry, tired, sick? Respond quickly to care for such needs.
- Tune in to your child's emotional needs. Does she need an extra dose of love today because her world has fallen apart? Make sure she gets it.

- Set aside a special time for each child at least once a week. Let the child choose what the two of you will do together during this time.
- Stop what you are doing to listen to your child.
- Have eye contact with your child while you listen, but don't stare. Smile and look interested.
- Make appropriate comments about what your child has said.
- Give your child sincere compliments. Find something to affirm him about several times a day.
- Connect your love (and God's love) with your child's value as a human being—not his performance. Never threaten to withdraw your love when your child misbehaves. When he fails is when he most needs your comfort and encouragement.
- Never abandon him by walking out the door or leaving the house when you are angry over something he has done.
- Forgive and forget. Don't keep bringing up past "sins."
- Make a "gallery" to display your child's art, homework, etc. Show that you are proud of her efforts.
- Give your child as many choices as possible during the day. Don't dictate every move and every minute.
- When your child is discouraged, offer a bit of help to get her over the hard part.
- Anticipate your child's needs. If she looks lonely, hug her.
- Give your child a second chance—or third or fourth, if needed. Let her know that you have confidence she will make it.
- Make your child a "special guest" at a meal honoring an achievement (good grades, winning a game, etc.). Use your special china and cook the child's favorite foods.
- Read Bible stories about God's love with your child. Talk about how God showed His love to the people in the story.
- Mention frequently how God has shown His love for your family— blessings, help when in difficulty, etc.
- Put a picture of Jesus in your baby's room. Frequently tell your baby, "Mommy [Daddy] loves you and Jesus loves you." Hug your infant while saying it and point to yourself and to the picture of Jesus. Pair your love with Jesus' love and associate them both with closeness and hugs from you.
- For older children, talk about the different ways in which God shows

His love. Love is sometimes soft and warm and cuddly, but it is also tough when we have done something wrong and need to learn a better way.

● Keep posters around the house that emphasize God's love (GOD LOVES YOU) or paintings that show Jesus loving and caring for the children, or playing with them.

KEYS TO LOVE

1. Be responsive to your child's needs.
2. Listen to your child.
    a. Stop what you are doing.
    b. Make eye contact and smile.
    c. Make appropriate comments.
3. Be generous with hugs and kisses.
4. Give sincere compliments.
5. Forgive and forget.
6. Read stories about God's love.
7. Connect your love with God's love.

CHAPTER 2

First Steps: Trust

"So, trust the Lord always.
Trust the Lord because he is our Rock forever."
—*Isaiah 26:4, ICB*

Tomorrow everyone's supposed to bring a picture of her family to put on the bulletin board at school. I need a picture of our family. Will you help me find one, Mom?'' The words tumbled out in a rush of excitement as Christie threw her backpack on the nearest chair. "You will, won't you, Mom?"

"Of course," her mother replied as she moved about the kitchen gathering the ingredients for the evening meal, "but I'm busy now. We'll look after dinner."

But after dinner Mom talked on the phone for a long time, the neighbor came over to visit, then it was time for bed. Christie was worried. How would she find the picture? Her mother promised to help her in the morning. But the baby was fussy half the night, and in the morning Mom was too tired and frazzled to look for a family picture.

"It won't matter, Christie. Just tell the teacher you'll bring it tomorrow."

"But Mom, you said you'd find it . . . and the teacher said to bring it *today!*" Christie wailed tearfully as she trudged off to school without the promised photograph.

At 4 Mike is a real handful. With energy to spare, he is full of questions about everything imaginable. One Sunday afternoon as the family was driving to go swimming, he and his sister started fighting in the back seat.

"If you don't stop that right now, there won't be any treats after swimming today!'' Dad yelled. But the fighting continued. Finally Mom reached back to stop the fuss, warning, ''That's it—no treats today!''

But after swimming, the child begged for a treat. ''I won't fight on the way back, honest!'' His parents relented, and everyone had an ice-cream cone.

Christie and Mike are absorbing an important lesson—that Mom and Dad can't be trusted. They are discovering that their parents don't really mean what they say and can't be counted on to keep their promises or word. Words don't mean much—actions are what really count. Someday, down the line, Christie and Mike may also have a hard time trusting God because they have learned their lessons well. If Mom and Dad—the most important people in their lives—couldn't be trusted, probably God can't be either.

Of course, as parents we don't have God's infallibility. We *do* forget sometimes, and things don't happen the way we intend. Children will forgive occasional lapses. It's the trend that really matters. Can our children count on us? Do we mean what we say? Do threatened consequences really happen? Do we give our promises to our children top priority? When we do, we are building trust in them about a God who truly never fails His children. We are teaching our children one of the fundamental spiritual lessons of early childhood.

How important is the spiritual lesson of trust? Love and trust go hand in hand. Without one we cannot have the other. Love sent the Saviour. Trust accepts His sacrifice. Love provided a way to deal with sin. Trust accepts His grace and His perfect life in place of our sinfulness. Love yearns to show us a better life. Trust accepts Him as the Lord of our life—a guide we can follow with certainty. The trust learned in childhood translates into faith and trust in God in later life.

Four-year-old Stephanie was demanding and aggressive, wanting to be in control all the time and refusing to cooperate with anyone. She trusted no one but herself. Her new adoptive parents—counselors who had worked professionally with many families—were at their wits' end. They couldn't believe anything Stephanie said. The child lied whenever convenient and then denied it. She appeared unable to distinguish between truth and falsehood.

In their late 30s, the adoptive parents had eagerly looked forward to having children. Stephanie seemed the answer to their prayers for a family of their own. But as they told me about their difficulties, they were seriously wondering about going through with the adoption.

As the story unfolded, I began to understand why they were having such problems. Stephanie's biological mother was mentally retarded and frequently did not care for her children. At 18 months of age Stephanie had already had to scrounge for herself if she wanted anything to eat. In order to survive, she became adept at opening the refrigerator door and reaching for whatever meager food was available. When neighbors finally discovered her plight, Stephanie was almost 2.

During the years when she should have learned to trust the adults in her world to care for her, she discovered instead that the world was unfriendly and uncaring, that she could not depend upon adults to care for her. Now, at 4, Stephanie trusted no one but herself. She had never experienced love or bonded to her mother. With such a serious gap in her early experiences she was well on her way to a lifelong personality problem.

Stephanie showed many of the signs of mistrust. She was sure no one would care for her, even though her new parents were doing their best to meet her needs. The child believed people were bad and tended to focus on what she didn't like about her new parents instead of the positive things they were doing for her. Constantly on guard, she refused to try to get to know them or let them get acquainted with her. Hiding all her new toys and clothes, she fought like a tiger when her mother wanted to wash her dirty clothes. The girl feared that they would disappear forever. It would take a lot of love and consistent care to get through to Stephanie that she could trust people.

Many children show some signs of developing mistrust, even though they received love and care as infants. They have learned over the years that they can't count on their parents and other adults in their lives when they need them most. Or they have experienced a severe break in their trusting relationship with an adult, such as occurs when a parent sexually abuses a child. And so the early trust learned during infancy erodes.

What can you do to help your children learn that God is trustworthy? Since children—and adults—tend to think of God in the same way as they do their parents, the first step is to be trustworthy yourself.

1. Always tell your child the truth—never lie. Don't tell her the shot won't hurt when you know it will. Instead, say, "I know the shot will hurt, but it will help you get better. Daddy will hold you. I know you can be a brave girl." When you are leaving, don't just disappear. Instead, announce to your child that you are going and when you will be back.

2. Keep your promises. Kathie has curly black hair, soft rounded cheeks, and big brown eyes. Her nose turns up just a wee bit, and she has a dimple in the middle of her chin. She looks adorable in her new blue Sabbath dress. The only real problem on Sabbath morning is that Kathie, even though she's almost 3, doesn't want to stay in Sabbath school without Mommy. If her mother even suggests leaving, Kathie starts crying and clinging. So one Sabbath morning Mommy decided to slip out the door when the girl was busy putting an animal on the felt board, even though she had promised the child she wouldn't leave.

Of course, as soon as Kathie discovered her mother wasn't there, she started screaming hysterically. No one could quiet her, and one of the teachers finally had to take her to find her mother. The next Sabbath she didn't even want to go in the door of the Sabbath school room.

Keeping promises is a vital part of teaching children to trust. Be careful what you promise so you can be trustworthy.

3. Follow through on what you say you are going to do. If you tell a child that he can't have dessert unless he finishes his vegetables, keep your word. If you tell your 7-year-old to stay in the yard and he goes next door to play, follow through with an appropriate consequence. Or if you promise that you will take the children to the park if they keep their toys picked up for three days, keep your word.

4. Show a high level of support for your child. Respect her feelings, help her over the rough spots of an assignment, listen to her stories about what happened in school. Never tease or berate her in front of other people. Don't bring up her faults to taunt her. Forgive and forget. Respect her opinions. When she confides in you that someone has mistreated her, investigate. All such actions communicate support, which in turn gives her the message that you are someone she can trust. She knows you are always on her side.

5. Communicate that you trust your child. Trust is a two-way street. When you show that he can trust you, you model how you want your child to act. He, in turn, learns how to be trustworthy. Assume your child will want to do the right thing and communicate that assumption, instead of giving the message that you really don't think you can trust him to make the right decision.

6. Teach your child when *not* to trust. Part of learning to trust is discovering when *not* to do so. Teach safety standards and how to get help if needed. In today's world knowing when to trust and when not can be a fine distinction. If you emphasize the evils in the world around us too much—that no one can be trusted—you run the risk of doing serious damage to your child's ability to trust anyone, including God. Trusting is an essential part of personality and spiritual development. Treat it with gentle care. In your efforts to protect your child from evil, don't crush the beautiful bud of trust. Your child will need it to develop healthy relationships with other people in later life and to accept salvation and a relationship with Jesus.

If your child's sense of trust has been violated because of sexual abuse by a family member, *run* to the nearest Christian counselor. You and your child need professional help. Get out of the situation immediately. Her future is at stake. But God can bring healing to your family and help your child learn to trust again.

As we have said, trust is an extremely important part of spiritual development. Without it we cannot have spiritual salvation. Jesus offers redemption, grace, and freedom from the tyranny of sin, but we must trust Him in order to take advantage of His marvelous offer. Helping your children acquire trust is an extremely important cornerstone of spiritual development.

KEYS TO TRUST

1. Always tell your child the truth. Never lie.
2. Keep your promises.
3. Follow through on what you say you will do.
4. Show a high level of support for your child.
5. Communicate that you trust your child.
6. Teach your child when *not* to trust someone else.

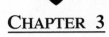

CHAPTER 3

Second Steps: Discipline

"If we obey what God has told us to do,
then we are sure that we truly know God. . . .
Whoever says that God lives in him must live as Jesus lived."
—1 John 2:3-6, ICB

Nineteen-month-old Jonathan was enthusiastically practicing swinging a plastic bat and then using it like a golf club to hit a small ball around the room as I sat at my desk. "Bawl, bawl," his baby voice lisped over and over again. Suddenly all was quiet. My mothering experience reminded me that when toddlers are quiet, I'd better investigate.

"Jonathan," I called as I turned just in time to see him jump. Hastily he responded with something that sounded a little like "Es?" as he withdrew his hand from the cabinet where his father keeps his favorite classical music CDs. Carefully and firmly I explained that "those are Daddy's" and he must not touch. "Daddy, Daddy," Jonathan responded as he pointed to the CDs. Several times he came back, reached toward the cabinet, and looked for my reaction. Each time I responded predictably. "Daddy's—Jonathan mustn't touch—Daddy's." He was learning about limits and self-control—tough but vital lessons for a toddler eager to investigate the world.

Acquiring self-control is part of learning about obedience—one of the indispensable childhood spiritual lessons that lay the foundation for a lifelong relationship with God. God's Word is quite clear that if we love Him, we will obey His commandments. The branches of our life tree will be covered with the fruit that grows from the roots of our love for Him. That love will trust God to make changes in our lives to draw us closer to Himself. Thus, obedience is our love response.

If children do not learn self-control and obedience during early childhood, later on the Christian life will seem restrictive. "Saying no" to drugs and peer pressure will be hard for them. They will come to prefer instant gratification of every whim and a "do it if it feels good" religion.

Obedience isn't a nasty word, although some people think it is. It doesn't mean a nonthinking, do-what-everyone-else-tells-you person. Nor need it lead to a "salvation by works" approach to God, either. *How* you teach obedience and Christian values makes the difference between a "grace" or "works" outlook toward religion. Fortunately, we have clear instructions about how to do it.

Researchers in child development have identified four parenting styles and their predictable effects on children. Hundreds of studies back their conclusions, and they are among the most reliable of all findings about child development. Interestingly, 50 years before the child development specialists began their research, Ellen White described parenting styles, using different names but identifying the same parenting behaviors and their results in the children's character. God knew all along what was best for children!

Control and support are the two main aspects of the parent-child relationship that lead to its success or failure, including how well children accept the values their parents have tried to teach. How much *control* you use with your child and how much *support* you provide him determine the type of parenting style used in your family.

On the diagram of the parenting styles you will notice that the horizontal line represents control. Control can vary all the way from almost none to a great deal. In between the two extremes fall many levels of control. Control describes how much influence you try to exert over what your child does. Do you feel that children need to be strongly guided and taught what is right and wrong? Or do you feel that children will usually make the right decisions on their own? Do you feel your role is that of a resource person to your child rather than a firm guide? Control describes who is in charge in the family—the parents or the children.

ADULT-CHILD RELATIONSHIPS

HIGH SUPPORT
(warmth)

Authoritative

Consistent limits
Firm, patient, loving, reasonable
Considerate of child's needs
Warm relationship with child
Adult is self-controlled
Teaches child to reason and make
*   choices*

Permissive

Inconsistent limits
Inconsistent discipline
Values not stated
Little control
Warm relationship with child
Child develops own values with
*   little adult guidance.*

HIGH CONTROL ———————————————— **LOW CONTROL**
(restrictive)   (permissive)

Authoritarian

Inconsistent demands
Excessive force and punishment
No concern for child's needs
Harsh and dictatorial
Unsympathetic and cold
Angry, uncontrolled adult

Neglectful

Inconsistent demands
No attempt to guide child
Ignores child
Adult may be abusive
No concern for child's needs
Uninvolved with child

LOW SUPPORT
(hostility)

The vertical line represents support. It can range from strong support at the one end to an almost total lack at the other extreme. We could better describe the lower half of the support line as hostility. When children do not feel supported by their parents, the relationship is generally hostile.

Supportive parents are child-centered. They understand that children have special needs because they are immature. But they also recognize that children need firm guidance toward maturity and clear standards for behavior. Such parents encourage independence and individuality. Parents and children talk with each other a lot, so both know how the other feels and the children understand the reasons for the family's standards. An atmosphere of respect for each family member pervades the home. Parents treat their children with warmth and love.

Nonsupportive parents engender hostility because they are primarily adult-centered, giving little consideration to the needs of the children. Dialogue between parent and child is either limited or nonexistent. Adults expect the children to obey but do not teach the reasons for their demands. Such parents are caught up in maintaining their authority. Afraid that if they let their children express an opinion they will lose control, they tend to use fairly severe physical punishment. Independence and individuality are taboo.

How the parents get along with each other and the support aspect of the parenting style create the emotional climate of the home, either an atmosphere of warmth and caring or one of coldness and hostility. The emotional climate of a home plays a significant role in determining whether children will accept or reject the religion and values of their parents. It colors everything that happens in the home, giving family life an aura of joy and happiness or of repression and sadness.

The control and support dimensions of parenting intersect to describe four different parenting styles: (1) **authoritative** (high support and high control), (2) **permissive** (high support and low control), (3) **authoritarian** (low support and high control), and (4) **neglectful** (low support and low control).

Seventeen-year-old Carl arrived home a half hour late from a Saturday night date. On the way home the car had a flat tire. Unfortunately, the spare wasn't in good shape and he had to pump it up twice before he finally made it home. When he tried to explain what had happened, his father cut him short, shouting, ''Don't give me any of that stuff! There aren't any excuses this time! You can't use the car for the next three weeks! Serves you right—you're totally irresponsible!''

Carl's shoulders sagged. He knew better than to try to explain—that would only get him a more severe punishment. But it didn't seem right. He had tried so hard to get back on time . . . and next week was the senior banquet, and he'd have to find another way to get there with his date. Resentment swelled inside and threatened to overwhelm him. ''I can't take this for three more months! I've got to get out of here . . . hey, next week's my birthday . . . maybe . . .''

When Ellen White talks about the authoritarian style she calls it "iron rod," a wonderfully descriptive phrase. Parents who use it are big on authority—theirs—and little on respect for their children's needs. Many times they are arbitrary and unduly severe. The least little indiscretion gets magnified into a mountain of "sin." The adults tend to be harsh, dictatorial, selfish, unsympathetic, and cold with their children. They use a lot of force and physical punishment. To them children are to be "seen and not heard," so communication between parent and child is strictly one way—parent to child, usually in loud-voiced commands that the children are expected to obey without questioning. Authoritarian parents rarely explain the reason for their commands or allow their children to develop the ability to make decisions for themselves. The parents are actually rejecting, unresponsive, and parent-centered. Their own need for power and control drives their relationship with their family. Unfortunately, the authoritarian style of parenting is quite common among conservative religious families, who often hide behind a misconception of God's authority as the mandate for their own actions.

Children reared under the authoritarian parenting style usually react in one of two ways. They either rebel against the values of their parents and get out of the home as soon as possible, as Carl was contemplating, or they become weak-willed, indecisive, spineless individuals incapable of dealing with difficult moral decisions.

Authoritarian homes usually produce children with poor self-concepts. They do not have a strong conscience and are apt to reject the values of their parents and embrace the negative values around them. Usually they reject religion. If they *are* religious, they may try to be "perfect" in every detail of the Christian life, hoping to earn God's favor and avoid His punishment through the effort of their good works. Their personalities many times lack warmth, compassion, and empathy for the plight of others. The God they worship is a wrathful, vengeance-seeking judge ready to zap anyone who doesn't measure up.

Carolyn is a cute, vivacious, dark-eyed beauty. At 14 she is popular with both guys and girls. She always wears the latest styles and has plenty of spending money. Her parents are both lawyers and have provided everything she ever wanted—except their love, time, and attention. They have placed no restrictions on the time she must arrive home after dates. Sometimes she comes in after midnight and one night she arrived at 3:00 in the morning. No one said a word—in fact, no one seemed to even notice. Anyone she dates is OK as far as her parents are concerned. They just don't have time to be bothered. Carolyn often cries herself to sleep because she is so lonely. She needs her friends at school desperately — they are really her family. When her friends suggested staying out late that night, she thought her parents would say something, do something — anything — that would show they cared about what happened to her. But they didn't. Carolyn cried for hours as if her heart would break. No one really cared.

The neglectful style of parenting hardly needs explaining — the name says it all. Tending to ignore their children, they show little concern for their needs and remain uninvolved in their lives. They keep their children at arm's length and do not want to sacrifice themselves and their own convenience. Usually they make only weak attempts to guide their children.

Neglectful parents can be the classic abusive parents who physically mistreat their children or do not supply their daily needs for food, shelter, and clothing. On the other hand, sometimes they can be well-educated, career-conscious men and women, like Carolyn's parents, who are so wrapped up in their own lives that they simply don't have time or energy for their children. Instead of teaching their children, they leave that task to the baby-sitter. Such parents usually provide well physically for their children but do not get emotionally involved or supportive. Unfortunately, their children recognize that they are not high on their parents' list of priorities. Consequently, they do not feel supported by their parents.

Children from neglectful homes often react in the same way as those from authoritarian ones — they rebel and embrace negative values. Usually they are not very religious, nor do they have strong values because their parents have not consistently taught or disciplined them. Such children also often have deep emotional problems related to the neglect they have experienced. Their God is a distant ruler of the universe uninvolved in His subjects' everyday lives. He is a God who really doesn't care what happens on earth.

The most damaging aspect of the authoritarian and neglectful styles of parenting is the coldness and lack of emotional support. It often leads to an "I don't care" attitude of open rebelliousness without respect for either God's or man's authority. Authoritarian parents generally force religion upon their children, while neglectful parents ignore the whole matter. The hostility that develops between parents and children usually leads to rejection of what the parents value most—their religion.

Three-year-old Susie whines and begs for a candy bar at the store. Her mother says she cannot have one, but finally gets tired of her whining and gets a candy bar. The same scene repeats itself every time they go shopping.

As far as their family friends are concerned, 5-year-old Mike is a terror. He sweeps into a house, runs through all the rooms, picks up whatever he wants to play with, and his parents never say a word of reprimand or attempt to restrain him. Instead, they usually say, "Well, you know how kids are . . ." Mike goes to bed when he feels like it. He also eats when he wants and isn't expected to show good table manners. "After all, he's just a kid," his parents sigh.

Permissive or indulgent parents like Mike's and Susie's are tolerant and accepting toward their children's impulses. Although generally warm and caring with their children, they don't make many demands to encourage more mature behavior. The children tend to do what they please without much adult input. The household has few rules and usually doesn't function on a schedule. Bedtime and mealtimes are whenever the children want them. Employing little discipline, such parents avoid authority, controls, or restrictions.

As a result of the parents' laissez-faire attitude toward child rearing, the children don't grow up with a strong set of values. They tend to be impulsive and want to do what they want now. Waiting for the rewards of tomorrow doesn't appeal to them. Since they have never learned to control their impulses, they can be aggressive and irresponsible and have a weak moral structure. Their God is an accepting and loving God who smiles indulgently and looks the other way when humans misbehave. To them sin isn't really a major problem in the universe.

Eight-year-old Jamie, red-haired and freckle-faced, rushes in the door from school, breathlessly calling, "Mom! The guys are all going to play ball. Can I go to the park with them?"

"Let's see," his mother responds, "have you completed your home jobs for today?"

Jamie hangs his head. He had forgotten to do them before he left for school.

"You remember our agreement, don't you?" his mother continues. "Work before play."

"Aw, Mom, just this once—I'll do them when I get back."

"I'm sorry, Jamie," she says as she puts her arm around him. "You can't go play with the guys this time. I know how disappointed you are. From now on I'm sure you'll remember to do your jobs before leaving for school, won't you?" Slowly Jamie nods, disappointment clearly showing on his face.

"Come, son, let's get those jobs done!" Mother encourages as she gives him a little hug. "I'll help you. It shouldn't take long. Maybe we'll have time to bat a few balls before I have to make supper."

The authoritative, child-centered parenting style sets clear standards and expectations for mature behavior for children while at the same time always considering their needs. It encourages children to be independent, to think for themselves, and to develop their own individuality. Parents enforce the rules and standards, using punishment when needed, but always in an overall climate of warmth and concern for the child. Such adults are not consumed with their own authority. Instead, they are concerned about guiding their children aright. Their children's needs are always important, and they respect their children's feelings. Such parents explain the reasons for their expectations and listen to their children's viewpoints. As a result their children generally feel whatever punishment they receive is deserved. And they know, beyond any doubt, that their parents care about them and support them.

Ellen White describes these parents as self-controlled and under the discipline of Christ. They show love and kindness and make friends of their children. While they display sympathy and understanding, they can, when necessary, also demonstrate firmness and strict discipline.

Children from authoritative homes are usually confident and competent. They have strong values that they are willing to stand up for. Responsible in outlook, they have a strong moral character and are helpful and caring toward others. Generally they are positive about the values and religion they have learned from their parents. In addition they have the strength to resist peer pressure and do what they know to be right because they have a strong, reasonable conscience that guides their actions. Their God is a caring and loving Being who forgives their misdeeds and continually helps them grow in grace and faith. Such a God is the perfect blend of mercy and justice, a God who continually draws them closer to Himself.

Only the authoritative parenting style truly represents the way God deals with us—loving and encouraging, but at the same time eager to help us grow. When we use this style of parenting we are assisting our children to develop a true picture of God. All of the other styles distort the child's picture of God and misrepresent either His goodness, love, or purity.

During 1989 the Department of Education of the General Conference of Seventh-day Adventists commissioned an extensive study of the youth of the Adventist Church. Approximately 11,000 young people ages 12 to 18 completed an extensive questionnaire for the Valuegenesis study. Their responses formed the data for the largest study of Christian youth ever conducted by any denomination. While this book largely deals with younger children, the findings from this study of teenagers tell us what we might expect as our children grow older. And so I would like to share with you some of the results of the Valuegenesis study that will help you to teach your children the way of the Lord.

One of the most striking discoveries is that the youth who had a growing, mature Christian faith consistently came from homes where the parents were not only loving and caring but also enforced SDA standards of behavior. The home is the place where children need to learn about the SDA lifestyle. When loving, caring parents teach standards, their children will accept them as part of their way of life. The study showed that young people will accept SDA standards better when those standards are taught by the home than when they are strictly enforced by the school or the church. The data fit perfectly with the authoritative style of parenting— love and caring combined with high standards for behavior.

As you read the descriptions of the four parenting styles, maybe you realized that you grew up in an authoritarian, neglectful, or permissive home, so you don't have a model of how authoritative parenting really works. All of us tend to parent the same way we were parented. That's the tape that plays in our head when we face a tough parenting decision. But you *can* change. The results of authoritative parenting are so far superior to any other style that it is well worth the effort. How can you make that shift?

First, **to get a clear understanding of how authoritative parenting really works, study how God deals with us**. Our heavenly Father models authoritative parenting perfectly. Think about God's personal character- istics, His requirements for us, the methods He uses to teach us, and how God deals with us when we fail. Of course, we don't have the infallibility or perfection of God, but we can seek to copy His ways.

GOD—THE HEAVENLY PARENT

Personal Characteristics
- God and His standards for us are the same. The embodiment of His law, He is a model for us (Ps. 119:68; John 13:15).
- God means what He says. He is the same yesterday, today, and tomorrow. Because He keeps His promises, we can count on Him. His standards do not vary (Heb. 13:8; 1 Kings 8:56; 2 Peter 3:9).
- God is always available when needed, but does not impose His presence on us or force His standards against our will (Matt. 28:20; Rev. 3:20; 2 Peter 3:9).

Requirements
- God has clearly stated guidelines for behavior (Matt. 5:48; 2 Tim. 3:17; Ex. 20).
- God balances mercy and justice. He is fair (Ps. 85:10; 89:14).
- God's requirements are realistic (Ps. 19:7, 8).
- God deals with each person on an individual basis. He considers the person's background and opportunities (John 3:1-21; 4:5-26).
- God's requirements do not vary. They are the same yesterday, today, and tomorrow (Ps. 119:89, 142, 144; Matt. 5:17).
- God expects high achievement and good behavior. He manifests trust in the individual's willingness to comply (Deut. 10:12-14; Matt. 18:14).

Methods
- God enlists the will and choice of the individual. He does not suppress the strength of the will. Respecting free will and choice, He does not force anyone against his or her wishes (Joshua 24:15).
- God provides encouragement, options, and guidance (Gen. 28:15).
- God considers the motives behind the action. He does not judge on appearances alone (1 Sam. 16:7).
- God is aware of our needs and anticipates them (Isa. 65:24).
- God assures that He is on our side (Joshua 1:9).
- God is consistent in the messages He gives through His Word and through His discipline (Job 5:17, 18; Jer. 30:11).
- God's discipline has a purpose. It is not to vent His anger, but to help us grow (Heb. 12:6, 7; Rev. 3:19).
- God frequently uses natural consequences to teach us (Hosea 14:1).
- God offers incentives in the form of rewards (Eph. 6:8).

- God sent His Son Jesus to show His love and to provide for our salvation (John 3:16; 1 John 4:9, 10).

Dealing With Failure

- God is always ready to forgive and forget and will erase the past forever (Ps. 103:3, 12; Isa. 1:18; Dan. 9:9) .
- God loves the person regardless of behavior. While He hates the evil deeds, God still loves unselfishly (Prov. 6:16-19; John 8:3-11; Rom. 5:8).
- God gives us a second chance, bringing us around to the same circumstances again to strengthen us (Joel 2:12-14; Zech. 1:3; Phil. 4:13).
- God's love is not conditional. Accepting us just as we are, He does not demand proof of changed behavior but loves through "thick and thin" (Jer 31:3; 1 John 4:10, 19).
- God is optimistic about our future. He focuses on what we can become through Christ (Jer. 31:17; Eph. 2:4-7).
- God is persistent. Not giving up easily, He actively seeks the wanderer. He has unending patience (Hosea 11:8, 9; 1 Tim. 1:19).
- God provides rest from the battle when needed—a change of activity and encouragement at the appropriate moment (Matt. 11:28; Mark 6:31).

God never gives up!

Second, **test your knowledge of the parenting styles** by completing the Temperature Check at the end of this chapter. It will also give you some ideas about how the different parenting styles really function in everyday life.

Third, **tell your children you are trying to change**. They will expect you to act as you always have and so will test you to see if you have really changed. Things may get worse before they improve, but in the end your relationship with your children will be much, much better. It's worth the effort.

Fourth, **pray every day for heavenly wisdom**. Pray many times a day that God will give you the love and warmth your children need. Also pray that He will provide you the strength to teach your children with firmness combined with love.

TEMPERATURE CHECK

After reading these brief descriptions of home situations, rate the emotional climate of the home as (1) authoritative, (2) authoritarian, (3) permissive, or (4) neglectful. The correct answers appear at the end.

Home Situation   *Rating*

Mother comes running to investigate the screams coming-   _____
from the living room and finds 2-year-old Melissa hitting
her 1-year-old sister. Quickly Mother moves over beside
Melissa and gently but firmly takes her hands away from
the baby and holds them in her own while saying, "No,
Melissa. That hurts baby sister. Let's find a toy for baby.
We want to be kind to the baby." After assisting Melissa
in finding a toy for the infant, Mother then suggests that
she help her in the kitchen.

"Please, Johnny, put your toys away before Daddy comes   _____
home," begs his mother for the fourth time in 15 minutes.
Johnny continues playing. Finally Mother feels desperate
and offers Johnny a piece of candy if he will only put his
toys away.

"You can't go to the beach because I said so—and no   _____
more of that back talk!" Marilyn's father proclaims in no
uncertain terms.

Mr. Jones believes in using the rod—it's the only way to   _____
make the kids mind these days, he says. Usually his
children get beaten eight or ten times a day.

Ten-year-old Heather rushes in from school, proclaiming   _____
loudly, "I don't want to sit next to Joe! He smells! Call the
teacher, Mom, *please*. Tell her I just can't sit next to him!
None of the kids like him. Why should I have to sit next to
him?" "Let's think about it, Heather," Mom responds. "It
does sound awful. I wonder why Joe smells so? Is there
something we could do to help him? How would you feel if
all the kids avoided you? Maybe when Dad comes home he'll
have some ideas. We could talk about it at suppertime."

Today is 6-year-old Kari's birthday. Daddy, who doesn't live with Kari and her mom anymore, promised to come for her party. But he never came. Kari cried and cried because she was so disappointed. The next day he said he was just too busy at work to come.

"Come on, honey, don't you think it's time to go to bed?" cajoles Mom. Four-year-old Justin shakes his head and continues playing with his blocks. Mom sighs and goes back to working on the papers she brought home from the office. An hour later Justin falls asleep on the floor of the family room. Mom carries him to bed.

(Answer key: 1, 3, 2, 2, 1, 4, 3)

KEYS TO DISCIPLINE

1. Provide clear standards for behavior.
2. Enforce clear consequences for misbehavior.
3. Be reasonable.
4. Respect each family member's individuality.
5. Provide an emotional climate of warmth and caring in the home.
6. Expect mature behavior; encourage personal responsibility and independence.
7. Respect the feelings of each family member.
8. Communicate clearly and frequently. Respect your child's viewpoint.

HTHYCRLJ-2

CHAPTER 4

Growing Like Jesus

"Jesus continued to learn more and more and to grow physically.
People liked him, and he pleased God."
—Luke 2:52, ICB

Raising roses is a lot like helping children grow spiritually. Where we live the roses must receive a lot of tender loving care in order to bloom. In the fall we must cover and protect them against the winter storms. When spring comes we must trim the rosebushes carefully so the new leaves will sprout. The bushes require fertilizer and plenty of water and sunshine to produce leaves and then flowers. If they lack any of those ingredients, it will stunt their growth.

Eagerly we watch for the first buds. Daily we look at them to see if the flowers are showing yet. Of course, we never say to them, "How terrible! You're just buds—you should be full-grown flowers. You aren't even pretty!" Instead we love the green buds. They are the promise of future flowers. Pretty soon a tip of color shows and just a few days later a few pink petals promise a full flower soon.

When Jesus was a child His life unfolded gently and beautifully, as do the roses in the garden. Although the Bible is quite brief—only one verse—about the early development of Jesus, Ellen White tells us much more in chapter 7 of *The Desire of Ages*. He did not mature supernaturally, but "the powers of [His] mind and body developed gradually, in keeping with the laws of childhood" (p. 68). "As a child, Jesus manifested a peculiar loveliness of disposition. His willing hands were ever ready to serve others. He manifested a patience that nothing could disturb, and a truthfulness that would never sacrifice integrity. In principle firm as a rock, His life revealed the grace of unselfish courtesy" (pp. 68, 69). Mary often marveled at the beauty of His character.

Although she did not fully understand His mission on earth, she took her responsiblity to nurture His spiritual growth extremely seriously. Gently she taught Him from the Holy Scriptures, adapting the lessons to His opening mind. She explained to Him God's goodness and greatness and His law. His human mother instructed Him in the ways of God and told Him the Bible stories about the history of Israel. And Scripture records that "Jesus grew . . . in favor with God and men" (Luke 2:52, NIV).

As Mary nurtured Jesus gently, in keeping with His development, so we must nurture our children spiritually. "Parents and teachers should aim so to cultivate the tendencies of the youth that at each stage of life they may represent the beauty appropriate to that period, unfolding naturally, as do the plants in the garden" (*Child Guidance,* p. 204).

Ellen White recommends no forced growth here. No excessive pushing toward maturity. Just the advancement in keeping with their stage of development. The beauty appropriate for each age: first the bud, then the flower.

In order to grow spiritually, children require the tender loving care of their earthly parents, the sunshine of God's love, the gentle rains of the Holy Spirit, the fertilizer of God's Word, and sometimes the discipline of pruning in order to produce the beautiful, fragrant blooms of a Christlike life. "In dealing with your children, follow the method of the gardener. By gentle touches, by loving ministrations, seek to fashion their characters after the pattern of the character of Christ" (*The Desire of Ages,* p. 516).

One of my favorite statements about growing flowers in the garden of God's children emphasizes the tenderness needed: "In our efforts to correct evil, we should guard against a tendency to faultfinding or censure. . . . Flowers do not unfold under the breath of a blighting wind" (*Education,* p. 291). So as you help your children develop spiritually, keep in mind the tenderness of God and the gentleness of the rain and sunshine.

Some of our rosebushes are quite resistant to disease. The insects don't seem to bother them as much. Other bushes seem to attract pests, and we have to use insecticide regularly. While some bushes survive the cold winters regularly, other varieties are more sensitive to cold, and we have to replace the dead bushes frequently.

Each bush, of course, produces a different kind of flower. One of my favorites has large, fragrant, deep-pink roses. Their fragrance fills a room. We have some miniature bushes planted beside a large rock. Their flowers are not showy, but if you look at them closely they have a special beauty in their smallness. Each bush is special and requires a particular combination of insecticide, fertilizer, sunshine, rain, and pruning to produce beautiful blooms.

So it is in God's flower garden of children. Each one is different, and each requires a special blend of care to nurture spiritual growth. Thus each child will approach God differently, and each will produce a different type of spiritual flower. God has no pattern—Simplicity Pattern No. 9478—for the perfect Christian child. Instead, the spiritual growth of each child is unique.

Furthermore, each of us comes to God and understands Him through our distinctive personality and life experiences, as well as with our own unique mind. Remember Peter and John and how unalike they were? Impulsive—maybe hyperactive—and sanguine Peter. Quick to accept Jesus, equally quick to deny Him. Afraid of the consequences of following the Lord. Transformed by the Holy Spirit into a powerful speaker whose words moved the hearts of thousands. Daring for the Lord.

John, quick-tempered, but loving. A true friend. Loyal to the end. A thinker, careful with words, meticulous with details. Articulate writer describing Christ's love in words everyone can understand. Entrusted with end-time prophecies, conscientiously recorded under difficult circumstances—details that probably would have overwhelmed Peter, the popular speaker.

Peter's writing is filled with action words—be ready, watch, be sober, go, believe, remember, be careful. John's Gospel and his Epistles exude relationship and love. While Peter doesn't ignore relationship and John includes action, each describes God from the viewpoint of his own personality. Each is right—God is action and God is relationship. The total enriches our understanding and provides a clearer picture of God. Peter and John each served God in the way best suited to his personality. And God used each one differently, again in keeping with his natural inclinations and Spirit-filled personality.

Each of our children has a unique personality, partially inherited and partially developed through life's experiences. Every child will experience salvation and God's love differently. An important aspect of helping children grow spiritually is to recognize how their personality affects their relationship with God.

Temperament is an important part of personality. Alexander Thomas and Stella Chess, well-known researchers on child development, have identified three types of temperament in children: easy, difficult, and slow-to-warm-up. They believe the three types account for approximately two thirds of all children. The remaining third display no clearly identifiable type. The Thomas and Chess temperament types are well known and respected among child development researchers. They help us to understand children better.

Thomas and Chess believe temperament consists of nine different traits. Each trait can be described anywhere along the line from one extreme to the other. Varying combinations of the traits form a child's temperament, which they believe is already present at birth.

TEMPERAMENT TRAITS

Activity Level
Quiet...Active

Regularity
Regular ....Irregular

Approach/Withdrawal
Withdrawn..Outgoing

Adaptability
High adaptability ....Low adaptability

Physical Sensitivity
Very sensitive...Not sensitive

Intensity of Reaction
High intensity ....Low intensity

Quality of Mood
Pessimistic ....Optimistic

Distractibility
Not distractible ....Very distractible

Persistence
High persistence ....Low persistence

A child's general level of activity can vary from slow to extremely energetic. Most children fall in the middle range, neither highly active nor slow. Approach/withdrawal describes how a child reacts to new situations and decision-making. Some children are ultracautious when confronted with a new situation, while others dive in headlong and seem to have no fears. Many children have a hard time making decisions, while others are impulsive in their decision-making. One group of children adapt to changes easily, while others require much longer periods of time to adjust.

Temperament differences affect children's reactions to spiritual matters also. David is usually the first to wave his hand to volunteer for a service activity.

Usually he doesn't give a thought to whether he has the time or if it conflicts with something else he has already promised to do. Jeff may not make up his mind until it is too late to join. The organizers have already made plans that do not include him because he appeared to be disinterested in helping others. In reality, it wasn't disinterest, but his cautious approach that excluded him.

Christine has intense emotional reactions to everything. Living life with great feeling, she will be deeply touched by the story of the Crucifixion and will appear to be "truly converted" because of her strong emotions. Melissa, on the other hand, is calm and cool. You really can't judge how she feels by her outward reactions. Because she does not appear to be so moved by the story of the Crucifixion, her parents and teachers may wonder about her salvation. Yet, deep inside she was just as "converted" as Christine.

A general attitude of optimism or pessimism also seems to be part of the inborn temperament. Mike has always been naturally happy. He smiles and laughs a lot and is confident that everything will turn out all right in the end. Just being around him makes everyone else feel happier. Michelle, on the other hand, thinks of all the "awful possibilities" around the corner and needs a lot of reassurance that things will turn out all right. Faith in God during difficulties will be a lot more natural for Mike than for Michelle because he is inherently optimistic. However, a solid spiritual experience can be a strong help to Michelle as she struggles with her inborn inclination to see the potential problems and to distrust the future.

Have you ever said something like "I wonder why Chris is so wild? His brothers get good grades and are real religious leaders. I can't believe they come from the same home"? In fact, they didn't. Each child in a family really grows up in a somewhat different environment. The oldest and the youngest child experience the family quite differently.

In addition to the differences the child's position in the family creates, the family may be living in another part of the country or Mom or Dad may have a more demanding job. Schools, churches, and neighborhoods may be different. Ask any teacher about how classes have personalities also. Some groups of children are much more spiritual than others, less inclined to "do drugs," and more interested in studying.

Even in the same place, experiences can differ greatly. Attending the same church school, four years apart, one of our children had a solid education from excellent teachers while the other had one weak year after another with marginally qualified teachers. It took years to catch up in some subjects. The same thing can happen in Sabbath school.

All of these differences—personality, family position, and life experiences—will shape a child's reaction to spiritual influences. As we try to help our children grow spiritually, we must adapt all our efforts to suit the individual child. No formula will work for all children. Salvation is an individual matter.

When my husband and I go to the garden center each spring, we eagerly anticipate getting a few more rosebushes for our garden. We know what we want—beautiful, fragrant tea roses that bloom on disease-and cold-resistant bushes. Quite an order for our Michigan climate! Happily we take home our new bushes, plant them carefully, water and fertilize, and wait for the flowers. As we do these things we look forward to enjoying roses all summer.

As we help our children grow spiritually, we, too, need to know what we want. Looking into the innocent face of your newborn baby, the main goal is clear: salvation and an eternity together with God. But you also need some plans for getting there, just as gardeners have plans for their gardens—goals for this year and ones for the future. Sometimes the gardener has to change his plans. A storm or disease affects some plants. Part of the garden may need replanting. But the gardener's main plan is always the same—an eye-appealing arrangement of nature's beauty.

While the main goal for your child remains the same—salvation and an eternity together with God—you need some more detailed plans in order to accomplish the main goal. I'd like to suggest that the first step of your plan might be to **help your children know God**. Satan has been misrepresenting God's nature and character since his days in heaven. One of his main efforts has been to give humans a wrong picture of God so that they will believe He is an unjust, severe, exacting judge who doesn't care about the plight of His earthly subjects and whose requirements are unreasonable and impossible to attain. If Satan can't get people to believe this picture, he has an alternate one to offer: God is so loving and caring that He wouldn't punish anyone for misbehaving. Any way of living is OK. God doesn't care what we do. He understands our human nature and knows it is impossible for us to overcome our evil inclinations.

So one of your most important goals is to introduce your children to the real God, the one who will be "our guide even to the end" (Ps. 48:14, NIV). How can our children learn to love God if they don't know what He is really like?

But we must first know God ourselves if we are to introduce our children to Him. When we know Him intimately, we will give our children an accurate picture. If the thought of God sends chills down your back as you picture an angry, confrontational judge, you need to meet the real Deity. Nothing would please Him more than to help you get acquainted with Him.

Yet, how do you get acquainted with God? How can you get rid of the distortions about His character that bombard us in our sin-distorted world? Start with a Bible concordance and look up all the New Testament verses that describe God and how He interacts with people. Then do the same thing with Psalms. Make a list of God's characteristics. Meditate on one each day during your private time with the Lord. The books *Steps to Christ*, *Thoughts From the Mount of Blessing*, and *The Desire of Ages* offer wonderful descriptions of God because they introduce us to His Son, Jesus, the perfect revelation of God. As you get to know God more intimately, you will reflect to your children a more accurate picture of Him.

A second main goal might be to **help your children develop Christian characters**. Solomon, the ancient wise man, had some most modern views when he wrote: "Even a child is known by his actions, by whether his conduct is pure and right" (Prov. 20:11, NIV). One of the big responsibilities of parenthood is to help children learn how to live in harmony with their family, friends, and other people they know and meet. Child development specialists call the process socialization—helping children behave in socially acceptable ways. Christians have a broader and deeper view when we call the process Christian character development because we are giving God His rightful place in the center of the child socialization process.

The third main goal for your children might be to lead them **to accept the salvation Christ offers**. While Christian character development begins during infancy, accepting Christ's personal sacrifice and grace occurs a few years later. Most children reared in Christian homes recognize Jesus as their personal Saviour sometime during the elementary school years (ages 6 to 14). Some children seem to have unusual spiritual insight at an early age and accept Christ's gift as their own during the late preschool years, while others do not make such a personal acceptance until middle or late adolescence.

The fourth main goal is closely tied to the third: **Make a commitment to an ongoing, lifetime relationship with God**. Such a commitment, permeating the entire life, leads us to "seek first his kingdom and his righteousness" (Matt. 6:33, NIV). It affects everything we do and all that we become. Becoming the central core of our life, our purpose for being, it causes us to walk so close to God that our thoughts and His become one and the same. When we act we are simply reflecting how He would if He were in our situation. Surely this is what we want for our children as well as for ourselves.

Children can begin their relationship with God before they are old enough to go to school simply as Jesus becomes their friend and companion. They can learn to trust Him to help in their difficulties. As they grow older, the relationship matures as their understanding of God expands.

Of course, these are not all the spiritual goals you could have for your children. They represent only a beginning—some of the big ones, if you please. But you are much more likely to be able to guide your child's spiritual growth if you have some clear goals in mind. Take a quiet time, after the children have gone to bed, to talk with your partner in parenthood about the spiritual goals you have for your children. If you are alone, get together with another single parent to discuss spiritual goals for each of your families. Write them down in a notebook. Review them frequently to see how you are doing.

Child development specialists often talk about developmental tasks for children of different ages. They consist of accomplishments important at each stage of development if the child is to progress normally. A child must attain or complete each task before he can move on to the next stage. For example, developmental tasks for the first two years include learning to walk and talk.

I have prepared a checklist of spiritual developmental tasks that will help children grow toward mature faith and spirituality. The earlier tasks prepare for the later ones. If early development was deficient, later spiritual development will be more difficult—not impossible but more challenging.

You will notice that the tasks fall into four main areas: faith in God's Word, faith relationship with God, faith for daily living, and faith relationship with other people. The first two areas relate to the main goals of knowing God and accepting salvation. The last two areas expand Christian character and build an ongoing relationship with God.

I have included two lists of tasks: one for early childhood (birth to 6 years) and the other for late childhood (6 to 12 or 13 years).

Put your child's name on the line at the top and then go through each task, keeping him or her in mind. Try to think of specific ways in which you know the child has accomplished this task. For example, can she forgive her brother when he teases her? Or does she hold a grudge against him and often bring up past misdeeds? Giving and accepting forgiveness are key components of understanding and accepting what Jesus has done for us. They lay a foundation for salvation. Learning to forgive is a hard lesson. Is she making steps in that direction? Don't expect perfection—just progress.

FAITH DEVELOPMENT
Developmental Tasks for Early Childhood

Child's Name _____

Faith in God's Word
_____ Enjoys Bible stories and considers some important Bible people as loved friends (Daniel, Noah, Jesus, and others)

_____ Knows many Bible verses from memory and can tell something about what the verses mean

_____ Uses some Bible verses to help with daily living (when afraid, when tempted to do wrong, etc.)

Faith Relationship With God
_____ Knows and feels that God and Jesus love her [him] all the time

_____ Shows that he/she loves God, is happy about his [her] friendship, and wants to please Him

_____ Acts guilty and feels sorry when she [he] has done something wrong

_____ Usually confesses or admits he [she] has done something wrong

_____ Profits from discipline (tries to do better in the future)

_____ Respects the wishes of parents and teachers and wants to please them

_____ Likes to talk with God through prayer

_____ Uses prayer to ask forgiveness for wrong and seek help when needed

_____ Trusts God to forgive and to help in distress

Faith for Daily Living
_____ Knows how to figure out the "moral" (what she [he] should learn) from a Bible or other character-building story

_____ Applies the story "moral" to his [her] life

_____ Knows a clear set of "do's" and "don'ts" to guide her [his] behavior and follows them most of the time

_____ Recognizes the voice of conscience (knows some things are wrong to do)

_____ Can follow the voice of conscience and refrain from doing something he [she] wants to do but knows is wrong

_____ Knows how to decide what is right or wrong in a new situation

Faith Relationship With Other People

_____ Recognizes how other people feel and wants to help them when they are needy

_____ Is learning to understand the effect of his [her] actions on other people (that the other child hurts when she [he] hits)

_____ Accepts forgiveness when he [she] has done something wrong

_____ Usually forgives someone who has wronged him [her]

_____ Usually obeys the rules (at home, with friends or grandparents, preschool or day-care center, Sabbath school, etc.)

_____ Knows about God's rules and wants to obey them

_____ Trusts [his] parents and teachers

Your children will have a strong foundation for faith, Christian character, and spiritual living if during early childhood they have learned to:

1. love, trust, and obey their parents and their God
2. empathize with other people and treat them lovingly
3. forgive and be forgiven
4. enjoy the friendship of Jesus
5. be self-disciplined

Because faith development is a lifelong journey, the spiritual developmental tasks for early childhood continue during late childhood. Each of the early childhood tasks deepens, expands, and matures through late childhood and into early adolescence.

However, faith development during late childhood brings in some new tasks. Knowledge of God's Word greatly expands along with more understanding of church doctrines. Acceptance of Jesus as a personal Saviour emerges, and prayer takes a more mature role. Christian self-esteem begins to be evident, and the child bases moral decision-making on principles. Identification with the church becomes clearer. Service to others helps link God with people.

The spiritual developmental tasks of early childhood are prerequisites to the more mature ones of late childhood because they provide the foundation for all faith development. Fortunately, gaps in earlier spiritual development can be filled in—though with greater effort—during late childhood.

FAITH DEVELOPMENT
Developmental Tasks for Late Childhood

Child's Name _____

Faith in God's Word

_____ Knows and believes that the Bible is the story of God's

relationship with human beings during the past and in the future
_____ Has a deepening understanding and knowledge of Bible history and prophecy
_____ Knows how the Bible was written and has a basic understanding of inspiration
_____ Knows and believes that the Bible is God's communication to human beings to guide them in deepening their relationship with Him
_____ Enjoys reading the Bible and turns to the Bible for help in daily living
_____ Knows the major doctrines of the SDA Church and accepts them as his [her] personal beliefs
_____ Has memorized many significant Bible passages
_____ Identifies with some Bible characters

Faith Relationship With God
_____ Accepts the Bible as God's personal communication to her [him]
_____ Turns to the Bible to develop a relationship with God and Jesus
_____ Recognizes that she [he] is a sinner in need of a Saviour
_____ Accepts Jesus Christ as a personal Saviour on an ongoing basis
_____ Communicates with God through prayer naturally and frequently
_____ Accepts God's forgiveness for sins and the grace offered by Jesus Christ to sinners on a daily basis
_____ Feels that God is her [his] heavenly Father and Jesus her [his] older Brother, forever Friend, and Confidant

Faith for Daily Living
_____ Believes that God and Jesus know best for his [her] life and is maturing a daily trusting relationship with Them to guide his [her] spiritual and character growth
_____ Is developing a positive self-esteem based on Christian values
_____ Is learning to make moral decisions employing guidance from God's Word and is developing the needed independence to follow through on those decisions
_____ Usually does what she [he] believes is the right thing to do
_____ Has some positive "heroes" she [he] wants to be like
_____ Is learning to apply God's Word to her [his] own life and actions
_____ Is developing principles to guide her/his behavior
_____ Shows remorse and guilt for wrong doing and attempts to "make things right"

Faith Relationship With Other People

_____ Identifies herself [himself] as a Seventh-day Adventist

_____ Is a baptized member of the Seventh-day Adventist Church

_____ Is beginning to understand the deeper meaning of the Ten Commandments (love God and love others) and is learning how to express that love through actions

_____ Thinks of herself [himself] as a helping, caring, empathic person and demonstrates it in relationships with other people

_____ Is beginning to have "dreams" of what she [he] may grow up to be and how she [he] fits into God's plan for the world

_____ Is learning how to cope when peers attempt to pressure her [him] to do what she [he] knows is not right

_____ Thinks of herself [himself] as a responsible person who can be counted on to fulfill her [his] obligations

_____ Shares her [his] friendship with Jesus naturally and openly with other people

As you read the following chapters, you will probably want to frequently refer to the spiritual developmental tasks in this chapter. If you keep them in mind, you will have a guide to what your children need to know and experience in their spiritual journey. They are an important key to helping your children grow up with Jesus as their close friend and companion.

KEYS TO GROWING LIKE JESUS

1. Nurture gently in keeping with your child's needs.
2. Consider your child's individual temperament.
3. Respect your child's current stage of development.
4. Consider your child's position in the family and his/her life experiences.
5. Keep the goals for spiritual development clearly in focus.
6. Review the spiritual developmental tasks. Decide which ones your child has accomplished and which ones need to be learned.
7. Keep your child's spiritual developmental tasks in mind as you plan for his/her personal growth.

♥

CHAPTER 5

Spirituality During Early Childhood

"You must accept the kingdom of God as a little child accepts things, or you will never enter it."
—Mark 10:15, ICB

When do children begin to grow spiritually? In a most enlightening statement Ellen White suggests that religion can begin when they are only babies. "Bring your children in prayer to Jesus, for he has made it possible for them to learn religion as they learn to frame the words of the language" (*The Adventist Home*, p. 321). By the time most children reach 2 years old, they are using words to communicate with other people. Language learning really begins even earlier as babies coo, babble, and in other ways get ready to talk during their first year. I have concluded from her inspired statement that children must be able to learn religion before they are 2 years old.

What kind of religion can babies and toddlers learn? Certainly not the 2,300 days or the seven last plagues! Their spiritual lessons are much more basic than the fine points of doctrine. The first steps in the religious life consist of love, trust, and obedience, and they remain the cornerstone of religion during all of early childhood. They are the spiritual lessons that eventually lead toward a saving relationship with Jesus Christ. If young children experience love and trust and learn to obey, their foundation for their spiritual experience will be strong. However, in addition, children absorb a great deal more about religion during early childhood.

Patterns of Living

First, they learn **patterns of living** vital to spiritual life. Two-year-old Jennifer fell asleep on the sofa waiting for Sabbath dinner. She looked so exhausted that our hostess decided not to waken her when we began to eat.

Caught up in the spirited conversation, all of us temporarily forgot about the sleeping child. As we cleared the table for dessert, in walked a sleepy-eyed but very hungry Jennifer.

Mom lifted Jennifer into her high chair, dished up her food, and placed the plate in front of her, all the while generally ignoring the child and continuing with our adult conversation. Puzzled, Jennifer looked all around the table at each adult busily eating dessert, then at her own plate. Again her eyes circled the table of absorbed adults and finally rested on her food.

Quietly, without any help or even encouragement from anyone else, she bowed her head, folded her hands, and mumbled something I couldn't hear from the other side of the table. Satisfied that she had solved her personal dilemma, Jennifer attacked her food with vigor. Why the adults were eating without praying would remain a mystery, but she had done what she knew she was supposed to do before eating.

I've thought of Jennifer often. Not born knowing that praying before eating is the right thing to do. She had learned it from her parents. Ever since she could remember, Mom and Dad had always prayed before eating, and they had helped her thank Jesus for the food, too. Day after day, month after month, when it probably appeared that Jennifer wasn't really paying much attention, Mom and Dad continued praying and helping her fold her hands for prayer. In fact, she couldn't remember a time when her family ate without saying "thank You" to God first.

And so when her decision time arrived, Jennifer was ready. She *knew* she should pray before eating, even though no one else seemed to remember. Having always done it that way, she would do it now, alone. Satisfied that she had done the right thing, she now thought the food tasted wonderful.

Jennifer was learning, at a beginning level, the patterns of living that will become part of the fiber of her being. They will become such an integral part of her way of life that she will not have to make a conscious choice over them. She simply would not consider doing otherwise. Her patterns of living—sometimes called habits—will make a big difference in years to come. They will be part of the strong foundation of her spiritual life.

You can teach many such patterns during early childhood: prayer before meals, before going to sleep, when in trouble, or when needing forgiveness; going to Sabbath school and church every week, wearing special Sabbath clothes, taking an offering, sitting quietly in church; gathering for family worship every day to read God's Word, learning the memory verse, singing and praying together; getting ready for Sabbath and welcoming God's holy day.

Such patterns, repeated every day (or every week), make religion part of the building blocks of a life. Your child will never remember a time when he or she did not pray and go to church. God's original plan for children included knowing Him from the very beginning so that He would always be part of their lives.

We teach children many patterns of living during their first six years—brushing their teeth, picking up their clothes and toys, helping other people. Doing such things every day ingrains them deeply until they become natural and automatic. The religious patterns of living are the same. A vital part of parenting young children is teaching them the patterns of living you want them to have for life.

KEYS TO PATTERNS OF LIVING

1. Decide what religious actions you would like to teach your child.
2. Do them regularly—don't ever miss.
3. Make learning fun. Pair it with your love.

Feelings and Attitudes

During the first three to four years young children are much more feeling than thinking creatures. Feelings are always front and center for them. They experience life through their emotions. You know immediately what is going on in their minds because they quickly show their unhappiness, fear, or displeasure. Children even remember events through feelings. Sally and Aunt Beth were talking about a walk they took through the woods. Aunt Beth recalled the big trees and the squirrels running about, while Sally remembered how tired and afraid she felt. As children mature, they begin to develop mentally and gain more control over their feelings. Reasoning, or thinking, comes to play a greater role by the time they get to be 5 or 6 years old.

Many early childhood memories are mostly emotional. Such feelings develop into attitudes—attitudes toward God, prayer, worship, and church. Young children sense our own feelings and attitudes and "catch" religion from the home and the church. When you look forward to going to church and joyfully participate in the services, your child will sense your joy and feel happy too.

A long and boring family worship that requires Junior to sit still for a long time listening to things he doesn't understand will probably produce negative feelings that will develop into negative attitudes toward the whole idea of family worship. If a Sabbath school room is brightly decorated with pictures of animals, flowers, and Jesus with children, the leaders are cheerful and friendly without being overpowering, and the program is fun, your 3-year-old will have happy feelings and memories of Sabbath school. On the other hand, if the Sabbath school room is a musty-smelling dark basement with dull, chipped paint, storage boxes piled willy-nilly in the corners, and one light bulb dangling from the ceiling, and the leader frowns a lot and doesn't have anything interesting planned, your preschooler will have negative memories of Sabbath school.

Children are extremely conscious of smells and atmosphere, of smiling faces and frowning ones. They read body language probably better than adults do and have a keen sense for knowing who really likes them and who feels children are a nuisance. All of this feeds into their memories and attitudes toward religious events. Preschoolers are extremely impressionable. They will naturally "catch" your own attitude toward religion. You don't have to try to make it happen—it will occur naturally, even if you don't want it to.

Thinking Processes

One day I was visiting the cradle roll division of an SDA church. After only a few minutes I realized the leaders were having an entire program on the seven last plagues. I was aghast! Two- to 4-year-olds have a lot of fears just because they are little and don't understand everything yet. At Sabbath school we should be helping children deal with their fears, not adding to them!

To end the program they had two children in front of the room sitting on the floor with an umbrella over them, and the leaders held a paper rainbow above the umbrella. One of the leaders said, "Now God's rainbow of promise will protect us!"

Young children think concretely. When teaching children this age you must say exactly what you mean in as literal a way as possible. Symbolism builds a wall between the child and you that he must climb over before he can understand what you are trying to teach him. What were these children learning from this activity? That when it rains you get under an umbrella, probably. Certainly the symbolic notion that the rainbow of God's promise protects us went right over their heads in more ways than one.

When you teach your young child at home, you will often run into this same problem of understanding. Biblical ideas are often symbolic and need clear, concrete explanations for young children. Just think of what the symbol means and present it that way. For example, the symbol of Jesus the Shepherd taking care of the sheep actually represents Jesus' care of us. Teach it that way to preschoolers. During the early years children do not understand things the way we do. They interpret differently because of their immature thinking processes.

For example, young children have difficulty recognizing that a person can be two different things at the same time. A classic example of such thinking is the story that came out of the White House when Carolyn Kennedy was a little girl. Someone asked her, "Is your daddy the president?" Carolyn shook her head vigorously and said, "No! He's my daddy!" In her mind he couldn't be her father and the president at the same time. The same way of thinking often also operates in the area of religion. To the question "Is your daddy an Adventist?" the typical response would be "No, he's my daddy!" Young children generally do not understand that they are members of a particular denomination. They think of themselves as boys and girls and members of a family. The idea that a person can be many things at once comes later.

Frequently young children will latch onto a little idea from a story and that concept will become the main thing they remember. Everything else will be lost to the one point. Rachel, one of my students, told me a story about her little boy that illustrates this principle perfectly.

It was children's storytime at Bobby's church. The minister started out by talking about insects. He explained a lot about insects and how God made them, going into great detail about different kinds and species. Finally he got to the story part.

One day, he said, a little boy playing in his yard saw a grasshopper hopping along. The boy followed the grasshopper across the yard to the fence. Of course, the grasshopper bounced through the fence so that the child couldn't reach it. But when the boy reached the fence and looked through it to the other side, he saw a baby sitting in the grass beside the crossroads. The boy knew the infant shouldn't be out there, so he went running inside to tell his mother. She rushed outside, picked up the baby, and took her inside their house. Then she called the baby's mother, who immediately came to get her. The baby's mother was so happy the little boy had found her baby. The moral of the story was that God uses even insects to help people.

At the dinner table that day Rachel asked Bobby, "Did you like the story about the grasshopper and the insects that the minister told in church today?" She thought he would have liked the story because he was fond of insects.

"It wasn't about a grasshopper," Bobby replied. "It was about the road to Jesus' cross."

My friend Rachel did a double take and thought, *The road to Jesus' cross? Where did he get that?* Not even the sermon was about that topic. So she asked him, "Are you sure?"

"Yes," Bobby said firmly, "it was about the road to Jesus' cross, and Jesus stopped along the way and picked some flowers."

What had happened? Bobby had evidently heard the word "crossroads," as the man telling the story had placed quite a bit of emphasis on the fact that the house was at a busy intersection. Recently Bobby had heard the story about Jesus carrying His cross. Impressed by it, as soon as he heard "crossroads," he latched onto the word and quickly made a mental connection to Jesus and the cross. Thus, the whole story went into that category.

Bobby's reaction was typical of that of young children. You might hear the same response from your own tiny tots. So when you are teaching your preschoolers Bible stories or other character-building stories, ask them to tell you what the narrative was about. Their response could be very enlightening and will give you an opportunity to help correct their thinking.

KEYS TO TEACHING TINY TOTS

1. Say it simply—avoid symbolisms. Say exactly what you mean.
2. Ask questions to find out what your child is thinking.
3. Concentrate on one thing at a time.

Belief and Faith

Young children are natural believers. They trust adults and accept what they hear. If you told 3-year-old Joey that the world is square and that if he walked far enough down the road he'd drop off the edge, he might believe you. Why? Because you are an adult, and he doesn't know anything different. He doesn't know enough about the universe to question what you say. Children don't yet have the ability to think and reason through a problem in the same way adults do—therefore, they are natural believers. Sometimes they put us to shame.

As Len approached the end of his graduate school studies, he spent many weeks preparing for his program's comprehensive examinations. He had a notebook full of data from his study and was working on mastering the material in preparation for the tests.

One day he could not find the notebook. He looked everywhere he could think of, posted notices on the bulletin boards at school, and told everyone he knew of the loss, hoping someone would find the notebook. Two weeks simply wasn't enough time to dig out all that material again. Besides, he hadn't finished mastering his notes. Desperate, he feared he would fail the examinations unless he found the material.

A week went by and the notebook remained lost. Len was feeling depressed when his little 3-year-old daughter said to him, "Daddy, have you asked Jesus to help you?"

His face flushed as he looked down, embarrassed. No, he hadn't prayed about the matter, and he didn't have a good answer for his daughter. How could he admit it when he had taught her that she should pray about problems? And why *hadn't* he prayed? Did he really think God didn't have time to bother with graduate school notebooks? On the other hand, if he said he had prayed and then the notebook didn't appear, what about his daughter's faith? He quickly decided truth was the best answer.

"No, honey, I haven't," he acknowledged reluctantly.

"Daddy, let's pray right now!" So together they knelt with the child praying first. Len followed, confessing his lack of faith and asking for divine intervention in his emergency.

Two hours after their prayers the telephone rang. A stranger had found his notebook. To this day Len wonders what would have happened if he hadn't prayed. Was God reminding him that He knew and cared about every detail of his life? It was a lesson he has never forgotten.

Len's daughter's religious experience is typical of preschool children. If their parents have taught them about God and prayer, their faith is strong. It's a nitty-gritty kind of faith. They are absolutely certain God cares and will help. Their trust is simple.

Since young children have such natural faith, I believe God has given us the first six years to nurture them with God's Word and to build their faith. It is our golden opportunity to ensure a strong foundation so when the winds of later years blow cold and faithless, our children's faith will be like the ''house upon the rock'' they have sung about so often. Nothing will be able to destroy it.

The child's simple trust and loving obedience are the model Jesus wants adults to follow in their own spiritual life. As He took the children in His arms and blessed them, He gently rebuked the disciples for thinking the little ones were not important. He made the point clear when He said, ''Anyone who will not receive the kingdom of God like a little child will never enter it'' (Mark 10:15, NIV). As you help your children grow spiritually, keep in mind that the trust and obedience of early childhood are the model God has given for spiritual growth throughout all of life.

KEYS TO BELIEF AND FAITH

1. Nurture your child's natural belief and faith.
2. Teach positively and clearly. Don't bring up doubts.
3. Build a strong foundation of faith and trust.

♥

CHAPTER 6

Conscience—
The Voice Within

*"If you go the wrong way—to the right or to the left—
you will hear a voice behind you. It will say,
'This is the right way. You should go this way.' "*
—Isaiah 30:21, ICB

Two-year-old Katie had just disobeyed her mother and was getting the scolding she deserved. "If I see you doing that again," Mother reinforced, "you'll get a spanking!"

Wide-eyed and serious, Katie responded, "That's easy, Mommy. Just shut your eyes!"

Katie's solution to the problem was simple: If her mother didn't see what she was doing, it wasn't wrong. As children learn the difference between right and wrong, they are almost completely dependent on the approval or disapproval of Mom or Dad. When their parents punish or scold them for something, what they are doing must be bad. But if they don't say anything, it's OK. If they don't see the action—and consequently don't do anything—it must also be acceptable.

Conscience develops slowly. All those "do's" and "don'ts" are like little building blocks, slowly but surely erecting a framework for right and wrong within the child's mind. If Katie gets basically the same messages about right and wrong from the important people in her world—Mom, Dad, grandparents, baby-sitter, teachers—she will build a strong framework that will help her choose her actions carefully as she grows older. On

54

the other hand, if Katie receives mixed responses about what is right and what is wrong, her conscience framework will be weak and will be an inconsistent guide in later life. She will have problems sorting out what she should or shouldn't do.

Sending consistent messages about right and wrong is probably one of the most important things you can do to help your children develop a mature conscience. If one day a parent disciplines Katie for being "sassy" and the next day the child gets away with the same behavior, it will only confuse the girl. Is it OK or isn't it OK to be "sassy"? Eventually she reasons that it must be OK—at least sometimes—because Mom or Dad didn't respond to it. And she will keep doing it.

On the other hand, if every time Katie is "sassy" she faces an immediate consequence, she learns rather quickly that such behavior isn't a good thing. And most likely she will learn to control how she reacts to her parents. Every now and then she may try it again, just to test out the rule she has learned. But if the consequence is again forthcoming, she quickly backs off and thinks, *Ah, they still don't like that. It's a bad thing to do. I better not do it again.*

Katie, like all children, has a real need to test the boundaries of behavior. She has to find out how far she can go and get away with it. And she will keep testing until she discovers where the boundaries are. If the "fence" keeps collapsing against her onslaught, she will continue testing and her conscience development will be fragile and undependable. But if the "fence" holds firm, she will back off. Secure in the knowledge of her boundaries, Katie can devote her energies to more positive pursuits. At the same time she is building a reasonable, reliable conscience to guide her in the future. As long as she is insecure about the "fence," she will feel emotionally insecure also and will keep pursuing the security she needs so desperately.

Conscience has input from many sources, including the Holy Spirit— the voice of God reminding us of His way—and the education and training received during childhood. Sometimes faulty early experiences make it difficult for a person to hear the Holy Spirit. Thus, as parents we have a vital responsibility to help our children develop a solid, reasonable conscience sensitive to God's voice.

Individual conscience develops most strongly during the early childhood years. Its foundation begins in infancy with the bonding between mother and baby. If the infant experiences love and warmth from her parents and knows someone will always be there to take care of her, the most important building block of conscience has already been put in place. The close bonding of babies with their parents develops into identification with Mom and Dad by the time they are 4 or 5 years old. With identification comes the desire to be like the parents, to do the things that please them. This desire, in turn, helps build the prohibitions that eventually form the educated part of the conscience.

Children denied the bonding experience of loving parenting during infancy often have great difficulty developing a reliable conscience. They become character-disturbed children without a conscience. Basically, at the core of their being, they are extremely angry at a world that has denied them the closeness with their parents that they so desperately needed. Unfortunately, because so many children have been abused and abandoned, professional counselors are seeing more and more children and adults who have not developed an appropriate conscience. Such individuals have a severe character disorder.

One day Gabriel, a student in one of my graduate classes, stopped to talk with me after one of our sessions. "I am so grateful for this class today! You can't imagine how relieved I feel. Today I learned why we could never get through to my cousin's boy who lived with us for several years. My wife, especially, blamed herself because she couldn't seem to help him. We tried love and more love, we tried consistent discipline, but nothing seemed to make a difference." The words poured out in a rush of feeling as Gabriel told me the following story.

Juan's mother died at his birth, leaving three children motherless. His father, Gabriel's cousin, overwhelmed with grief and unable to cope with a newborn, gladly accepted the offer of relatives to care for the child. For the first eight years of his life Juan passed from relative to relative. Sometimes he was in a home for six months, other times it was only a few weeks before he went to another family. Each family loved Juan and tried to do their best for him, but he received no consistent care, no one bonded with him, and there was no one he could really consider his own. As the years went by, his relatives became more and more reluctant to take him because he was difficult to manage and disruptive to their family life.

When he was 8 years old Gabriel and Suzanna agreed to take him into their home. They realized Juan was out of control but thought that with consistent love and discipline they could make a difference in his life. Within the first week Suzanna knew she had real problems on her hands.

Juan was angry and hostile much of the time, although he could be a real charmer if he wished, especially around strangers. When Suzanna or Gabriel tried to hug him, he pushed them away and ran off. He had a hard time making friends at school or in the neighborhood. Other children would play with him for a while because he was charming at first, but soon he became hostile, and they ignored him. The boy lied about almost everything. In fact, he couldn't seem to tell the difference between truth and lies. Whenever he could he grabbed the cat and swung it by the tail. One day Suzanna caught him hitting the animal with a hammer. She had to watch him constantly or he would seriously hurt their baby or set fire to anything that would burn.

By now Suzanna and Gabriel were desperate. What could they do to help Juan? Suzanna prayed many times a day, continued trying to show the boy that they loved him, and used all the disciplinary methods she could think of. Sometimes things would go better and he seemed to be making progress. Then, without warning, he would revert to his former ways. Over the years Juan did improve, but he never got to the place where they could trust him. His influence in their family was disruptive to their younger children. Finally, when he was 11 years old, they reluctantly decided, for the sake of their own children, that Juan would have to live with someone else.

That day in class during our discussion about conscience development, Gabriel had finally realized what he and his wife had been dealing with. The boy was no ordinary child with a few behavior problems capable of being solved with consistent discipline. He was severely character disordered, a child without a conscience. No wonder things had been so difficult!

Juan displayed many of the classic characteristics of a child without a conscience. Children like him often deliberately injure themselves and seem to be abnormally preoccupied with fire, blood, and gore. Sometimes they have severe problems with stealing, hoarding, or gorging on food. Such children eventually grow up to be adult psychopaths, the terrors of society. Unfortunately, the psychopathic pattern is set early, usually by 7 years of age, and seems to be strongly related to the lack of bonding during infancy and toddlerhood, although some authorities think there may be a genetic tendency also.

Prevention is the best cure. If you want a solid foundation for normal conscience development, provide lots of opportunities for strong bonding

with your baby and young child. In every way possible be your son or
daughter's primary caretaker during infancy and early childhood. Attend
to your child's needs, both physical and emotional. Provide plenty of
loving physical contact and lots of opportunities for emotional closeness.
Be there when your child needs you.

From a secular point of view the outlook is extremely bleak for
children and teenagers without a conscience. The social sciences know of
no way to make up for the early deficiency in conscience development.
However, another year a different student shared his story with the entire
class.

Alex was born with a crippling physical problem that meant he spent
most of the first four years of his life at a well-known major medical
center. For reasons unknown to him as a child or even as an adult, his
parents came to visit him at the hospital only two or three times a year.
The nurses and hospital personnel were kind and loving, but he had no one
as close to him as his own mother would have been. So, of course, he
grew up without the intimate bond of affection between mother and child
that babies and toddlers need. He had a difficult time adjusting to his
family when he finally went home with them.

During grade school and high school Alex was the typical child
without a conscience. Destructive and mean-spirited, he was fascinated
with blood and fire and a constant liar. The boy hoarded sweets in huge
caches in his room. Of course he had no close friends. In my class he told
us how he delighted in pushing girls down the stairs at school just to see
them get hurt and hear them scream. He loved injuring other kids and
animals.

Alex was well on his way toward becoming a menace to society when
he met a young woman who was a Christian. Why she even dated him,
he's never been able to figure out. But date him she did, and gradually,
over the course of several years, she introduced him to Jesus Christ as his
Saviour. In time he was converted and came to know Jesus as his Best
Friend and the Lord of his life. Today Alex feels that he bonded to Jesus,
who provided the love and security he needed. The transformation did not
happen overnight, but gradually Alex changed. Eventually he married the
young woman who introduced him to Jesus. Today Alex is a minister,
living proof that the Lord has a solution for every problem!

The opposite of the child without a conscience is the one with a
neurotic conscience that constantly condemns. She has a vague, almost

continual feeling of never doing anything right. Such a conscience usually develops from faulty parent-child relationships during childhood. If you are constantly berating your child and giving her the impression she can never do anything right, or punishing her severely for minor infractions, her conscience development will be defective. It will condemn her for almost everything she does. To grow a reasonable conscience, children need reasonable requirements. Don't expect perfection. Allow for childish mistakes and learning. Keep the consequences in keeping with the severity of the infraction. If you punish severely for something minor, your child will think it is a major mistake and conscience development will be distorted. Let your children know when you are pleased with what they have done. They need your compliments because they motivate them toward ethical growth as well as let them know what is good behavior. Without such compliments, children often are not clear about what is right or wrong. They know plenty about what is wrong, but can be hazy about the right way unless you point out the direction clearly.

During early childhood children often have difficulty understanding and acquiring general principles to guide their behavior. They actually learn much better when taught what specific behaviors are right and wrong. The principles will come later. For example, when you say to your 3-year-old "Be kind to your sister," what do you really mean? You probably want Mr. Three to share his toys with his sister, not to hit or to bite her, to play with her without fighting or yelling, and who knows what else! He will learn standards for behavior much more easily if you are more specific about what you want him to do.

You can begin to build understanding of the general principles by pairing the principle statement with a specific action you want the child to do and then explaining the reason for the behavior. For instance, you might say to Mr. Three, "Please don't hit your sister. That hurts her. You want to be kind to your sister." By stating your requirements in this way you have accomplished four important things: 1. Told your child exactly what you want him to do. 2. Given a reason for that behavior that helps your child understand the effects of his actions on other people. 3. Paired the specific action you want with the general principle—kindness. 4. Let your child know that you believe he wants to be good. All four things are vital if you want to help your child to develop an internalized conscience as he grows older, one that will be a suitable guide for his life.

When you pair the specific action you want (don't hit) with a statement of the general principle (kindness), you are assisting your child in developing principles to guide his behavior. In time, as he gets older, such principles will sink in and become part of his conscience and will aid him in making decisions about what to do in different situations.

Children who have learned about the effects of their actions on other people are much more inclined to treat them unselfishly and with respect. Always help your child understand how what he does affects others. As your child gets older, instead of telling him how his sister feels, ask him how *he* thinks she feels. Teaching children to put themselves in someone else's shoes is one of the most effective ways of enabling them to grow up to be empathic, unselfish, and caring adults.

Last, you want your child to think of himself as a kind person, to accept it as part of his personal self-concept. If he does, then he is much more likely to act that way in real-life situations. Keep encouraging him in that direction instead of making him think he is an unkind and selfish person. Children quickly accept the labels we give them and make them part of their self-identity. Give him a good label. Youngsters are especially sensitive to incorporating your labels into their self-concept from 5 to 9 years of age. Because of changes in their thinking processes during these years, they are pulling together their feelings and experiences to form the self-concept they will carry with them for some time to come—perhaps most of their lives.

Guilt is a sign of conscience development. When your 2 or 3-year-old shows signs of feeling guilty when he has done something wrong, you are seeing the beginnings of conscience. Guilt is part of God's plan for alerting us to wrongdoing and should be heeded. But, like many other areas of life, Satan has introduced his own counterfeits for the real thing. He wants to either overwhelm us with guilt (neurotic conscience) or quiet the voice of conscience completely so we will not hear the whisperings of the Holy Spirit ("dead" conscience, or no conscience).

For many years non-Christian psychologists have tried to tell us that all guilt is bad. That we shouldn't make our children feel guilty or have guilt ourselves. After all, we're wonderful people and we're OK. Guilt only makes us feel bad. When you read or hear such ideas, however, please remember that they have in mind Satan's counterfeit for the real thing—neurotic guilt. True guilt is vital in leading people to acknowledge that they are sinners in need of a Saviour and results from the "quickening" of the conscience by the Holy Spirit. Without feelings of guilt for the sin in our lives, we would feel no need of the grace of Jesus Christ. God's type of guilt leads to confession and repentance, keys to a real relationship with Christ. Only His forgiveness erases the guilt.

Some children seem to naturally have a more tender conscience. Be careful with that fragile bud. Occasionally the guilt feelings are all such a child needs to change her behavior. If you punish her severely, you may destroy the guilt feelings and in their place she may feel resentful and angry.

Other children show less guilt, and are less willing to admit they were wrong. Their pride is stronger, and they need much more of the softening influence of the Holy Spirit to respond to the voice of conscience. Pray much for the Holy Spirit to speak to them. You will need to be firmer in your own responses to their behavior, be very clear about right and wrong, insist on a time to "think and pray about it," and be willing to wait patiently for the child to acknowledge his guilt.

Your own role model is an important part of conscience development for your children. If you say to your children, "Always tell the truth," and then try to get your child into the zoo without paying because she is small for her age, she will not miss the unintended lesson. She will hear loud and clear that it isn't always important to tell the truth. Future messages from her own conscience will urge, "Tell the truth only if it is convenient."

Conscience can also be educated through stories from the Bible and other character-building sources. Stories provide a wonderful model for children to follow. A well-told story has great emotional appeal. Children identify with the hero or heroine and want to do what he or she did. Also, stories give children a chance to try out different solutions to problems without actually having to live with the consequences, allowing them an opportunity to learn vicariously. Stories will help a child deal with something that is bothering him. They help introduce a topic and make it all right to talk about it. In moments of temptation, stories flash their insights to help with the decision.

Do you remember those things your mother used to say, such as "Birds of a feather flock together" or "Pride goeth before a fall"? Probably she said them so many times they pop into your mind automatically in certain situations. Your mother was smart. She knew that if she repeated it often enough, somehow it would stick and rise up as a dictate of conscience to guide you later on. Do what your mother did.

Don't pay any attention when your child wiggles his nose and pretends not to hear. He does. Those little guiding principles are slowly but surely being stored away in his little mind, to pop up at the most inconvenient (for him) times!

God's Word is the best conscience builder of all. Fill your child's mind with Bible stories and memory verses. Use Bible passages as key thoughts. As your child grows older, help her find guidance for puzzling things in God's Word. Teach your children that "conscience is a safe guide as long as the Guide of conscience is safe!"

Comparing conscience to something the child has seen or heard makes it easier to understand. You might say conscience is like a whispered voice telling you what to do; a traffic light that flashes stop, go, or be careful; a gong or a bell straight from the throne of God to you; or Satan's voice and God's voice telling you what to do. Use whatever illustration your child best understands.

One of my favorite promises for parents has a lot to say about conscience development, although it doesn't specifically mention conscience. "If we will live in communion with God, we too may expect the divine Spirit to mold our little ones, even from their earliest moments" (*The Desire of Ages*, p. 512). I believe we can claim this promise as we teach our children and help them develop a conscience attuned to God's voice.

KEYS TO CONSCIENCE DEVELOPMENT

1. Strong bonding between infant and parent
2. Reasonable requirements
3. Compliments for right actions
4. Consistent do's and don'ts
5. Consistent consequences for wrong actions
6. Consequences fit the misbehavior
7. Parents model desired behavior
8. Scripture and character-building stories
9. Key guidance thoughts expressed frequently

♥

CHAPTER 7

God and the Child

"The Lord's love never ends. His mercies never stop.
They are new every morning. Lord, your loyalty is great."
—Lamentations 3:22, 23, ICB

Late one afternoon, as I was trying to work through a pile of papers on my desk, a man appeared at the door to my office. He had two boys with him, probably 4 and 6 years old. All three were handsome and attractively dressed. But that is not why I remember their visit.

The man began asking questions about our graduate programs, and soon we were engaged in a lively discussion of the pros and cons of certain courses of study and his personal career goals. In the meantime the two boys began playing in the reception area. Gradually their voices grew louder and louder until suddenly a brotherly quarrel erupted. Obviously we could no longer ignore the boys, and our conversation came to an abrupt halt.

The father responded immediately, but in such an unusual way I was momentarily aghast. Many parents I know would have gone to the boys and reprimanded them firmly, ending with a threat intended to get good behavior. Other parents would have revealed their aggravation and said something such as "Why can't you two behave yourselves while I'm talking? Now sit down, and no more quarreling!" And still others would have yelled at the boys, jerked them over to a chair, and thrown them on it.

My visitor did none of the usual things. Instead, he turned and walked toward the boys, saying in a calm, gentle, and courteous manner, "Gentlemen, please sit here," then pointed to the chairs. The effect was magical. Both boys instantly stopped hassling each other, walked over to the chairs, and sat down, acting, indeed, like the gentlemen they had been called. Until the end of our visit the man's sons remained seated, quietly conversing with each other.

It was obvious the boys were accustomed to being treated with courtesy and smiling gentleness. Their father had no need to yell and scream to be heard. Nor did he need to jerk or shove to get his point across. He made his point quietly, with a smile, and in the most courteous manner possible. I suspect that back of his quiet courtesy were some occasions when his boys had learned that he meant what he said.

Gentle words and loving actions. Calling our children "gentlemen" instead of "brats." Treating each family member with utmost courtesy and kindness. Is that what God meant when He said, "I have loved you with an everlasting love; I have drawn you with loving-kindness" (Jer. 31:3, NIV)?

Introducing our children to the God of the universe is a real challenge. Satan has worked diligently to distort people's ideas about God, to paint a picture of God that makes humans run in the opposite direction. Our job as parents is to create an image of God that will attract our children to Him.

Just as children's thinking changes as they mature, so do their ideas about God. Their concepts about God have fascinated researchers in religious education and child development since the early decades of the twentieth century. Such research conclusions can aid us in understanding our children better and give us ideas for helping them learn about God.

Two- and 3-year-olds often think of God and nature together. Thunder is God being mad. They think God lives in churches or perhaps in heaven. Joy's cradle roll teacher had emphasized that the children should be quiet in church because it was God's house. When Joy arrived in the sanctuary, she eagerly looked all around the building. After a while, with a disappointed look on her face, she whispered loudly to her mother, "Mommy, where's God? I don't see Him." Three-year-old Kevin wanted to know where God sleeps because he didn't see any beds in the church.

Young children also strongly believe that God is magical—He can do anything they want. This leads to a simple belief in God and His care for them. Not questioning how God can do it, they just believe in the magic. He can—that's all that matters. "God can make the rain stop so we can have a picnic." "God can put my dolly back together again."

Four- and 5-year-olds recognize that God is powerful and that He watches over human beings. In their view, God also punishes the bad things people do. They want to get to know God and desire to please Him. Preschoolers describe God in extremely human terms, viewing Him in the same way they do other people.

This is the ideal time to emphasize God's care through the angels. Miss Three and Mr. Four often have a lot of fears—big dogs, thunder and lightning, shadows at night, loud noises. Believing in God's power and the watchfulness of angels can aid them in coping with their fears.

You can motivate Mr. Four and Miss Five to do the right thing because they want to please God. They are also afraid He might punish them for doing something wrong. We need to be careful that this idea doesn't get carried too far, however, because it is easy for young children to associate two totally unrelated events and come up with God as the cause. It's the nature of their thinking during these years.

Five-year-old Allen and his dad were enjoying a weekend camping on the shores of a beautiful mountain lake. Sunday morning they packed a small picnic lunch and took off paddling across the crystalline waters. Gently rocking in the middle of the lake, they stopped to eat a sandwich and a banana. After finishing, Allen threw his banana skin and sandwich bag overboard.

"You shouldn't do that, Allen," his father scolded. "Trash makes the lake yucky. You wouldn't want to camp here if everyone threw trash all over! God wants us to keep everything clean and beautiful."

Allen looked crestfallen. An unexpected clap of thunder drowned his response as a sudden squall began brewing on the horizon.

"Guess we'd better head back for camp," Dad decided as he turned the boat around and began paddling rapidly. But before they could get to shore the rain poured down. Dashing for their tent, they crawled in, wet and cold. Shivering in the dark as the storm thundered and crackled around them, Allen shook his head and sadly announced, "All that because of a banana peel!"

Wanting to please God because we love Him begins with wanting to please Mom and Dad because we love them. Sometimes it is absolutely essential to say there is a rule and if the child breaks the rule, he will be punished. That is the "tough love" side of parents and of God. If the heavenly rules didn't matter in the universe, there would have been no need for Jesus to come and die on the cross because Adam and Eve—and everyone since—disobeyed God's law. However, love sent the Saviour.

HTHYCRLJ-3

We want our children to respond to that love. So we need to emphasize, as much as possible, pleasing God because it is how we show our love for Him.

Beware of religious words. Few children understand the terms churches commonly use to describe God. Even 3- and 4-year-olds may repeat the words, so they appear to understand, but most likely they are only parroting something they have heard adults use. Check up on their understanding all through childhood.

Six- and 7-year-olds still describe God as if He were a human being, but the first traces of their sense of God's divinity now begin to appear. They start to think of God as spirit or as love. Also, they begin to understand that God is not confined to one place, as people are. Mr. Six and Miss Seven find themselves fascinated by the orderliness of God's activities. The details of creation and the way nature functions in orderly fashion intrigue them. They feel secure in the predictability of rules and orderliness. God's rules have great appeal, and they feel close to Him.

Teach your child with nature activities emphasizing the marvelous details of God's handiwork and describe how nature follows the rules He set up. Now is also a great time to introduce the Ten Commandments, God's rules for how people should live. Children need to learn the essential meaning of each commandment and how it applies to daily living. Explain each "rule" in child language.

Emphasize both the "do's" and "don'ts" of each commandment because it helps children understand more clearly what each one means. Take the sixth commandment, for example. Both sides are important: To take care of life is the counterbalance to do not kill.

Miss Six and Mr. Seven are also not too young to learn about the two great rules for life: Love God and love people. They help put the commandments within the perspective of love.

Introducing the Holy Spirit as the third member of the Godhead is appropriate as children begin to think of God as spirit. If your child doesn't seem interested or clearly doesn't understand, wait another year or two.

Eight- and 9-year-olds have much clearer ideas about God as a spirit. They also think of God as a loving all-powerful and all-knowing father. In addition they have a sense of responsibility to work with God and want to participate in church activities. Their personal relationship with God is growing, and they are beginning to feel responsible for other people close to them. Clearly their ideas about God are maturing and their relationship with Him is strengthening. At this stage they are still believers.

Ten- and 11-year-olds have an increasing sense of relationship with God. Their questions clearly indicate they are still searching to understand who God is and how He relates both to them personally and to the rest of the universe. Sometimes their questions reflect an element of doubt as they move toward adolescence.

Twelve and 13 years mark a time of great change in a child's understanding of God. No longer do they describe Him in the specific, concrete words they would have earlier applied to people. They are more likely to employ attributes they have learned from their family and church—loving, just, harsh, critical, benevolent.

God's relationship to nature is less important to them than His dealings with people. Clearly they want a God who cares about people. Their expressions of faith reflect the culture of the church they attend. Eager to participate in church and to contribute to its life, they now see it as a place to learn about God.

As children move into adolescence, the search for meaning in life begins. It may lead to blaming God for the troubles in the world or in their own lives. Other times they may see trouble as a result of not cooperating with God. Some adolescents express continuing faith, while others start to doubt. A number express theoretical or hypothetical questions that seem far removed from a personal relationship with God. Others clearly view God as a guide for their actions.

During early childhood, the fantasy or fairy-tale stage, children tend to think of God as a magical being who can supply all their wants—the Candy Man, as Jack Rodgers put it. But even young children can experience reverence and awe for God.

During the early elementary school years children's ideas about God reflect anthropomorphic concepts. They describe Him in extremely realistic terms as a human being. As children move into preadolescence, however, they begin to understand that God is not like humans, but has His own divine attributes. They start to regard Him as a spirit. At the same time their relationship with God becomes very important.

How Children Get Their Ideas About God

Most children develop their ideas about God during early childhood, mainly from their relationship with their parents. Most of the research studies have concluded that ideas about God come from children's interaction with both parents and are a combination of paternal and maternal characteristics. Sometimes their ideas seem to be more like what they wish their parents were than the reality of what their parents actually are. The styles of parenting described in chapter 3 also influence children's concepts of God.

Children of authoritarian, domineering parents tend to view God as a punishing judge ready to zap them whenever they do anything wrong. Permissive parents often have children who envision God as a gift giver, who showers them with goodies but never expects anything in response, not even a "thank You." The child from a neglectful home generally regards God as an ice sculpture king, impressive in exquisite, cold detail, sitting on a throne high above the clamor of daily needs. Authoritative parents tend to conjure up God in images of a heavenly friend, warm and comfortable like a teddy bear, but also protective and helpful when the child is in distress.

Extremely young children see God reflected in the mirror of their parents' lives. Since they cannot read about God for themselves, their ideas about God get formed by their human relationships. As they grow older they begin to learn about God from their Bible lessons and from other people important to them—their teachers, their pastor, their youth leader, or the parents of their friends. The early ideas about God may change some as they mature but will probably never entirely be obliterated. Throughout life we almost always carry a remnant of the image our parents gave us of God during our early years. We also carry with us the ideas about what we wish our parents had been for us and transfer them to God.

So during adolescence and adulthood our ideas about God become a mixture of early experiences with our parents, our "ideal vision" of what we wish they had been, and what we have learned about God both through studying His Word and through our personal experiences with Him. Culture and the ideas heard from others at church or school get thrown into the mix, too. All this provides great opportunity for Satan to distort our ideas about God—and he makes great use of his chance!

The best remedy for misguided images of God is to study His Word so that we can come to know Him as He describes Himself. It is also an excellent counterbalance to human foibles for our children. Introduce them to the God of the Scriptures. Talk about what He is like and what the different Bible stories tell us about Him. During middle and late elementary school, keep asking your children what the Bible story or lesson tells them about God. Encourage thoughtful ideas. Listen carefully. Respond with some thoughts of your own to keep the dialogue going. Never disparage what your child says about God. Keep your shock to yourself. Simply ask, "What makes you think that?" Then listen for feelings and offer additional ideas for him to think about. Find some Bible verses that might be helpful.

Differences Between Boys and Girls

As children enter adolescence boys' and girls' ideas about God begin to show a striking difference. Boys relate more to God's power and authority. They often don't see Him as a heavenly father unless it involves an authority role. Also, they more often think of God as spirit in an abstract way. Their God seems to be more distant, a powerful being with great authority in the universe but remote and more nebulous.

On the other hand, girls respond more to God's love. They focus on their relationship with Him and much less on authority and power. Theirs is a warmer, closer, more caring God.

The differences between boys and girls have serious implications for helping adolescents grow spiritually. It seems to me that if we emphasize only the relationship and love of God, we may fail to reach the boys. And if we stress only God's power and authority, the girls may be less interested. Obviously, we need to integrate our views of God to include His power and authority as well as His loving relationship with each one of us. Only then will we present the total divine picture.

I have really been struck by how well the results of research in spiritual growth fit with the first steps in spiritual development—love, trust, and obedience. When we combine all of them we are truly presenting a more complete, integrated picture of God. Both boys and girls will be learning that He is loving and caring as well as powerful and the King of the universe.

God always forgives, never gives up, constantly searches for ways to draw each person to Himself. At the same time He is the Creator of the universe, all-powerful and all-knowing. He is the judge and authority in the universe, concerned about the happiness of every one of His created beings. The Lord had to deal with the sin problem in a forceful way the entire universe would understand. And He is ultimately responsible for creating a perfect, sinless universe once again.

God During Difficulties

"Why did God let my mommy go away?" Kevin questioned in a voice filled with anguish. Just a month before, his mother had evidently decided caring for her family and being a doctor's wife was not her idea of a fulfilling life. One day the children came home from school to an empty house and a note saying she did not intend to come back. Now Kevin's dad was struggling to keep his medical practice going and to care for three children at the same time. No wonder 7-year-old Kevin wondered why God had let his mommy go away.

A drunk driver killed Patti's twin sister as the girl crossed the street in a pedestrian crosswalk. Steve's baby sister died of leukemia. Carl and his family came home from vacation to an empty house—robbers had taken everything of any value while they were gone. Maria's father lost his job because a fellow worker misrepresented his work. Where was God when all these tragedies happened? "Where was my angel?" one child demanded. "Doesn't God care about human suffering?" all of them wanted to know. Adults have wrestled with such tough questions through centuries of suffering. How can we possibly explain them to children when our own hearts are bleeding and bruised? But explain we must. We cannot let our children grow up believing God is to blame for all the evil in the world!

One of the best answers to the question "Where was God?" I have ever heard is a very simple one. "Right beside you, crying too!" God is not a spectator to human suffering. Sin wasn't His idea. He is a fellow sufferer, weeping with us, carrying us in His arms when the going is too hard. He goes through the darkness with us and does not stand at the other end waiting for us to emerge from our dark night of despair. Because He cares. Because He loves. Because He feels our heartache. If we can give our children this message, they will come to know the God who cares.

Young children can have extremely distorted ideas about the reasons for the serious difficulties they go through. Their limited thinking abilities create garbled explanations for divorce or death, for example. Because they have difficulty differentiating between fantasy and reality, they believe their thoughts are as powerful as their actions. Thoughts are powerful, sometimes overwhelming. They also have a tendency to pair two events, or a thought and an event, that occurred close together in time as cause and effect. Because of their thinking limitations, most children younger than 7 or 8 years believe that they are personally responsible for the divorce of their parents, a serious illness of a parent, or a death in the family. Even older children conclude that they are to blame for the divorce, although probably not the illnesses.

It works this way. Most children, at some time, get angry at their parents and wish they were dead or at the very least, gone. Some children will actually say it openly, others will only think it. When Daddy leaves the family or Mommy gets sick, they believe those "bad thoughts" were the cause. Most likely they will not acknowledge it, so you will not know how they feel. They will, however, act out their feelings, perhaps get aggressive or withdrawn or misbehave frequently.

You can safely assume that preschoolers have such feelings. So the first thing you must do in dealing with a personal family tragedy is to reassure young children that they are not to blame for what happened. Hug your child and say, "You didn't make Mommy get sick. Mommy got sick because . . . (fill in the correct answer, simply stated). It isn't your fault." Children need to hear such reassurance many times.

Children can get the same type of warped thoughts about God, especially if told repeatedly that "God gets mad (or sad) when you do that." It isn't unusual for preschoolers to think that thunder and lightning are "God being mad" at them because they didn't finish their cereal or they hit baby brother.

Eight- to 12-year-olds may be afraid they will die too. They understand much better than their younger siblings that death is final, but they are still a little vague about the reasons. Thus they need reassurance. Little children need reassurance that someone will continue to take care of them. When one parent has disappeared—for whatever reason—maybe the other one will too. Statements that God will take care of him are not enough. He needs to know there will be a human being.

One day when I was a houseguest at the home of Keith, Karen, and Kris—ages 14, 12, and 8—Keith was in a bicycle accident. A man on a motorcycle had tried to run him off the path. Keith was bruised and scraped but not seriously hurt. That evening I asked the children to each make me a drawing of their family. With paper and pencil each retreated to a separate corner of the house to complete the task. The accident of the day surfaced in each of the drawings, although only Keith actually drew a picture of the event itself. Kris drew herself riding a bicycle with an angel flying above. Karen took 45 minutes drawing a detailed picture of Keith polishing shoes on Friday afternoon and then drew all the rest of her family in five minutes. Each had expressed anxiety about the bicycle accident in different ways, though Keith was more direct. Kris expressed her anxiety through the image of an angel, while Karen symbolized her feelings by concentrating most of her effort on the drawing of Keith, the accident victim.

One of the best ways to find out your child's concerns and worries is through art. Most children love to draw. They don't have the vocabulary to express their feelings, but they can communicate them through art. You could suggest drawing a picture of the accident, the hospital, the funeral, God, the family, etc. Leave the child alone while she is drawing. After she completes the drawing, make a simple comment of approval, such as "O-o-oh, I like your drawing." Then ask her to explain it. "Tell me about your drawing." Never express disapproval, horror, or shock. Accept what your child has drawn as an expression of her feelings, but use your new insight to help her deal with her feelings later.

There is no easy path to learning how to deal with difficulties. God and Satan both work in our world. Understanding their interaction sometimes takes more wisdom than human minds can have. As you yourself discover more about the wisdom of God's ways, you will be more capable of communicating your understanding to your children. Life experiences teach us and our children a great deal. Children can grow through difficulties during childhood to emerge as thoughtful adults who confidently trust in their Lord to lead them through life.

As your children grow older, they need to expand their ideas about God. The God of their early childhood will not be sufficient for later life. As children begin to understand symbolic ideas, usually between 9 and 14 years, you can purposefully help enlarge their understanding of God. The Scriptures are full of God's attempts to help us grasp Him through comparisons to familiar objects. Each illustration has wonderful possibilities for enlarging your child's comprehension. For example, God is the great healer (Ps. 147:3); God is like a potter (Isa. 64:8); God is like a fire (Heb. 12:29); God is a counselor (Isa. 9:6); God is like a mother (Isa. 66:13); God is like an eagle (Deut. 32:10, 11). Todd Temple in his book *52 Simple Ways to Teach Your Child About God* provides 52 different illustrations of God along with activities to help children understand God better. You could learn about one illustration each Sabbath afternoon for a year! Or your children themselves could think of an illustration to expand each Sabbath afternoon through hunting in their Bibles during the week, taking turns proposing the illustration everyone would study the following Sabbath. That could be a lot more fun than just reading one that someone else has had the fun of creating. Generating the ideas won't be hard if you have a computer whiz at your house. A good Bible program could search for God words paired with other words. A Bible concordance would help, too. Or if your children are reading the Junior Bible Year, everyone could look for illustrations of God in the chapters assigned for that week.

Little do we really understand about the God of the universe or even the God of our hearts! We see "through a glass darkly" with our earthbound minds. Every day, through all eternity, we will be learning more about God. No wonder we sometimes find it difficult to explain God to our children when we can hardly explain Him to ourselves. But our eternal understanding begins today. God is eager to help us communicate Himself to our children.

KEYS TO LEARNING ABOUT GOD

1. Children's ideas about God begin with their feelings about their parents.
2. Introduce God in ways appropriate for a child's stage of development.
3. Use Bible stories to introduce children to God. Emphasize what the story tells us about God.
4. Be careful to present a balanced picture of God—loving and merciful as well as powerful and authoritative.
5. Help children realize God is with them through difficulties.
6. Be careful not to distort God through inaccurate descriptions.
7. Purposefully expand children's ideas about God through biblical analogies and descriptions of God.

CHAPTER 8

God and His Word

"Your word is like a lamp for my feet
and a light for my way."
—Psalm 119:105, ICB

Childhood is a once-in-a-lifetime opportunity to fill our children's minds with thoughts of God and His Word. Their curiosity about the world and eagerness to learn can easily be channeled into a lifelong discovery about God and the Bible. How can we introduce children to Scripture so that they will develop a real love affair with God's Word?

First, **show your child how much you personally love and respect God's Word**. Ruth Graham, wife of the world-famous evangelist Billy Graham, decided when she was 10 years old that she wanted to read the Bible for herself because all the adults in her family seemed to gain so much pleasure from God's Word. She desired to find out for herself what it was they enjoyed so much. Her missionary parents never missed reading the Bible early in the morning. Even the Chinese servant who lived and worked in their home seemed to love reading her Bible. And so Ruth was irresistibly drawn to God's Word because of the example of the adults most important to her.

Traditionally Adventists have been known as "people of the Word." We talk about the importance of the Bible and preach glowingly of the wonders found in its sacred pages. However, our lives often deny our words. Children learn what we live, not what we preach. If you want your child to really love God's Word, show your own love for the Scriptures in unmistakable ways.

Having to hunt all over the house for your Bible as you rush out the door to Sabbath school because you haven't used it since last Sabbath sends the clear message to your child that it is only important when going to church. It has no relevance for everyday living. On the other hand, if Mom and Dad reverently and lovingly read God's Word each day at the family altar, openly turn to the Bible for answers to problems, and frequently claim its promises for the family's needs, the implication is quite different.

Demonstrate your respect and love for the Scriptures by having a special place of honor where you keep the family Bible. Show your child how to place the Bible on top of other books, in the place of honor because it is God's Word. As a small child my parents taught me that the Bible was not like other books. It is God's Word and should be treated with respect. We should never carelessly throw the Bible on the seat of the car or toss it on the floor. Place no other book or object on top of it. (Note: some cultures might place the Bible at the bottom of a stack of books because it is the foundation of everything else. It is their way of showing respect.) That childhood lesson has stayed with me all my life. I believe it has added immensely to my respect for God's Word.

Refer to the Bible with love and joy. Show your own pleasure in reading God's Word. Frequently share with your family a special insight gained from Scripture during your time with the Lord. With your children, turn to God's Word when your family faces a problem. Claim a special Bible promise and seek God's guidance. If you freely share your joy in God's Word, your children will eagerly want what you have.

Second, **associate Bible learning with your love and care**. God intended childhood memories to provide a lasting association between parental love and God's love. Make Bible learning a special family time. Each day read a short passage from the Bible for family devotions. Use a modern version children can more easily understand and explain what the verses mean. Make it a special time for family togetherness and closeness.

Never use the Bible as a "hammer" to beat a child into submission. Certainly God's Word has specific instructions for how a Christian should live, but the manner in which we teach the Bible will make the difference between acceptance and rejection. Children must learn about God's way of living in an atmosphere of loving support, never one of angry confrontation and put-downs.

Third, **make Bible learning fun and interesting**. Your goal is to create many happy memories associated with God's Word. Bible games, role playing, audiotapes, pictures, video tapes, and other visuals all help make Bible learning fun for younger children. Choose a modern version of the Scriptures that children can comprehend more easily.

Use Bible-learning activities adapted to the age of the child. Introduce older children to Bible customs and other background material that will make the stories more interesting. Give your child a special Bible of her own—one of the children's editions, such as the *International Children's Bible* or a large-print edition for young readers. Create opportunities for her to use the Bible during family worship and encourage her to take it to church.

Angry and negative feelings engendered by bad experiences with God's Word can close the door to any future desire for hearing the voice of God through His Written Word. By letting your child see your own love and respect for the Scriptures, associating Bible learning with paternal love and care, and making Bible learning interesting and fun, you will be setting the stage for helping your children want to be involved in a lifelong relationship with God and His Word. They will have positive feelings about Scripture.

Bible Study Developmental Tasks for Children

Several of the developmental tasks that help children grow spiritually involve the Scriptures. They include:
1. Understanding why the Bible was written
2. Getting to know the people of the Bible as friends and admired heroes
3. Enjoying reading the Bible
4. Seeking help from the Bible for daily living
5. Memorizing significant Bible passages
6. Understanding how the Bible was written
7. Learning how people lived in Bible times
8. Knowing and accepting the major doctrines of the SDA Church as personal beliefs
9. Beginning to learn about Bible history and prophecy

Of course, all such developmental tasks are at a beginning level suited to children. The depths of God's Word can be endlessly explored. During childhood we can only introduce children to the wonders of a lifelong love affair with God's Word. As in all great love affairs, the relationship will deepen with the passage of time.

Keep these developmental tasks in mind as we explore in more detail how to acquaint our children with the Divine Word.

How to Teach the Bible to Children

Presenting the Bible to your child is fundamentally different from teaching math or history facts. The Bible is God speaking to human beings so they might know and love Him. We cannot leave the encounter to chance but must use the best methods possible.

Ellen White has given us rich insights into how to open the Bible to children so they will accept its principles and come to love God and His written message. Some have to do with a knowledge of the Bible, some with attitudes or feelings about it, and others with our action response to Scripture.

Each of the three areas is important to a total response to God's Word. Knowledge forms the foundation for what we believe about God. But it is not enough. Many people know what God says but do not act in accordance with it. In order to have a vibrant relationship with our Lord, the end result of a knowledge of God's Word must be a life response. Without it, knowledge is of no value.

When children memorize verses from the Bible or learn about the life of Joseph, they add to their biblical knowledge. But they must go beyond that. For them to use a Bible verse to help when confronted with a problem in living or to follow the example of Joseph when deciding about moral living is an action response to the Divine Word.

Attitudes or feelings often determine whether or not a person will make that response. If children have generally negative experiences with biblical teachings, they will more likely reject what they have been taught and thus will not respond to the prompting of the Holy Spirit. So as we teach our children from God's Word, we must keep in tune with their attitudes and feelings. Unless our children respond to the "still, small voice" speaking to them through the Scriptures, we have failed. They have not really met the living God through His Word. Instead, they have only memorized words in the same way they acquire history or geography facts in school.

The following chart summarizes the ideas Ellen White suggests for teaching the Bible. You will observe that many of them apply to more than one area of learning. Notice how many concepts have to do with attitudes or feelings toward the Bible. Obviously it is vital that we teach our children in such a way that they will develop positive attitudes toward Scripture.

Long speeches and prayers, tedious remarks, hard-to-understand words, and negative feelings turn children off. Cheerfulness, happiness, love, tenderness, and sympathy inspire them. The Bible is more interesting when we use nature objects, music, everyday events and objects, attractive visual illustrations, and stories in our teaching.

Children are more likely to make an action response to the Bible's teachings when we emphasize positive principles rather than attack their wrong habits. Showing the Bible reasons for faith, relating Scripture to the child's interests, helping children think independently about what the Bible teaches, and making an application of what they have discovered to their own lives all encourage a positive action response.

As we explore more about how to introduce our children to God's Word, we will expand and clarify some of the following ideas to make them practical for teaching in the family.

PRINCIPLES AND METHODS FOR BIBLE TEACHING

Principle or Method	Area of Learning
Teach simply. Use easy words.	Knowledge/Feeling
Don't rush learning. Use short, frequent periods of instruction.	Knowledge Feeling
Show Bible reasons for faith.	Knowledge
Use nature to teach spiritual truths.	Knowledge
Use music to teach Scripture.	Knowledge
Use familiar objects and everyday events to clarify the Bible.	Knowledge Feeling and Action
Use audiovisual aids to keep interest and explain teaching.	Knowledge Feeling
Let children explain in their own words what they have learned.	Knowledge Action
Use stories and illustrations to impress truth upon the heart.	Feeling and Action
Teach with a cheerful, happy spirit.	Feeling and Action
Teach with love, tenderness, and sympathy.	Feeling and Action

Teach positive principles rather than attacking wrong habits.	Feeling and Action
Relate the Bible to child's interests.	Feeling and Action
Avoid long speeches and prayers, tedious remarks.	Feeling
Help children think independently about Bible truths.	Feeling and Action
Be a model of your teaching.	Feeling and Action
Help child make a personal application to own life.	Action

If you are interested in exploring these ideas as Ellen White herself explained them, you will find them in the following references:

Counsels to Parents and Teachers, pp. 169, 181-183, 434

The Ministry of Healing, pp. 23, 24

Education, pp. 114, 120, 167, 168, 185-192

The Desire of Ages, pp. 516, 517

Fundamentals of Christian Education, p. 390

Child Guidance, pp. 496, 505-516, 534, 535

Testimonies, vol. 1, p. 157; vol. 5, p. 330

Counsels on Sabbath School Work, pp. 77, 114-119

Christ's Object Lessons, p. 25

Memorizing Scripture

Since the Bible is such a special book, quite different from all other books, it can have a profound effect on how we think and act. According to Ellen White, studying and memorizing the Bible can expand our ability to learn other things, improve our reasoning abilities, and give us clear comprehension and judgment as well as balance. Certainly studying God's Word improves our understanding of Him and His way.

One day I came across the following Ellen White statement: "Children should be so instructed that they will be familiar with God's Word, and be able to know when part of a scripture is read and part left unread in order to make a false impression" (*Evangelism*, p. 591). All I could say was, "Wow! What a lot of Bible memorizing . . . to know when something is left out!'' No slouchy mumbling the verse on Sabbath morning just to get a sticker. Learning Scripture is clearly a vital part of children's spiritual development.

Learning the memory verse is a long-time tradition in the Adventist Church, even for young children. One Sabbath morning, while hostessing at one of the entrances to our church, a young mother stopped to talk with me. Her face lit up enthusiastically when I asked about her two small sons, ages 1 and 2-and-a-half years. As we conversed she told me how hard she was working to help her older son learn Scripture verses.

"As you know," she elaborated, "it's really important for him to learn many Bible verses while he's young. I've hit upon a method that really works. When I go to get him out of his crib in the morning or after a nap, I won't pick him up until he has said a Bible verse. And when we're eating, he has to say a Bible verse to get another bite of banana, for example. We do that all day. Whenever he wants anything, he has to say a verse before he can have it. It really works. You'd be amazed how many verses he knows!''

After she went into the sanctuary with her children I felt troubled. While I applauded her desire to help her son learn Scripture passages, her method bothered me. I wondered if her son was learning some things she hadn't counted on—"Mommy only loves me when I say Bible verses," for example. "I have to earn my hugs and my food by saying Bible verses," "Bible verses get me what I want," or "If I don't say the verse right, Mommy won't love me."

Of course her method worked—conditioning has always been highly effective. But what was she conditioning her son to think and feel about the Bible? As children memorize Bible verses they also experience feelings and emotions that get paired with the Bible verse, also through a process of conditioning. In years to come, those feelings can encourage or discourage their reading of Scripture.

Offering children incentives to learn a Bible verse is a time-honored way of encouraging Bible learning. At Sabbath school and day school we often give stickers to children who know the memory verse as a method of recognizing effort. What bothered me about my young friend's method was withholding what is every child's right—food and love—unless the child said the Bible verse. Feelings of rejection or a need to earn Mommy's love—or Jesus' love—could easily get paired with Bible learning and later lead to either feelings of rejection by God or to a need to earn His favor.

Learning Bible verses and stories should be fun and interesting and be associated with family togetherness and love. Young children can absorb the Bible just as eagerly and joyously as they do the rest of their world. And as they do so, then they will be associating joy and happiness with God's Word.

Young children pick up things easily. They can memorize a Bible verse with only a little effort. However, they forget just as rapidly. Easy come, easy go is the way it is for preschoolers. Because they have not developed strategies to help themselves remember, they are simply dependent on hearing the verse. If you want your preschoolers to remember Bible verses, you need to review them frequently. Children quickly associate a verse with a picture. Remember the memory verse booklets they used to give out in Sabbath school when you were a child? They are now available as a set of cards at your local Adventist Book Center. Each week make a game of reviewing all the verses for the current quarter using the memory verse booklet. Explain the meaning of the passage and employ it in a real-life situation in which it can bring comfort or instruction to your child. Sing the Bible verse (music, tapes, and videos are available through your local ABC). Encourage 4- to 8-year-olds to draw a picture about the verse. Say the verse yourself, but leave out key words and let your child "fill in the blanks." If your child learns in all these different ways, he will remember the verse for the rest of his life.

The golden years for memorizing biblical passages are from second or third grade through high school. Most children memorize easily during those years and have developed memory strategies that help them retain material. Memorizing the Bible will never be so easy again. During the primary and junior years you should take advantage of their ability with a planned program of acquiring key Bible passages. If your child is not learning significant Bible passages in school or Sabbath school, take charge of your child's religious education and do it at home. Following is a list of Bible selections that should be part of the memory bank of every child growing up in a Christian home:

Psalm 23   Revelation 12:6-12
Psalm 91   Matthew 6:9-13
Exodus 20:3-17   Matthew 5:3-12
1 Corinthians 13   Psalm 27:1-5
John 14:1-3   John 3:16
Revelation 22:1-7

Memorizing Scripture can be fun if you make it a game. Divide the passage into smaller sections. Illustrate them with pictures that clarify the meaning. Many Bible passages have been set to music. If you have ever sung in Handel's *Messiah*, you know the power of music to impress Scripture upon the mind. Make the memory project a family affair with Mom and Dad joining in too. Offer an incentive for completing a memory project.

An effective way to help children learn longer passages of Scripture is to make an illustrated booklet. Use an attractive picture on one side and the words for one verse or phrase opposite the picture. Illustrated Scripture booklets are available for selected well-known Bible passages from Thy Word Creations (Route 76, Box 28, Glenville, WV 26351). The packets come with the illustrated booklet and an audiotape of the Bible passage set to music.

Select a Bible version for memorizing and stick with it. Use it for family worship and elsewhere around the home. When your family employs a different version each time the Bible is read, you will lose the effect of repetition and your children will find it much more difficult to memorize Scripture. For family worship it would be helpful to have a copy of the same version of the Bible for each family member so everyone can follow the reading. By the time your children reach their earliteen years they will probably enjoy using different versions for family worship. They like variety and will enjoy hearing the Bible thoughts expressed in different ways.

Your child will have a more solid foundation for later years if you select a translation rather than a paraphrase. The translations attempt to be faithful to the original languages of the Bible. The paraphrases are rather freewheeling in the way they interpret the thought of the verse. Key Adventist doctrines sometimes get muddled in the process, although the paraphrases are wonderful to read devotionally to gain new insight into the meaning of a passage.

The newer translations take advantage of more information about the original manuscripts than was available in 1611 when the King James Version first appeared. I'm sure your pastor would be happy to discuss the merits of the different versions with you. Generally the King James or the New King James Version, the New International Version, and the Revised Standard or the New Revised Standard Version are well respected. While you will find other reputable translations, the Sabbath school quarterlies and the Bible curriculum for the elementary school generally employ these three main versions.

Making the Bible Live for Children

One day 3-year-old Kevin is a mooing cow and the next an airplane zooming around the house. He has several imaginary friends—people and animals—he delights to play with, making up all the conversation, performing the actions for everyone, and pulling his mom into the drama. He doesn't need many props—many times the whole dialogue is totally imaginary. Kevin isn't unusual—most 3- to 5-year-olds have imaginary friends and love to make up stories. You can use their vivid fantasy life to help your child learn to love the Bible and delight in its stories.

During early childhood children naturally tend to think of an anthropomorphic God—a God who has human form and acts like a human being. They imagine Him as being like themselves or their parents. So pretending to be a Bible character is natural and easy for them. After children start school they gradually become more self-conscious and playacting disappears along with the imaginary friends of earlier years.

For Friday evening worship, or on Sabbath afternoon, your whole family could playact some of the Bible stories. Costumes aren't important. Two- and 3-year-olds usually don't like to dress up, although 4- to 6-year-olds generally do. You can easily transform an oblong piece of plain or striped cloth into a head covering by making an elastic circle to go around the child's head and holding the cloth in place with the elastic. It will look surprisingly like the pictures of Bible people. A basket and a doll easily become Baby Moses. A large cardboard box converts to an ark with stuffed animals lined up to enter.

Let the story dialogue flow naturally. Don't demand too much reality from the children—they will have their own creative ways of imagining what Moses or Noah said or did. That's part of the fun. Getting into the feelings of Bible people brings Scripture to life.

A sandbox is wonderful for Bible drama. Sticks for people, folded paper for tents, a few small branches for trees, tin foil for rivers and lakes, a bit of Play-Doh, and—presto!—a Bible scene appears. A blanket becomes Samuel's bedroll as you playact God's call to a small boy, and a basket carries the loaves and fishes to share with the crowd. Imagining what heaven and the new earth will be like encourages children to want to live there (see *Child Guidance*, p. 488).

Five- to 10-year-olds enjoy painting, coloring, and cutting. You'll love their interpretations of Bible stories as they draw, paint, or make a collage. Again, don't insist on absolute accuracy—let them enter into the mood of the Bible stories. What you want to discover is what they think and feel, so let creativity take over. Never make a disparaging remark about their efforts, because you want to generate an atmosphere of acceptance and love to associate with Bible learning.

Eight- to 12-year-olds will enjoy hearing about Bible times and culture so they can understand the Bible stories better. A number of books provide wonderfully descriptive pictures of life in Palestine during the period of the Old and New Testament. They will add immeasurably to bringing the Bible to life for your children. Today most children in modern metropolitan areas have no idea what a shepherd does when he takes care of the sheep. Yet the Scriptures repeatedly use it as an illustration of Christ's love. To fully understand the meaning of the shepherd analogy, children need to learn about sheep and shepherds. Many other Bible stories remain relatively meaningless until children understand about the Bible culture and way of living.

Older children love to play Bible charades in which they act out Bible stories and let the rest of the group guess the story they are portraying. They also enjoy putting themselves in the place of a Bible character and writing or acting out how the person felt at a particular moment. You can set the stage by telling a Bible story and stopping at the crucial moment and asking the children to fill in how the person felt. For example, pause when Joseph's brothers throw him into the well. How did he feel? What was he thinking? Have each member of the family write out what he or she thinks is going on in Joseph's mind, then share with each other.

Creatively imagining the Bible story leads into a love affair with God's Word. The Bible becomes more than a dry book about ancient people. It comes alive with boys and girls, men and women who have the same feelings we do, who face the same temptations, and who have conquered the same way we do—through Christ. Entering into the lives of Bible people lays a strong foundation for spirituality—that intimate relationship with God that bonds us to Him forever.

The children's Sabbath school lessons provide a systematic way of learning about the most important stories of the Bible. They select 16 Bible stories for children under 2 years, 52 Bible stories for children ages 2 to 4 years, and 156 Bible stories for children ages 4 to 10 years. Each week the quarterly has a new Bible story. Studying the Bible story with your child every day will have a great impact on her learning. The quarterlies also contain related activities that emphasize the main points of the Bible story and make it more interesting.

As the week progresses, older children especially like some variety. After studying from the quarterly for three or four days, you might introduce some new material. Read the story from the Bible itself (a modern version). Then read it from another book of Bible stories, such as *My Bible Friends*, *The Bible Story*, *Bible Pageant*, and *Forever Stories* (all available at your local Adventist Book Center) or other books of Bible stories you might find at your local religious bookstore. Older children might enjoy hearing the story from the Conflict of the Ages Series by Ellen White. Children usually love the dramatized Bible stories available on audiocassette tapes. Another day you might dramatize the Bible story yourself, as suggested earlier. Additionally, the children might teach you the Bible story or draw a series of pictures that they could staple into a booklet. Video producers are taking advantage of the interest of Christian parents in Bible stories for their children by producing video versions. But don't rush out to buy just any Bible videos. Many are purely commercial ventures by people who have little respect for the Word of God. Recognizing a potential market, they have gone after it. So don't be an unsuspecting sucker!

Before you make your decision, let's take a look at videos through a child's eyes. Research on television and children has clearly revealed that most children don't distinguish well between fantasy and real life until they are 6 or 7 years old. Young children tend to think of TV or videos as "real life," not fantasy. If real life disagrees with TV, then real life is wrong and the TV story is right. In other words, children get their facts from TV or videos.

While 8- to 10-year-olds can more readily distinguish between fantasy and real life, they can easily get confused about facts. During these years children are acquiring information about the world and learning the rules by which the universe functions. Videos that present a distorted view of reality confuse them.

Getting the facts straight is crucial in learning about the Bible. If Bible facts are "crooked," we have helped children build a "house upon the sand" belief that will not withstand the storms of later questioning. Therefore, the first questions to ask when selecting Bible videos are: **1. How accurately do they portray the Bible story?** A Bible video I watched recently showed the Israelites digging a tunnel beneath the walls of Jericho to help them conquer the city. Would this video tend to confuse a child about the facts of the Bible? Most likely. Nowadays Sabbath school teachers sometimes hear children protest that the Bible story ''isn't that way'' and then describe what they have seen on some video. Confusing facts tend to undermine faith in the Bible.

2. What role does God appear to have in the affairs of earth? Some of the Bible videos I have watched recently minimize God. The imaginary modern children introduced into the story seem to be actually controlling the outcome. I believe that such a device has the subtle, but faith-damaging, effect of downplaying God's role in the universe. As adults we can easily toss such fantasy aside, but children believe the video message. Ask yourself, does a particular video tend to create greater confidence in God's leading in the affairs of the universe? Or does it imply that humans are the ones really in control? The answer is vital for teaching children to trust in God.

3. How true-to-life is the role of the Bible and the modern characters? When the child characters control the affairs of nations, as some Bible videos portray, we are teaching our children an unrealistic view of life. Again, the impact of the Bible story suffers. Bible biographies are the most true-to-life narratives available. God evidently intended for us to learn from real-life experiences.

When fantasy takes a major role, it may cause children to think of the Bible story as ''just another cartoon.'' Obviously, we want our children to learn that the Bible is God's Word and truthfully tells us what has happened in the past. It is not a cartoon. Confidence in God for the future rests largely on knowing that His Word is truth and that He is in control of the universe.

Expanding Bible Understanding

As your children grow older, just teaching Bible stories is not enough. They need to put a solid foundation under their knowledge of Scripture by learning about the background of the Bible. If your children do not attend church school, you will need to take a carefully planned approach to religious education or they will be shortchanged. Even if your children are in church school, you need to check up to be sure they are getting the foundation they need for understanding the Scriptures.

The following areas are all important in building a solid foundation for the Scriptures:

1. views of biblical inspiration
2. how and why the Bible was written
3. how we got the Bible

4. Bible geography, customs, lifestyle, and culture

5. using the Bible—finding a Bible reference or books of the Bible by sections

6. using reference books to help in Bible study (Bible concordance, atlas, dictionary, commentary, encyclopedia, *SDA Bible Students' Source Book*)

7. beginning principles for interpretation of the Bible:
    (a) context
    (b) unity of Scripture
    (c) important themes of Scripture
    (d) Bible as final authority

8. referencing or cross-referencing subjects in the Bible (e.g., What does the Bible say about friendships?)

9. overall view of historical events period by period

10. most important key texts for doctrines of the Adventist Church

Sounds like a lot, doesn't it? It is, but the Bible is worth the effort! When your 10-, 12-, or 14-year-old protests that the Bible is "boring," bring out one more new thing from the list above.

Remember, you are in charge of your child's religious education and his introduction to God's Word. Sabbath school teachers and day school teachers are only your helpers. Check up on what your child is learning to be sure she is getting the needed tools to make Bible study exciting and meaningful.

Personalizing the Bible

If the Bible is going to speak to your child, it must have personal meaning. It must be something more than a collection of stories about ancient peoples and strange symbols written in archaic language. Instead, it must settle itself squarely into the middle of your child's life *today*. What can you do to help it happen?

First, **relate the Bible to your child's interests**. Is your child a "bug" fan right now? Help him find Bible passages about insects. Make a collection of pictures of Bible insects. Read Bible stories in which insects played an important role (e.g., plagues on Egypt). Help him figure out what God wants to teach him from such verses and stories.

Is your preteen girl absorbed with her appearance? Find all the Bible references to women and their personal appearance—not just injunctions about appearance but actual descriptions of biblical women and how they looked. If she is artistic, have her draw pictures of them based on how the

Bible depicts them. Go to the Bible encyclopedia to find illustrations of dress in Bible times.

Since the Bible relates stories about real people in real times, you will usually be able to find a counterpart to most modern interests. You may have to use some creativity of your own to make the connections, but I believe God will give you ideas. After all, He is exceedingly interested in helping your child love His Word. Maybe your child's big interest is computers. Obviously the Bible doesn't mention computers, but it does talk about the mind and how it functions. Computers are a kind of mind, and you might make a connection in this way. Computers are also a way of communicating with other people. How did people communicate in Bible times? Your miniature computer hack might like to write programs to study the Bible or for Bible games.

Second, **relate the Bible to your child's needs**. My earliest clear memory of using the Bible to meet a serious personal need happened when I was in fourth grade. As a child I was shy and many times almost overwhelmed by fears. When I was 9 years old, the daughter of one of the employees of the Adventist publishing house near where we lived was murdered. Two masked men shot her when she opened the door in response to their knock. Additionally, in our neighborhood two children had been kidnapped. The events had left me terrified. As I ran the two blocks to school every day with my heart pounding in my throat, I kept repeating "The angel of the Lord encampeth round about them that fear him, and delivereth them" every inch of the distance. For many months it was the only way I could gather enough courage to walk to school. Our family didn't own a car, so I had no other way to get there. Gradually, over time, my fears subsided, but Psalm 34:7 remains indelibly imprinted on my mind.

God's Word responds to all human needs. Help your children find solace and comfort, courage and love in the divine words. If your child is fearful, assist her in finding a verse that speaks to that concern. Memorize the verse together and remind her of its promise whenever she is fearful. God's Word has power to help her cope with her fears. Low self-esteem, difficulty with studies, the desire for friends, loss of a friend or family member, lack of confidence, anger, courage to share Jesus with someone, and the drive for love are only a few of the childhood concerns that can be met through the assurances of God's Word. A book of Bible promises will aid in finding just the right verse to meet your child's needs.

Before children can read, they can find reassurance in Bible promises they have memorized. When your 4-year-old doesn't want to go to bed because he is afraid of the ''monster'' in his room, repeating a Bible verse about protection can be comforting. After children learn to read, you or they can copy the promise on a card to keep with them all day long or to post on their bulletin board.

Here are a few Bible promises to get you started:

Fearful	Psalm 56:3; Psalm 34:7; Psalm 50:15; Psalm 118: 6, 7
Lonely	Hebrews 13:5; Matthew 28:20
Tempted	1 Corinthians 10:13
Helpless	Isaiah 41:10
Weak	Isaiah 40:31; Deuteronomy 33:27
Studies	James 1:5, 6
Divorce	Psalm 27:10; Isaiah 49:15
Self-esteem	Romans 8:38, 39; Jeremiah 31:3; 1 John 3:1
Sleep	Psalm 4:8 (TEV)

A number of years ago I read in *Guideposts* magazine about a family who took the injunctions in Deuteronomy 6:6-8 literally when they built their new home. Each person selected a Bible verse he or she especially liked and had it woodburned into the ceiling beams in that person's bedroom. The family together selected the verses they used for the joint living areas of the house. You could do the same with posters or a beautifully lettered version of your child's favorite verse.

Third, **turn to the Bible for direction in puzzling situations**. Suppose your son comes home one day shaking and visibly frightened. After much coaxing, you finally get him to tell you that a bully who lives down the street beat him up and threatened to do it every day if he told anyone. You feel enraged and angry. How can you comfort your son? Does the Bible provide directions for what to do in such a situation?

The next day your daughter comes home from school upset because the teacher has just assigned new seats and she has to sit next to a girl who cannot control her bladder and ''smells awful.'' What can you tell your daughter? Does the Bible provide directions for what to do in a situation like this?

Helping children learn to find Bible principles to help solve everyday problems is an important key to aiding them in developing a real relationship with God's Word. Searching together for God's answers provides not just the solution to the problem but a close tie between you and your children. As your children approach the teen years, study together to find Bible principles to deal with teenage problems such as dating, personal adornment, and entertainment. Such principles will help smooth the turbulent seas of the teen years.

Most important of all, personalize God's call to repentance and salvation for your child by helping him find Bible verses that deal with sin, repentance, forgiveness, and salvation. Such passages begin to take on more individual meaning when your child inserts her name in the verse. "For God so loved Becky that He gave His only begotten Son . . ." Another way to personalize the verses is for the child to write his own paraphrase. Depending on your child's verbal skills, 10- to 14-year-olds usually enjoy doing it once they get the hang of it.

Obviously the Bible has endless possibilities. In this chapter we have only begun to touch the proverbial "tip of the iceberg." I hope it has inspired you to mine deeper in God's Word and to introduce your child to the joy it provides. You will always be glad you did.

KEYS TO BIBLE LEARNING

1. Show your own love and respect for God's Word.
2. Associate Bible learning with your love and care.
3. Make Bible learning fun and interesting.
4. Teach for knowledge, feeling, and action.
5. Have a plan for memorizing Scripture. Make it fun.
6. Make the Bible stories live.
7. Teach your child how to use Bible study tools.
8. Personalize the Bible for your child.

CHAPTER 9

Doctrines for Children

"The one who reads the words of God's message is happy.
And the people who hear this message and do
what is written in it are happy."
—Revelation 1:3, ICB

- Johnie's friend said Jesus was going to burn all the bad people when He returns. Now he feels afraid, worried that maybe God will burn him up.
- Kristi's Sabbath school teacher said Jesus would come soon. When Mommy and Daddy leave for the evening, she wonders whether Jesus might arrive while they are gone. How would He find Mommy and Daddy?
- Mommy said everybody would see Jesus when He comes back. Joey wonders if He will be on TV.
- Sharon's kindergarten teacher said people would go up in the air to meet Jesus. The girl wonders whether the people will travel in airplanes or helicopters.

Theological doctrines and religious concepts are really complex ideas. They develop through a process of comparing different passages in the Bible and attempting to logically reach clear conclusions about what the Scriptures teach on a certain point. The theological discussions that erupt from time to time in all churches remind us of the complexity of understanding Scripture.

So how can we teach doctrine and other religious concepts to children? First, we need to understand a little about how their thinking develops. Babies and toddlers learn by trying to make sense of all the sensory experiences that bombard them: hearing, seeing, touching, and tasting. From their sensory experiences they eventually learn that stones are hard and fur is soft or that a round ball will roll down the hill away from them. It takes many, many experiences to figure out complex ideas.

Preschool children have difficulty putting all the facts together to form a concept. For example, a young child might call every four-footed creature a "doggie" until he sorts out the differences between dogs and cats and rabbits. Eventually he realizes that all of them are animals, a more inclusive category. We would then say a child has formed the concept of "animals." Facts can be especially disjointed for preschoolers, and even for children during the early years of elementary school. Unrelated facts get paired together and create confusion.

Theological and doctrinal concepts develop in the same way. Many different experiences enter into a child's evolving ideas. A child learning about the second coming of Jesus might have some of the following thoughts or experiences influence her:

- Tommy saw a picture of Jesus' return and noticed the open graves. He felt afraid.

- Jack sees a picture of a smiling Jesus with a boy on His lap. They look happy. He wonders whether he will sit on Jesus' lap when He comes.

- Daddy said Jesus was mad at James because he told a lie. Now James doesn't want Jesus to come, and is afraid.

- Daddy read a story about heaven that had a picture of a family in white robes. Peter thinks that wouldn't be very much fun—he couldn't play because his robe would get dirty.

All of these ideas—and many more—may form a part of the child's thoughts about the second coming of Christ. The more a child hears religious ideas, the easier it will be for him to learn theological concepts. Only then will he have many opportunities to "put the pieces together." As children get older they begin to understand better because of the many life experiences they have had.

Understanding theological doctrines has a direct relationship to the child's maturing thinking processes. A highly intelligent child may understand doctrinal ideas earlier. By the time most children reach a mental age of 10 or 12 years, they are capable of beginning to deal with the key text approach to Bible doctrines. They are learning to think logically and come to conclusions based on putting together facts from many sources.

Before then they have a rudimentary understanding of some of the more important ideas related to religious doctrines, but the total picture can be inaccurate or incomplete. By the time most children start school, if they have been reared in a Christian home and taught lessons from the Bible regularly, they have ideas about many doctrines. They know Jesus is returning again to take people to heaven with Him. The Sabbath is a special day. Jesus made the world. He died on a cross to "save" people (but they probably have only the vaguest idea of what this means). God sends angels to take care of people and hears and answers prayers.

During the early elementary school years ideas about doctrines become clearer but can still be quite inaccurate. Children at this age do not identify doctrines as the beliefs of a particular church. Even 10- to 12-year-olds have a hard time identifying the beliefs of their church. This understanding does not usually come into focus until the teen years. If you were to ask your 10-year-old "What do Adventists believe?" you might be surprised at the response. Unless children have specifically been taught that Adventists have certain beliefs, they do not put the things they know about religion together with being an Adventist or with the concept of church beliefs. Generally they are not aware of the doctrinal differences between churches. The exception might be a child whose parents belong to different denominations and have emphasized doctrinal perspectives in the home. Or a child in a public school who must explain why he can't come to the band concert on Friday night. You can help your child grow in understanding of church doctrine, for example, by frequently mentioning that Adventists believe that Jesus is coming again because the Bible says so. And you can do the same for all the doctrines you want your child to know.

During the preteen years begin to teach your child key Bible texts related to church doctrines. You could use the junior baptismal materials or *Good News for Today—Kid's Lessons* (by Marjorie Gray), a workbook about SDA doctrines written especially for junior-earliteens. Both sets are available through your Adventist Book Center. They are designed to teach children the most important doctrines of the Scriptures and to lead them to make a decision to accept the salvation Christ offers. It is important that every child have some formal exposure to doctrine before adolescence.

Children form misconceptions about scriptural ideas for many reasons. One involves information overload. Too much television can clutter a child's mind with ideas that she doesn't really organize or assimilate. Sometimes we mistake quantity for quality. Our children really learn better when they do not have an overdose of material. It might be better to know fewer memory verses and really understand their meaning and use in daily living than to be able to repeat many passages but not have any understanding of what they say.

Sometimes children misunderstand what adults are trying to say and don't have the mental capacity yet to check their own observations with what they have been told. They depend a great deal on their senses because of their still-limited ability to make judgments and to reason clearly. But the senses can be deceptive.

In addition, children may have had previous experiences that lead to incorrect conclusions. Susie told her Vacation Bible School teacher that she was sure there wasn't any God. When her teacher asked why, she responded, "There isn't any Santa Claus, and so there isn't any God!" In her mind God and Santa Claus were the same.

When words have more than one meaning, children can easily become confused. We may be clear about what we mean, but the child may interpret our words in a quite different way. Children interpret in the light of their own experiences. One little boy thought Peter walked on water covered with ice—a logical conclusion for a child from a cold climate, but certainly not the biblical view! Children also sometimes hear words incorrectly and fill in the missing information in any way that seems logical to them. Like the little girl who thought Adam and Eve had a boy and a girl—Cain and Mabel (from *Faith, Hope, and Hilarity*, by Dick Van Dyke). Children's friends can also be a source of misinformation because they understand at the same immature level.

To lessen misunderstandings of biblical ideas, listen carefully to what your child thinks. Get him to tell you the story, ask questions about religious ideas and Bible stories, pay attention when children talk to each other, listen to how they sing songs, and ask him about common religious words and ideas. Children will often give pat answers they have previously learned but have no idea of the real meaning. Pursue your questioning if the answer sounds like an adult talking. Ask the child what he *really* thinks it means.

Religious ideas can easily be expressed through art or role playing.

You may often be surprised at what you discover about what is going on in your child's mind. Norman Wakefield and Robert Clark tell the story of a little boy who drew a picture of a car with three people — a driver with two passengers in the rear seat. When questioned about the drawing, he said it was God driving Adam and Eve out of the Garden of Eden — a perfectly logical notion as far as he was concerned.

When giving instructions you will elicit more of your child's thinking if you are purposefully vague in your directions. If you have been studying the story of Elijah on Mount Carmel, simply say, "I'd like you to draw a picture of the story we've been reading this week." After she completes the picture, get her to tell you about it. Don't guess at what the child has drawn but leave the interpretation entirely up to her. You could say, "Oooh, I like your picture! Tell me about it." Never say, "What's that?" because it often offends children. To them the drawing is perfectly obvious, and they wonder why you can't see it too.

If you note a misconception, never belittle or berate or embarrass the child. To do so will most certainly cut off future communication. Just make note of the misunderstanding and remember to bring it into your teaching later on.

As you teach your child doctrines, begin on a simple level for preschoolers. But don't make things so simple that the child will have to unlearn it later on. Children should be able to build on the foundation they have already been taught, not have to reconstruct the whole building as their mental capacity grows.

Many times preteens will say a Bible story is "boring" — one of their favorite words. "I've heard that story before!" they protest. I believe one of the reasons juniors and earliteens think the Bible stories aren't interesting is because we haven't adjusted our teaching to the child's age and understanding. We have a mental list of the traditional message to get from each Bible story, and don't vary it.

Actually, each Bible story contains many different lessons. Let us look at some well-known Bible stories and see how we can adapt their main emphasis for children of different ages.

FEEDING THE FIVE THOUSAND

Ages 1-3   Jesus gave food so people would not be hungry. He cared.
Ages 4-6   A boy shared his lunch with others. We should share too.

Ages 7 -9   We cannot do what Jesus did. It was a miracle. Jesus is God.

Ages 10 -14   As the food was multiplied, God will multipoly our talents when we use them for His service.

ABRAHAM AND ISAAC—THE SACRIFICE

Ages 1 -3   Not suitable for this age level.

Ages 4 -6   Isaac was obedient to his father (no drama of death).

Ages 7 -9   Abraham obeyed God's voice. How does God speak to us?

Ages 10 -14   Full symbolism of the lamb and Christ, Abraham and God.

DAVID AND GOLIATH

Ages 1 -3   Not suitable for this age level.

Ages 4 -6   David was not afraid. He knew God would help him.

Ages 7 -9   The Holy Spirit is our helper, just as He was David's helper.

Ages 10 -14   David wanted to vindicate God's honor. What are the giants in your life?

When you attempt the impossible for God, He makes it possible.

For younger children you need to emphasize concrete ideas and things that are important to them in addition to what they can understand. As children grow older they begin to grasp symbolic ideas, and their world expands. Our Bible teaching should reflect such change.

Expanding the focus of the Bible story as the child grows in understanding keeps the Bible fresh and interesting. You can do this many ways: learning about how people lived during Bible times, reading passages related to the story, comparing the versions written by the different gospel writers, or studying the reasons for writing each of the gospels, including the different audiences the writers sought to address.

Another good way of combatting the "boring" response is to introduce little-known Bible characters. The Bible is full of fascinating stories about people we never hear about. They make marvelous bits of knowledge for Bible trivia games and quizzes, but they also teach lessons for our daily living. Do you know about Ebed-melech (a Black man from Ethiopia), an official in the king's court who rescued Jeremiah from the cistern and saved his life? You and your children can read about him in Jeremiah 37-39. When the Babylonians captured Israel, God saved him because he trusted in the Lord.

Theology for Children

What theological ideas should children learn? Rather than guess at an answer, I made an intensive study of the ideas of Ellen White on the topic. I discovered that she had plenty to say about the theological and spiritual lessons children should acquire. Each idea in the following paragraphs comes from a passage that specifically mentions that we should teach it to our children. The first section summarizes the ideas she emphasized and that appeared more frequently.

God Is Their Father. The first lesson children should learn is that God is their loving Father. Children are to give loving obedience to God. All Bible study should stress that God is love. God cares for children and the holy angels help Him (*Child Guidance*, pp. 487, 548; *Testimonies*, vol. 8, p. 320; *The Adventist Home*, p. 321).

Life of Jesus. Tell children the story of Jesus as soon as they can understand. Teach them about His life, death, and resurrection and how God shows His love through Him. Every spiritual lesson should be associated with Christ. Make it part of the child's daily experience (*Child Guidance*, pp. 487, 494; *The Adventist Home*, pp. 320, 321; *Testimonies*, vol. 8, p. 320).

Scripture. Children should learn to love the Bible as their rule of life and that the Holy Spirit will help them understand God's words. The Bible should have a vital place in teaching children (*Counsels to Parents and Teachers*, pp. 171, 172).

Law of God. Children should love God and obey His law and understand what is right and what is wrong. God's law should be the child's rule of life. Teach them from babyhood to keep the commandments (*Child Guidance*, pp. 43, 81, 489, 490).

Salvation. Present the plan of salvation simply for children. Stress that disobeying God's law is sin but that Jesus will forgive their sins if they ask Him, something they should do every day. Teach them to believe that Jesus does forgive sins. Encourage children to give their hearts to God. Jesus loves us greatly and came to live on this earth and to die so that we might be forgiven. Always present the subject with love and tenderness (*Counsels on Sabbath School Work*, pp. 78-81; *Child Guidance*, pp. 490, 491; *Messages to Young People*, p. 15).

Victorious Life. Tell children to look to God for strength. He hears prayers. If they will believe and trust in Him, He will help them. They should thank God, remember the wonderful things He has done for them, and use the Bible as a guide and help. Children should clearly understand the terms of entrance to the City of God. With His help they can be true to God under all circumstances and in all places (*Counsels to Parents and Teachers*, pp. 109; *Testimonies*, vol. 2, p. 287; *Child Guidance*, pp. 146, 147, 172, 173).

Again and again Ellen White indicates that we should impress upon our children that God is their Father, that He and Jesus love them very much, and that they should study the Bible and obey God's law. When they do wrong, Jesus, who died to save them, will forgive their sins and help them to do what they should. These are the basics of salvation.

In addition, she mentions other theological concepts that we should present to our children. I have summarized them below.

Prayer. Teach children how to pray clearly, distinctly, simply. They should learn to pray as young as possible and to repeat the Lord's Prayer also (*Child Guidance*, pp. 522, 523).

Sabbath. Children should learn how to keep the Sabbath holy, to prepare for it beforehand, and to help their parents get ready for it. They should attend worship services. Parents should be with them on Sabbath, especially out in nature. Every child should grasp the fact that the first day of the week is not the true Sabbath and that it contradicts the law of God (*Child Guidance*, p. 530; *Testimonies*, vol. 6, pp. 193, 356; *Education*, p. 251).

Stewardship. We should teach children self-denial and benevolence. They should deny self and give to others, or earn money to help others. Each child should begin paying tithe and giving offerings. On birthdays and holidays they should offer thanks to God rather than being the center of attention (*Counsels on Sabbath School Work*, pp. 139-143).

Healthful Living. As children mature they should acquire habits of self-control and self-denial, and discover the laws of health in eating, drinking, and other areas of living. They should learn about their bodies and how they function, that a cause-and-effect relationship exists between what they do and illness (*Testimonies*, vol. 3, p. 567; *Child Guidance*, pp. 104, 362).

Reverence and Worship. The highest reverence for both God and His house includes proper deportment in the sanctuary and in meetings (*Child Guidance*, pp. 541, 542; *Testimonies*, vol. 5, p. 494).

Heaven. Encourage your children to imagine the glories of heaven, and teach them God's requirements for entrance into the Holy City (*Child Guidance*, pp. 487, 488).

Service. Children should understand that they should be helpful to others, starting with their own families. They should have opportunities for missionary activities (*The Adventist Home*, pp. 285, 286, 486, 487).

Creation. Nature is God's second book, and children should learn much from it. It presents many different spiritual lessons, including God's care and love, the creation of the world, sin and suffering, and the potentialities of the new earth. Children should have a strong foundation in creationism (*Testimonies*, vol. 8, pp. 326, 327; *Counsels to Parents and Teachers*, pp. 185-190).

Day of Atonement. Primaries and older should gain an understanding of what the Day of Atonement meant—that it was a special time for confession of sins to be sure all sins were forgiven (*Testimonies*, vol. 5, p. 520).

Pillars of Faith. Every Adventist parent should present sound doctrine—the pillars of our faith, reasons why we are Seventh-day Adventists and why we are to be separate and distinct from the world (*Testimonies*, vol. 5, pp. 330, 331).

If our children enter adolescence with a basic understanding of the above points of faith, they will have an excellent foundation on which to build an ongoing, lifelong study of God's Word. The crucial point to remember in teaching doctrines to children is to present them simply but accurately. As the child's understanding grows, add more complex ideas.

KEYS TO DOCTRINES FOR CHILDREN

1. Teach simply, but accurately.
2. Increase complexity as child's thinking matures.
3. Check for misunderstandings.
4. Teach Bible stories differently for different ages.
5. Teach main doctrines so children understand what they believe.

♥

CHAPTER 10

Communicating With God

"I love the Lord because he listens to my prayers for help.
He paid attention to me.
So I will call to him for help as long as I live."
—Psalm 116:1, 2, ICB

Five-year-old Heinz was worried. He'd heard Mom and Dad talking about moving—something about Dad having a new job at the union office, whatever that was. As he wondered where they would live and if he'd get to take his toys with him, he wished that they could have a house with a yard. He didn't like the tall apartment building they lived in now. It had no place to play outside. In fact, he couldn't even go outside unless Mom or his older brother went too. Wouldn't it be nice to have a house with a yard?

But then Heinz sighed. No one he knew had a house with a yard. All his friends lived in tall apartment buildings. But he knew that some houses did have yards—he'd seen them one day while riding on the bus. Maybe he'd ask Mom if they could move to a house with a yard.

"Oh, my no!" his mother declared emphatically. "Those are only for rich people with special connections to someone in the government. We could never live in a house with a yard! No, we should be happy we have such a lovely apartment."

But Heinz's father could not find even a small apartment for his family in the city where the union office was located. Housing was hard to find in Germany during the years following World War II. So reluctantly he began the new job alone, staying in the home of a fellow employee in the union office. Because of weekend speaking responsibilities he got home only once every two or three weeks. Every free evening he searched for an apartment for his family. Weeks went by. No apartment appeared on the market.

Meanwhile, back at home, Heinz grew more and more upset at not seeing his father. Every day he asked, "Why can't we go where Daddy is?"

The answer was always the same. "We don't have any place to live in that city."

"Why can't Jesus find us a place?" And so Heinz began to pray about a place to live. Only he had definite ideas about the kind of home he wanted. The first time he prayed about the matter during family worship, he said, "Dear Jesus, please help us find a house with a yard. Thank You. Amen." Every night he prayed the same prayer.

"I told you we can't have a house with a yard," his mother remonstrated. "It would cost too much money. That's only for rich people." But Heinz continued praying for a house with a yard anyway. He was sure Jesus could answer his prayer. Besides, he really wanted a home with a yard.

Several weeks later Heinz changed his prayer. "Dear Jesus," he prayed, "please help us find a house with a yard with some trees." His mother sighed. How was Jesus going to answer her son's impossible prayer? And what would happen to her little boy's faith when God didn't respond in the way he asked?

She felt she had to say something to protect her boy's faith. "Heinz, you know Jesus doesn't always answer prayers the way we want. Sometimes He says no because what we want wouldn't be best for us. Jesus knows best."

"But Mom, why wouldn't Jesus want us to have a house with a yard with trees? I think it would be wonderful!"

"Jesus knows we don't have enough money to pay for a house like that," she responded. "He wants us to be happy with what we have."

"But I think Jesus could figure out how to pay for a house with a yard," Heinz said firmly. "I'm going to keep praying. I know Jesus wants me to have a house with a yard."

"Just remember that Jesus might not do what you want."

Weeks went by and still no apartment. The family was becoming discouraged. But Heinz kept on praying every night at worshiptime. One night he confidently added an additional request. "Dear Jesus, please help us find a house with a yard with trees and a sandbox."

The next weekend Heinz's father arrived home. He had heard his little boy's prayers and was also concerned about the trauma to the child's budding faith. But he decided Jesus was going to have to take care of the matter in His own way.

Saturday night the phone rang. On the other end of the line a mysterious male voice asked, "Do you have an apartment for rent or sale? I am looking for something in this city."

"Yes, we do." And Heinz's father went on to describe their apartment.

"May I come to see it tomorrow? It sounds like just what I am looking for." After inspecting the apartment, the man offered to make an even exchange—the apartment for his place in the city where the union office was located. The family was elated. Finally they might get to move. So the father made arrangements to see the place one evening the next week.

As they drove through the city to see the man's residence, the minister became a little concerned. They were in a rather exclusive part of town when the man stopped in front of a house and opened the door of the car.

"Sir, I'm afraid there has been some misunderstanding," Heinz's father said. "I am a minister on a very small salary. I could not afford to live in this section of town. I think we are wasting your time."

"Oh, no," the man replied. "I said we would make an even trade. I meant it. Your apartment suits me perfectly. Come in and see my place." Hesitantly, the pastor followed the man through an iron gate into a beautiful yard with large trees.

"Trees!" he gasped. As his eyes scanned the beautiful grounds he thought he must be dreaming, for there in the corner of the yard stood a sandbox!

"Come, let me show you the inside."

A house with a yard with trees and a sandbox . . . a little boy's voice seemed to echo through every room of the house. "And you thought I couldn't handle a small boy's prayers?" another voice seemed to whisper.

"What do you think of the place?" the man inquired.

"Perfect. Absolutely perfect! Are you sure you want to make an even trade? It doesn't seem very even to me. My apartment is really quite meager and plain compared to this place."

"Your apartment suits me perfectly, and I am pleased to have someone of your caliber in my place here in the city."

"Isn't a special permit required to live in this section of town?" the pastor asked.

"Yes, you are right. A permit is required. However, I will arrange all the paperwork. You don't need to concern yourself with that aspect. As soon as I have it done, I will contact you."

As they shook hands the pastor still could not believe what he had just seen and heard. A house with a yard with trees and a sandbox. It was too good to be true! Why had he ever doubted that Jesus could answer a small boy's prayer?

Heinz was ecstatic. "He did it! He did it! He did it! Jesus did answer my prayers. I knew He would." Why were the grownups so worried about finding a house? Jesus could handle anything.

After the pastor and his family had resided in the house for two months, a loud knock at the door revealed two government officials. "Do you have a permit to live in this house?" one of them brusquely asked.

"Yes, I do," the pastor answered.

"Show us the permit!" they demanded.

After the pastor produced the required document, the officials stepped to one side of the porch. As they inspected the permit, they talked excitedly to each other. After what seemed like an eternity, they returned to where the pastor stood waiting.

"You should never have received this permit! But since you have it, you may as well stay." And they left as abruptly as they had come. The pastor sighed with relief and gathered his family for a thank-You prayer. Apparently the owner wanted to transfer hastily for political reasons and had arranged all the necessary paperwork through his contacts. God, who knows the future, bent down to listen to a 5-year-old boy who wanted a yard with trees and a sandbox. The pastor and his family lived in that house for seven years.

Connecting our children to God through prayer is one of the most thrilling aspects of helping them grow spiritually. We can give them a direct line to the central switchboard of the universe. In order to have real spiritual life and energy, we must actually connect to God through prayer. Meditating on God's works and His blessings, although important, is not communicating with God in the fullest sense, Ellen White tells us in *Steps to Christ*. We must have something to say to God about our everyday life—our joys, our hopes, our fears. Children must gradually grow into this aspect of prayer.

In prayer I open my heart to God. He already knows me intimately, so I don't do it to tell Him who I am. Rather I open myself up to receive Him. "Prayer does not bring God down to us, but brings us up to Him" (*Steps to Christ*, p. 93). Prayer helps me see things His way. It pulls me out of my self-centeredness, the aspect of prayer most difficult for children to understand. Such awareness comes to them gradually, but generally not until near the end of childhood.

Prayer is also "the key in the hand of faith to unlock heaven's storehouse, where are treasured the boundless resources of Omnipotence" (*ibid.*, p. 94). This is the part of prayer children grasp most easily. Heinz, in his simple childish faith, unlocked the treasures of heaven. Young children often think of God as the Candy Man or Santa Claus—just pray and God will give you what you want. Their requests are usually quite self-centered. In their own minds they are the center of the world and everything revolves around them. Naturally their prayers reflect their way of thinking. It is one of the earliest stages of a prayer life. But their prayers change as they grow older. The development of prayer life during childhood has definite stages.

Stages in the Development of Prayer

Researchers in child development and religious education have explored how children mature in their prayer life. Various studies with children of different ages and religious backgrounds have come to the same conclusion that they go through at least four stages in their prayer life. Each stage reflects changes both in their thinking processes as they mature and in their experiences with prayer itself.

Studies have found that children even from different religious faiths go through the same stages, but they may progress through them more rapidly if they have many experiences with prayer, thus reaching each stage at a younger age. Understanding the steps through which children progress as they develop their ideas about prayer will enable you to know how to help your own child to reach a more mature understanding of it. Also, it will guide you in knowing how to relate to his prayers at each stage.

Young children, ages 5 to 7, have only vague ideas about how prayers get to God. Many of them think prayers fly or float or jump up to heaven. Unanswered prayers distress them more than older children. They often think that God did not answer a prayer because they didn't say it right. A child believes that what he says makes the difference between good and bad prayers. Also, he assumes that the more people pray, the quicker the response. Many children this age believe that even animals pray. Because such children pray themselves, they conclude that all others do also.

Children ages 7 to 9 years realize that animals don't pray, and have discovered that not all children do either. Some are too sleepy or forget or don't want to or don't want anything. In their minds, God has only a limited capacity to hear prayers and thus cannot hear everyone at once. It is sort of like standing in line for your turn. If prayers don't get answered, it might be because the children were naughty or they prayed too quietly or they were silly. Although their requests are for specific things related to their lives, children now also become more altruistic and begin to pray for peace, for the poor, and for the sick. During these years the first traces of doubt appear—does God really answer prayer? Younger children believe implicitly, but by 8 years of age many of them have lost some of their unquestioning belief in prayer. They may have a tit-for-tat idea about prayer. That is, if you respect God, God will respect you and answer your prayers.

By ages 10 to 12 children believe prayer is a private conversation with God about things you wouldn't talk to other people about. They share intimacies and confidences with Him. Prayer becomes intensely personal, as they believe prayer originates within oneself and is heard directly by God. Spontaneous prayer comes about because a person is feeling lonely, worried, upset, or troubled, or in response to other people's feelings.

By the earliteen years many children recognize that prayer changes the person who is praying, too. Prayer, they learn, is valuable in and of itself—not just a means for asking God for favors. As teenagers grow older, their belief in the efficacy of prayer declines, but they continue praying anyway. Their requests are specific and mundane—about everyday concerns, exams, dates, etc. Many look upon God as a personal friend to whom they communicate through prayer.

Many of the studies show that children who have had many religious experiences have a much different understanding of prayer than those with few such experiences. Here is one area in which it really pays to teach your child well and to give him many opportunities to develop a relationship with God through prayer. Maturity in prayer is not just dependent on cognitive or intellectual development. Experiences and teaching really make a difference. Now that we know how children form their ideas about prayer, what can we do to enable them to mature?

Helping Children Grow in Prayer Life

For children growing up in a Seventh-day Adventist home, I would like to add another stage to the ones described above. It would be the earliest stage—for children under 3 years of age. Because we teach toddlers to pray spontaneously as soon as they can talk, their prayer life evolves more rapidly. Most other churches teach their children memorized prayers during the early childhood years. In fact, the idea of children praying spontaneously shocks many people. They have a hard time believing children can do that.

So I believe the first stage in the development of prayer life begins when Mom and Dad help Baby hold his hands together while they say a blessing for the meal. Or they might cradle their infant in their arms while they say their evening prayers or pray for the child. Baby experiences prayer through the prayers of Mom and Dad. I believe the Holy Spirit is present during those prayers, and the child senses the warmth and closeness of God and her family surrounding her like a blanket of love. Prayer comes to be associated with love and closeness.

Even babies quickly learn to relate events that occur together repeatedly. It doesn't take too many months for them to begin to put their hands together in anticipation when they see food appear. They have discovered that prayer precedes eating and now imitate the actions that go with prayer. I don't think they actually know what prayer is, but they have learned, by association and imitation, to put their hands together and to expect someone to say something before they can eat. Often " 'men'' is one of their earliest words, said with some relief and joy—now I can eat!

All in all, it is a fine introduction to ''talking to Jesus.'' Observing the family pray at worshiptime and participating in a short nightly before-bedtime-prayer also form part of Baby's introduction to prayer life. As such prayer experiences continue during the first two years, children come to accept prayer as an expected part of life.

Some children, even though they are capable of kneeling or folding their hands for prayer, refuse to do so. Don't be discouraged. Continue praying. After a while, just when you are about to give up, suddenly your child will kneel and fold his hands for prayer, just like he has seen you do so many times.

Sometime along the way, Mr. Toddler may exert his independence and refuse to fold his hands for prayer. Proceed with prayer anyway. If you don't make a big issue of it, in time he will decide to cooperate.

Often 2-year-olds who have been cooperative about prayer during family worship and at bedtime will suddenly refuse to pray. ''No!'' they say with flashing eyes and stubbornly set jaw. Don't pay any attention or make a big issue of the matter. Just proceed with your prayers as usual. You might say something like ''That's OK if you don't want to pray. Just sit quietly while Mommy and Carole pray.'' Be pleasant, but firm. Insist that your child remain quiet while you pray, but don't insist she pray. She shouldn't run around the room yelling during prayer, however. Such a display of independence is normal for 2-year-olds and even some 3-year-olds. Give her a little time, and she will be cooperative again.

A number of children who have experienced many prayers during this imitative stage will want to pray before they can really talk well. They want to do what everyone else in the family does. You can help them by saying a finish-the-sentence prayer. Start out with ''Dear Jesus, thank You for Daddy. Thank You for _____'' and let your child complete the sentence. Probably she will say ''Mommy'' or the name of a sibling or favorite pet, and in so doing she will feel like she is praying and loved by you and God.

Another way to help a beginner is to say a short, one-sentence prayer your child can imitate word by word or phrase by phrase. He will love it and feel grown up. Of course, you wouldn't insist on proper pronunciation or that every word be exactly right. That would take all the joy out of the experience. I'm pretty certain God loves to hear ''baby talk.''

It won't be too long before your 2-year-old will want to make up his own prayers. And then the fun really begins! Young children pray about anything they think about. They will also pray the phrases they have heard others say. Even though you want to laugh at their candid prayers, restrain yourself to a smile. If you laugh, your child will get the idea that it is ''cute'' to say funny things, and prayer could easily become a show-off time.

Some 3- and 4-year-olds really get into long prayers. They will pray for everyone they know, including all their pets, toys, and imaginary friends. If it gets out of control so the blessing for a meal seems interminable, you might suggest the idea that there are different kinds of prayers.

The prayer for a meal is a short one thanking Jesus for the food. Waking-up prayers and bedtime prayers are longer. In the morning we say good morning to Jesus and tell Him all about what we are going to do that day. We say thank You to Jesus for keeping us all night. At bedtime we tell Him all about everything that happened to us during the day. That is the time to pray for all our family and friends. Sometimes during the day we pray a short help-me prayer when we are in trouble. Other times we might say a short thank-You prayer when we want to show appreciation to Jesus for something especially nice we see or for helping us. Every time we pray we don't have to say the same thing.

Four-, 5-, and 6-year-olds will be fascinated by the different types of prayers. They may ask you, "Is this a thank-You prayer?" Or they may announce proudly, "This is a help-me prayer." You might also introduce the idea of public prayers, such as your child hears every week in church. Explain that the person who offers the prayer is really praying for everyone in the congregation. Children will enjoy the church pastoral prayer more when they understand the different aspects of public prayer. Point out to your child the different parts of pastoral prayer: praising God, thanking Him, making petitions, confessing sins, and requesting forgiveness. If your church gives members an opportunity to make prayer requests before the pastoral prayer, help your child be aware of what is going on and maybe participate when she has a special request. After the prayer, you might whisper quietly in your child's ear, "Did you hear the thank-You part?" That will help him learn to listen to the prayer and feel more included in the worship service.

The prayers children hear at home when they are learning to pray give form and shape to their own prayers. Prayer, like much of what a young child learns, gets copied from what she hears. When your child first begins to pray, she needs to hear short, one-sentence prayers. "Dear Jesus, thank You for the food. Amen." But don't get stuck in that pattern.

When teaching your child, you can either "go with the flow" or challenge his thinking, as Tom Lickona points out in his book *Raising Good Children*. When you "go with the flow," you explain things in terms your child can easily understand. You teach in the way most naturally suited to his stage of development, appealing to his way of thinking. Intuitively it seems like the "right" thing to do. And for many things it is. But not for everything.

Your child needs challenge as well as security. Encourage her to think differently, to mature and to grow. To challenge your child, teach in a way that is slightly "out of his reach" at the moment. Make her stretch and stand on mental tiptoe to grasp the meaning. Confront her comfortable way of thinking by throwing in a new idea.

"Going with the flow" helps children understand clearly and matures their thinking in their present stage of development. Challenging urges them to move forward toward greater maturity in the next level of growth. Children need both for balanced development.

Let's see how it works with prayer. Teaching and modeling simple one-sentence prayers using a child's vocabulary "goes with the flow."

Children understand them clearly and can learn to pray that way themselves. But if you are still praying simplified, two- or three-sentence prayers with your 5-, 6-, or 7-year-old, you are missing the opportunity to challenge and advance your children in their prayer life. They need to hear prayer models that will help them grow. Don't get stuck on the infant level, but don't skip to the adult model, either. The steps in between will help your children grow.

Teach your children a model for prayer. An easy way to do this with 5- to 7-year-olds is to make a scrapbook about prayer. On the cover paste an attractive picture of children praying or a picture of Jesus. The scrapbook should have a section for each part of a prayer. The following model is simple and easy for children to remember. When we pray for worship or at bedtime, we want to include the following:

1. Thank Jesus for the blessings He gives us.
2. Ask Him to help us and other people.
3. Confess the bad things we have done and ask forgiveness.
4. Ask Jesus to help us love Him more every day.
5. Thank Him for loving us and for preparing our home in heaven.

In the thank-You section you could have pictures of a house, toys, car, friends, food, etc.—the possibilities are endless. The second section on asking for help could include pictures of someone in trouble or of individuals who especially require assistance—children who need food and clothes, the elderly, or a family in trouble. The confessing section could have pictures of boys and girls doing things they shouldn't be doing. A picture of Jesus could close that section.

The fourth section on asking for love could have illustrations of children doing kind things for other children or adults, such as hugging, playing together, etc. The thank You for loving section could have three pictures: Jesus with some children, Jesus on the cross, and a heavenly scene.

If you have a camera, you could take pictures of your children, their friends, your family, and the things they are thankful for. It would personalize your prayer scrapbook and make it meaningful for your children. Pictures of Jesus and the heavenly scene can usually be purchased from your conference ABC or Children's Ministries Department. The rest of the pictures your children and their friends could pose for.

The prayer book doesn't have to be completed all at once. You could introduce the book with only a few pictures at the beginning. Explain the different things to pray about. At first, select only one thing. Gradually, as your child gains understanding, add more items to the prayer. Thus your child will grow in comprehension of prayer as communication with Jesus and God. You will be helping her move toward a deep, life-changing prayer life.

Heinz is a perfect example of the strong belief young children have that Jesus will answer their prayers. Not having experienced enough of life yet to question and doubt, their faith is simple and childlike. Jesus can do anything—and will in response to their requests.

As children head toward the end of early childhood, their thinking processes begin to change, and they may begin to express some doubts about prayer. By 8 years of age many children have lost some of their simple faith of the early years. They have discovered their Candy Man God doesn't always give them what they want.

You can help children over this transition by modeling a more personal, heart-changing approach to prayer. Confess your own wrongs and ask forgiveness of God. It is a prayer He always answers positively. Request help in personal spiritual growth. You can also model a more open approach to personal problems and requests. Instead of telling God how you want Him to respond, you can present the problem and ask for His solution. Also begin to model prayers in which you intercede with God for other people and their needs. The use of such kinds of prayers will help your children move toward a more satisfying understanding of "talking to Jesus," one more in keeping with their maturing lives.

You can also assist their transition by helping children begin to grasp the fact that praying is like talking to a friend. Jesus is their special friend, one who never abandons them, never quarrels, never moves away. Constantly there, He always loves and wants to help them. During the early elementary years children begin to be more conscious of friends and of making friends. They understand the idea of friendship better than when they were younger. Jesus as their friend fits perfectly into their maturing ideas about friendship.

If the prayers your child hears you offer remain mostly on the Candy Man or Santa Claus level, your child will remain stuck at this stage. He doesn't know about your individual, heartfelt confessions and struggles during your private time with God. But he needs to know that this is what mature prayer is all about. Model it for him. Give him a taste of real communication with God, and he will want more. Show him what God is doing in your own life.

If you don't help your child make the transition during the latter part of elementary school, she will become disillusioned with prayer as she moves into the teen years. The Candy Man approach simply is not enough to carry the relationship. Her prayers must become part of a friendship with Jesus, a sharing of intimacies, joys, sorrows, desires. A pouring out of her heart to Jesus. Nothing less will enable her to cope with the questions of the teen years.

By age 10 many children would be interested in a prayer journal—some perhaps even as young as 8. A prayer journal makes prayer come alive. My own prayer journal has two main parts. In one section I write a list of people or concerns I am sharing with God. Sometimes it has been only a list. Right now I have a book just for my prayer list in which I can write each request on a separate page so I can include notes about progress in that area. The second section is for the insights God gives me during prayer and daily study time with His Word.

For children I suggest the simpler plan—a list of prayer concerns. Children who don't write well could draw pictures or compose on the computer, if that is easier. Each day the child can pray for some or all of the concerns on the list. It's a good idea to leave a little space after each concern to write how God answered. Be sure to date each entry and the answer.

Your family might want to keep a prayer journal for family concerns that you pray about together. Such a journal is a constant reminder that God hears and responds to our needs and interests. If you start a family prayer journal when your children are young, by 10 or 12 they will be eager to have their own private one.

In another chapter we'll look at how to help children really experience the grace of Jesus in their own lives through prayer. We'll see how to help them get rid of the guilt forever and really feel Jesus' love in everything they do—again, through prayer.

This step is absolutely essential if your children are to make the transitions through adolescence. I believe this is one of the most powerful ways of assisting children through the turmoil of adolescence. Before entering the teenage years, your child must meet the Saviour as a personal friend who can enable her to deal with all the problems in her life. The key to that friendship is prayer.

Help your children move away from the Candy Man model of prayer to the friendship model—the God who cares deeply and offers real solutions to our problems.

Just one more vital point—if your own prayers are vibrant and you enjoy a really close relationship with your Lord, your children will catch your own enthusiasm. But if you limit your prayer life to childish prayers to bless the food and for family worship, your children will sense that prayer is really not that important. Again, your own model is vital to your children's spiritual growth. It is hard to lead children down unknown paths. Leaders must already know the way.

KEYS TO PRAYER

1. Begin praying with your baby as soon as he is born.
2. Be regular about prayer for meals and other times so prayer becomes an expected part of your toddler's life.
3. Begin teaching your child with simple prayers.
4. As your child grows in understanding, introduce more aspects of prayer.
5. Help your child experience prayer as a friendship with Jesus.
6. Before the teen years, help your child experience the joys and security of real communication with Jesus.
7. Model the kind of prayers you want your child to experience.

CHAPTER 11

Spiritual Development

"It always gives me the greatest joy
when I hear that my children are following the way of truth."
—3 John 4, ICB

Mike shivered as he plodded home from school. Head down, he pulled his cap over his ears and hugged himself as protection against the biting wind and snowflakes. *Winter is definitely on its way. Sure wish Mom could have picked me up. No use fussing about it. She had to work at the hospital today, and we need the money.*

Suddenly a male voice interrupted his thoughts. "Want a lift, sonny?" Mike glanced over at the road. The voice came from an elegant black car that shouted money. The man looked pleasant enough. Maybe it would be all right this time despite his mother's warnings about taking rides with strangers. After all, the man looked OK, and it was so-o-o cold.

"Thanks, sir! It's really cold today!" Mike settled himself in the front seat of the luxurious vehicle. Cautiously he looked around. He'd never ridden in a car like it before. *Wouldn't it be great to own something like this!* Again the man intruded in his thoughts.

"What's your name, sonny?"

"Mike Eastwood."

"Where do you go to school?"

"At the Seventh-day Adventist church school on Division. I'm in the third grade."

"Where do you live?"

After Mike gave his address, the man responded, "I'm going that direction myself. I'll just drop you off at your home."

"Thanks, sir!"

Silence enveloped the two as the car hummed through the slush of newly fallen snow. The well-dressed man puffed on a fat cigar as Mike looked out the window. Shortly the boy had had all the smoke he really wanted to smell. Looking up at the man, he asked, "Sir, don't you know you shouldn't smoke?"

"Why not?" the man countered as he flicked the ashes from his cigar and tried to keep from smiling at such a direct approach.

" 'Cause the commandments say so."

"Which commandment says that?"

Mike was stumped. He knew the commandments said a person shouldn't smoke, but which one was it? For a moment or two he paused, trying to decide.

"The one about adultery," he finally stated firmly.

This time the man smiled but decided to guide the conversation in other directions. The matter of smoking did not come up again. After letting Mike off in front of the boy's house, he continued on his errand.

But he couldn't get his mind off the topic of smoking. He knew he should quit. After all, he had read the surgeon general's reports on smoking. The more he thought about it, the more he determined to quit. And he did. But quitting himself wasn't enough. He became an antismoking crusader. Every client who came to his law office smelling of tobacco received his persuasive lecture on smoking. In fact, for a while he wouldn't accept clients who smoked unless they would quit. A little boy's brash question had indeed changed his life.

Mike's experience with the lawyer describes religion during the middle childhood years very well. Concerned about doing what he knew was right, he wanted to please God. He knew God has certain requirements and that those requirements are important. You have to mind those rules. But he was a little vague about their meaning. Still he was not afraid to tell a stranger about the rules and how he should live because living right is important.

In this chapter we'll take an overview look at spiritual development during late childhood and early adolescence, similar to the overview of spiritual development during early childhood in chapter 5. Both chapters seek only to give you the big picture. Most of the how-to-do-it details appear in the other chapters on specific topics.

Seven to 9: The Activity Years

Seven- to 9-year-olds are extremely practical and realistic. They want a clear "this is right" and "this is wrong." Now is the best time to teach children about God's rules—the Ten Commandments—and how they help us live right. Children this age are just learning about the laws that govern the natural world. Conscious of rules and their effects, they are also beginning to classify things and group them in categories. Thus they understand that the Ten Commandments are God's rules for living happily. Parents can also use them to remind children of categories—love God and love people. In fact, when you teach the Ten Commandments this way, you will help your child get past the hurdle of negativism many people have toward them.

Despite Miss Seven's or Mr. Nine's focus on rules, you would be wise to emphasize that we obey God's rules because we love God (challenge their thinking). God doesn't "zap" boys and girls who disobey them. Instead, He tries to get them to understand that He loves them and wants them to love Him in return.

When teaching their children to be morally responsible persons, many parents find themselves using three basic appeals: (1) You'll get punished (or rewarded), (2) there's a rule, and (3) there's a principle involved. The first appeal ("you'll have to go to your room if you can't play nicely with your brother") is the one best understood by preschoolers. The second appeal ("our rule is that you must come straight home from school unless you ask permission") children grasp during elementary school. It is usually the most effective one to use with this age, although rewards and punishment continue to be helpful. The third appeal (principles) is much harder to grasp, and children do not generally understand it until the late elementary or early high school years.

While children develop and begin to understand more mature reasons for their behavior, the earlier appeals still continue to be effective. In fact, governments and businesses—and churches, by the way—often use them to motivate adults. Traffic rules are a good example—straight punishment when you hear the police siren behind your car. Commissions for sales reward hard work. Some churches use this type of motivation a great deal in their "hellfire" preaching or "you-can't-be-saved-unless-you're-perfect" approach to salvation. God often employed it when He was trying to take a slave nation and transform it into a nation of leaders. The Israelites, just emerging from 400 years of slavery, were really infants spiritually. So God began with "baby" methods.

The Lord used a rule-type appeal with the children of Israel when He gave the Ten Commandments and the Levitical laws. At the same time He tried to challenge them to more mature ways of thinking when He declared "thou shalt love thy neighbour as thyself" (Lev. 19:18) and "thou shalt love the Lord thy God with all thine heart, with all thy soul, and with all thy might" (Deut. 6:5).

Not ready for His principles of love, they persisted in their rule approach. When Christ came as Redeemer He found many of them still deeply entrenched in rules. Again He tried to articulate the principles of love, quoting these same passages from the Old Testament, tying love to His eternal principles for living. Many people think of the God of the New Testament as a more loving, merciful God than the Deity of the Old Testament. But God used the appeal of love way back in the beginning!

As parents we can take a lesson from God. While young children best understand the rewards-and-punishment appeal, let's tie it with our love and God's love. During the elementary school years, when rules are most appealing, let's not forget to bind them to both our love and God's love. Only in this way can we successfully teach our children about God's love. If we leave off the love part, we will end up with legalists who truly believe they must be "perfect" before God will accept them. Forever bound by the rules, they cannot grasp God's grace for themselves. Remember the most important spiritual lessons of early childhood? Love, trust, and obedience. They are still inextricably bound up with the character of God and with spiritual growth during late childhood.

Children need a strong foundation of "this is right" and "this is wrong" upon which they will later build principles for life. Without a foundation of right and wrong there can be no principles. The foundation is absolutely indispensable in order to support the principles. Children during this age need lots of practice with the virtues they have been taught so this way of living will become automatic.

Give your child lots of opportunities to make choices. Help him think about why the action is right or wrong (building the principles). In order to get him to ponder the whys, ask him what they are—don't tell. In other words, get *him* to say what he thinks. Offer him opportunities to consider the issue. If necessary, guide his thinking with leading questions, but allow him to come to his own conclusion.

Your child also needs to learn about the reasons for being "good." Explain why you have said no or yes about some situation or issue. That way you are beginning to build the principles that Mr. Seven or Miss Eight will need to guide their behavior later on. "I said so is all the reason you need!" completely stifles growth toward principles. Ultimately children cannot depend on a set of rules. Because it is impossible to learn a rule for every possible decision, they must acquire principles that will enable them to deal with different situations of every possible kind. Helping your child understand the reasons behind your prohibitions is the first step in assimilating principles.

Your 7- to 9-year-old has rapidly expanding ideas about God and religion. He recognizes God as the supreme authority and power in the universe although he is probably puzzled about where the Deity came from and how He began. The child has a hard time understanding how God can love everyone good *or* bad. It doesn't seem fair. In his scheme of life fairness is important. People love you when you are good—that's fair. So how can God love bad people? People are either good or bad, nothing in between. His thinking is either/or, all or none. Hazy areas in between simply do not exist yet to him. Something is either good or bad. Truth is important at this age. One of the quickest ways to lose your child's respect is to be wishy-washy about truth, especially during these crucial years.

Mr. Eight and Miss Nine are beginning to understand the simple religious symbolisms that baffled them during earlier years. Now when you talk about ''giving your heart to Jesus'' it makes more sense to them. However, don't assume they grasp all the symbolisms. Check to be sure they really understand. You can challenge their thinking with additional simple religious symbolisms.

They memorize easily and are capable of learning a great deal about the Bible. Take advantage of this golden time for memorizing Bible passages and learning about Bible stories and characters. Play ''Twenty Questions'' with Bible characters while traveling in the car. Simplified Bible Trivia games are great, and Bible quizzes reinforce learning of facts. You are really cheating your child of something valuable if you do not encourage her to memorize Scripture.

Eight- to 10-year-olds also need help in learning to use the Bible. Don't assume they will acquire the ability at school or at Sabbath school. The teacher will probably present the ideas, but it takes a lot more repetition than Sabbath school can give for a child to learn the names of the books of the Bible and how to find Bible texts.

During the first years of elementary school children love to learn. Take advantage of it and teach them about the Bible. Begin with the most familiar books: Genesis, Exodus, Psalms, Matthew, Mark, Luke, John, and Revelation. That would be enough for most 7-year-olds. Add more books as they grow older until they can find their way around the Bible with ease. I have made some suggestions for Bible memory projects in chapter 8. You will have your own favorite passages you will want to pass on to your family.

Around 7 or 8 years of age children become more conscious of the characteristics of other people. Before that, if you asked a child to describe his friend, he would probably say, "He plays ball with me." Your child viewed his friend with reference to himself. Now children will depict their friends by talking about personal characteristics without referring to themselves. A child might speak of his friend as "a super ball player." With the new viewpoint also comes the realization that other children in turn can evaluate him. He himself is thus different from other kids. Self-consciousness dawns and self-concept begins to gel. But watch out! Self-concept is extremely fragile and disintegrates easily.

Now is an important time to help children understand that they are special to God. That each child is truly unique because God created no one else exactly like her—unless she has an identical twin! You can influence the self-concept by giving her a positive image of herself. Say "You are a helping person" if you want your child to be altruistic and helpful. During this period such words will have the greatest long-term effect on your child's way of acting. "You're so kind and gentle to animals." "You are so loving!" Such phrases create a self-image that will stay with your child for years to come. And she will live up to that self-image. Take advantage of the special window of opportunity between 6 and 9 years to help your child feel her specialness to God and to build a positive self-image. It will never be easier.

Because kids this age love action, encourage your child to help others and be involved in service projects. Since she is probably earning some money or has a small allowance, it is a good time to introduce stewardship concepts. Tithing means more now that your child has some money of her own. Setting aside her own offering money has more significance than being handed a dollar bill on the way into the Sabbath school room. She needs many opportunities to sacrifice for others if she is to mature into a loving and caring person.

As children advance through the late childhood years, their focus on rules gradually fades. You will see a glimmer of principles emerging in their thinking and a leaning toward a relationship with Jesus. Their emerging understanding of the meaning of salvation anticipates their decision to accept Jesus as Saviour.

Ten to 14: The Transition Years

Although some precocious children give their hearts to Jesus during early or middle childhood, most of those reared in Christian homes accept Jesus as their Saviour between 10 and 14 years of age. Twelve is the peak age for baptism of SDA children.

Church membership is important, as children need stability to cope with the years ahead. Cooperate closely with your pastor and church school teacher. You are all working together for the salvation of your child. Be sensitive to the Holy Spirit's wooing of her. Encourage her to open up to His influence. See to it that your child has had an opportunity to respond to an invitation to accept Jesus as a personal Saviour. What greater privilege could you have than to bring your child to Christ!

"Wait a minute!" I can hear you saying. "I'm not a minister! I've never asked anyone to accept Jesus as his Saviour. I wouldn't know what to say. Don't tell me parents have to do *that?*" Don't panic. I will give you some ideas that will make it simple. (See chapter 12, "Jesus, the Children's Saviour.") You can learn how to share Jesus with your child. It isn't difficult.

The expanding mental capacity of 10- to 14-year-olds helps them understand many religious ideas that previously were too abstract. Religious symbolisms, such as the cross and the sanctuary service, can be a meaningful part of their spiritual nurture now. Because they can understand historical sequence—which before was a mumble-jumble of isolated facts—Bible prophecy and its fulfillment become interesting and important. Current signs of fulfilling prophecy intrigue them because children this age are now much more aware of the world around them than their younger brothers and sisters.

Preparing a family collection of newspaper or news magazine clippings about fulfilling prophecy is an exciting project for this age level. Start by helping your children find Bible verses about signs of Christ's second coming. Make a list of the signs with the appropriate Bible verses. During the week encourage your children to collect clippings about the topics. Then on Sabbath afternoon as a family arrange the clippings in a scrapbook, manila folders, or clear plastic protector envelopes. You will be encouraging family togetherness as well as aiding your children to grow spiritually. What signs have not appeared yet? The urgency of getting ready for Christ's coming really strikes home when you work on a project like this.

Ten- to 14-year-olds need help making the bridge between the simplified religious ideas they absorbed when they were younger and the more abstract ones, such as charity, salvation, and faith, that they are now capable of understanding. If you use examples from everyday life, you can enable your child to make the transition to the more abstract terms used in religious services and the Bible. Start with vocabulary your child understands and then challenge his thinking by gradually moving from the known to the unknown. As you do so, you will be helping your child enter the adult world of religious thought by challenging him to learn many new ideas in school. If he doesn't advance in religious knowledge, he will sooner or later consider religion "babyish" and beneath him.

If your child is not attending a church school, you will need to have a careful plan to help him acquire a history of the Bible and its organization. Now is the time to introduce how to study a Bible topic and how to use Bible study helps as described earlier in chapter 8. During the latter years of elementary school, children still memorize easily. Continue the memory projects you started earlier. You could now work on key Bible doctrine texts, studying and memorizing several passages for one doctrine every month. It would take more than two years to cover all the doctrines at this pace, but it would be worthwhile for your children.

Ten- to 14-year-olds want a practical, realistic religion with a clear "Thus saith the Lord." Unfortunately this is not always easy to give. Some of today's problems don't have simple answers, but your children have a real need to discuss real-life situations and their solutions. Don't hide behind your own insecurity about the answers. If you can't support what you believe—or you don't know what you believe—now is the time to dig into the Bible and find the answers for yourself. Maybe you and the children can do it together.

Don't pretend to have answers when you really don't. Kids will see it immediately. Simply say, "I really don't know. Let's try to find out. God's opinion, not ours, is what really counts." As you point your children to the Bible, you will need to help them. After all, they are just beginners in Bible study.

Your children will want to know how *you* deal with temptations and problems. They need to see how Christianity works in real life. You must model for them what to do with sin and guilt in their lives, how to gain spiritual victory. If you don't know yourself, get on your knees and find out. God will be thrilled to show you so you can pass it on to your children. Juniors and earliteens can spot a phony from a long distance, but they also recognize the real thing when they see it—and respect it.

Perhaps your child may have high ideals for himself and get easily discouraged when he falls short of his own standard. If he confides in you about a personal struggle, never betray his trust. Take him seriously. Don't laugh or make light of the problem. It is intensely real and serious to him, and he is particularly sensitive to betrayal. Don't make a joke of whatever he is struggling with and tell the neighbors. That will effectively cut off all communication with your child. In years to come, you will desperately need that channel of communication to help him navigate the turbulent waters of adolescence. Keep it open no matter what.

You can help with discouragement by showing him how to set reasonable goals for Christian living, what to do with the resulting guilt when he fails, and how to personalize religion. Show him that God will help him in just the way he alone needs. God has a plan for his life and a special place of service. By now he may be having thoughts about a lifework. Some children make a career choice even before they start high school. Your child needs to know how God guides in decisions—how to hear His voice leading him or her.

Children this age need examples of Christian living—heroes to dream about, if you please. They especially require Christian heroes, as the media and their friends often entice them to secular heroes with almost overwhelming force. Be sure your junior-age child has lots of books with stories about pioneer missionaries, Bible heroes, present-day stalwarts of faith and service, and boys and girls who were daring and faithful under difficult circumstances. You might read some of the stories together as a family on Friday evenings or Sabbath afternoons. If your child finds reading difficult, obtain stories on tape or read with him. Invite potential "heroes" to your home—the pastor, visiting missionaries, a church member known for outstanding service to the Lord, visiting college students, etc.

During these years children have extremely strong self-doubts. They desperately need to know they are special to God and to you, that God loves them no matter what. Never condemn them in any way. Be open to discussion and reassurance. A sense of specialness to God can see your child through many turbulent moments. Help her learn to cope with peer pressure and to live the Christian life. Aid her in making the transition from a childhood religion to a more mature viewpoint.

At times you will feel very discouraged or go through intense soul-searching. To all outward appearances, your child may seem to have forgotten everything you ever taught him. But pray often for your child. Rely on the Holy Spirit to help you guide his spiritual development. Above all, don't give up. God never does. Lead your child day by day to a fuller understanding and commitment to his Saviour.

The Difficult Passage: Grandchild to Child of God

While the main thrust of this book is spiritual development during childhood, in order to understand how to prepare your child for the adolescent years you need to know what happens spiritually then. I will not attempt to present a detailed description of how to help a child grow spiritually during adolescence. Many others have done that. Rather, I will give you an overview of the most important issues to surface during adolescence.

Spiritual development during the teen years can be compared to crossing the North Atlantic Ocean during the winter storms. Many ships have perished in that venture because it is a difficult passage. Unpredictable winds and storms buffet the vessel with uncontrolled fury. Only the most prepared and skilled mariners with the best equipment can hope to make the passage during that season. Most don't try it.

Our children, however, must attempt the difficult passage from grandchild to child of God. They have no choice. Adolescence inexorably urges them toward maturity. We must do our best to prepare them for the journey. Solid preparation will make it a success.

The changes begin during preadolescence. Hormones create an unfamiliar body and new feelings toward the opposite sex. By early adolescence most children have acquired a new set of mental skills. The ability to think logically and test hypotheses begins for most children sometime between 11 and 14 years of age. Be patient if your child's thinking doesn't seem logical at times. It takes time to develop the full skill. Many college freshmen have not yet attained this level of conceptual thinking. But the process begins during preadolescence and early adolescence.

Along with the new thinking skills comes the ability and desire to question everything, especially what others have previously taught them. It is a normal and natural part of growth and development. School should be teaching children to cross-examine ideas in order to arrive at truth. By middle adolescence, or earlier, the questioning of religion will be in full swing. "But my child was just baptized, and here he is doubting everything!" you say. "Seems like just yesterday he was such a strong believer! What happened?"

Until his change in thought processes he was mostly an uncritical believer. Oh, now and then, he'd raise a question, but mostly he accepted. You were lucky. Now if he didn't raise any questions, you might wonder about his mental development. Mentally gifted kids often raise many questions long before their friends do. It's part of the process of growing up.

During the childhood years children accepted the information their parents gave them as well as their adult standards and values. Parents work hard to impart their spiritual values to their children during early and late childhood. And well they should. Such teachings form the foundation for lifelong values. However, during adolescence children must rework the values and make them their own. Going into adolescence, children have a spiritual values system largely acquired from their parents and their teachers at school and church. Now the major spiritual developmental task of adolescence is to sort out what others have taught them and translate it into their own perspective. Each teenager must decide whether the religion presented to him or her is worth keeping and worth living by.

Ellen White describes how the prophet Daniel made this choice: "Daniel and his companions enjoyed the benefits of correct training and education in early life, but these advantages alone would not have made them what they were. The time came when they must act for themselves — when their future depended upon their own course. Then they decided to be true to the lessons given them in childhood" (*Child Guidance*, p. 167).

Each individual must make the passage from grandchild to child of God because for the long haul God has no grandchildren—only children. Mom and Dad's religion will not carry a child through life. Only a *personal* religion, hammered out of the insecurities and questions of adolescence, will stand the test of time. Each youth must decide for himself or herself "to be true to the lessons given them in childhood."

And so the questions of adolescence are important. Treat them gently and carefully. Help your teenager find answers for himself. He doesn't need an authority to proclaim the answers—that was what happened during childhood. Now he needs a guide who will gently point the way, who will sit down with him and search, who will help him read the compass and navigational charts so he can find his way through the unchartered waters of daily living, who will help him find his *own* answers. You will be richly rewarded for your time and patience at the end of the passage.

Many times I've heard young people say, "I've been an Adventist all my life, but I've only been a Christian for the past two months." And I often wondered, What do they mean? Was everything that happened before wrong?

And so I decided to study what happens during adolescence and young adulthood. Out of that study came the realization that the young person had had a new encounter with Christ, an adult encounter far different from his childhood conversion. The realization of what Christ had really done for him on the cross had finally dawned.

During a panel discussion on righteousness by faith one Sabbath afternoon on our campus, a respected member of the seminary faculty told how one day when he was a junior theology student, during his private devotions, the realization of what Christ had done for him and what righteousness by faith really meant came through for the first time. Elated, he wanted to shout it from the rooftop, to tell everyone he met. The sun shone brighter than it ever had before, and his whole life took on new meaning. He wondered why no one else knew. As time went on, and he shared his discovery with others, he found that many people did indeed know. *He* was the one who had just had a life-changing encounter with His Lord!

That is what I mean by a new "encounter with Christ" on an adult level. The childhood conversion was right for a child. The commitment during the transition just before adolescence helps steady and give focus to the passage. But it is a child's commitment with a child's understanding. Throughout adolescence and youth, understanding must grow and eventually mature into an adult's faith. A child's comprehension will not suffice for adult life.

As I have observed teenagers and youth during the 25 years I have taught on Adventist college campuses in the United States and overseas, I have seen many, many young people experience the "adult encounter with Christ." I've observed it happen as young as 14 or 15. But I've also seen many young people coast through college on their childhood commitment. They graduated and went on to graduate school or out into the working world. Then they came face-to-face with the decisions. Would they follow their Lord or would they take the easy way out? What did Christ really mean to them? Some have followed Him and others have turned away. I suspect that Adventist churches have many adult members who are still living with their childhood understanding of the Saviour. They have not experienced the fullness of joy that only a realization of what Christ has really done for each of us can bring. Their faith is immature.

The chart at the end of this chapter is a simple illustration of how children grow spiritually. Development begins with the early lessons of love, trust, and obedience. They form the foundation. During early childhood children are credulous, natural believers. If we point them toward God, they will believe in Him. They have not experienced enough of life and their thinking processes are not mature enough to even think of doubt.

As children move through late childhood their spirituality matures. They learn more of the meaning of sin, forgiveness, and salvation. Although their understanding is still incomplete, it is sufficient for a child. During the transition years between childhood and adolescence they experience a childhood conversion and make a childhood commitment to follow their Lord. All heaven rejoices over the finding of a "lost lamb" (see Matt. 18:14).

Not too long after that childhood commitment, the questions of adolescence begin. And it may seem to others that their commitment meant nothing. But it did. The questions now come *because* of that commitment. Without their childhood commitment and the previous teaching, they would have little reason for questioning and sorting. Adolescents not exposed to religious influences earlier generally have little interest in religion later.

The questioning-and-sorting process may go on for many years, or may resolve itself rather quickly. Whichever way, the new "encounter with Christ" at a more adult level is the beginning of commitment for adulthood. Glancing at the following chart, do you see the faith line on the right side? Notice how strong and solid it is throughout early and late childhood. Notice the breaks during adolescence. Those are the questioning years. But also observe how the faith line solidifies again with the "encounter with Christ." The decision has been made to be a believer. But the person is no longer the young child believer who knows nothing else. She is the thinking, near-adult believer who could have chosen to turn her back on Christ. Instead, she elected to place her trust in Jesus and to believe with the faith of a little child. Did not Christ say, "Except ye become converted, and become as little children, ye shall not enter into the kingdom of heaven'' (verse 3)? Mature faith is really childlike implicit trust in our Lord's saving grace.

Faith has emerged full bloom from the two-leafed plant of babyhood, the bud of childhood, and the half-open petals of adolescence.

SPIRITUAL DEVELOPMENT

EARLY CHILDHOOD

- **INFANT**

- **TODDLER**

- **PRESCHOOL**

FOUNDATION YEARS

- Habits of Living

- Conscience

- Feelings and attitudes

LOVE, TRUST, OBEDIENCE
Relationship to parents

CREDULOUS

Strong belief in
prayer, faith, love

Learning about
sin
forgiveness
confession
salvation
doctrines

MIDDLE CHILDHOOD

- 6-9 years

- 10-12 years

- Practicing Values

- Conscience

CONVERSION
CHILDHOOD COMMITMENT

ADOLESCENCE

- 13-15 years
  Transition

- 16-18 years
  Aspiration

- Cultural versus
    moral issues
- Peer pressure
- Thinking

- Developing a
    personal philosophy
    of life

REASONING   questions

sorting/
solidifying

"encounter with Christ"

A sound belief
based on
scriptural proof

YOUNG ADULTHOOD

- Self-assurance

ADULT COMMITMENT

faith line

KEYS TO SPIRITUAL GROWTH DURING LATE CHILDHOOD

1. Build a strong foundation for understanding right and wrong. Make your instructions practical.
2. Explain the reasons for right and wrong actions. Deal with everyday situations.
3. Give many opportunities to make choices.
4. Link rewards and punishment with your love and God's love.
5. Encourage memorizing Scripture.
6. Explain religious symbolisms carefully.
7. Give lots of practice in learning to use the Bible.
8. Emphasize each child's specialness to God.
9. Provide opportunities for service projects.
10. Encourage personal devotions.
11. Provide opportunities for accepting Jesus as a personal Saviour.
12. Prepare your child for baptism. Study church doctrines.
13. Introduce Bible study skills.
14. Emphasize what Christ does for each person.
15. Provide Christian role models for your child.
16. Prepare for adolescence. Prepare for peer pressure.

KEYS TO SPIRITUAL GROWTH DURING ADOLESCENCE

1. Respond thoughtfully to questions.
2. Help your teenager find biblical principles to guide his life.
3. Be firm for right. Give a clear message for living God's way.
4. Emphasize Christ's righteousness and what this means personally.
5. Help your teenager deal with the discrepancy between her ideals and her daily life.
6. Show your teenager how to deal with guilt, receive forgiveness, and trust in Christ.
7. Be open to discussing difficult issues. Study to know what you personally believe.
8. Strongly encourage a personal friendship with Jesus.
9. Gradually increase personal responsibility for choices.
10. Show in your own life how God helps you grow spiritually. Be willing to share your personal walk with the Lord.

CHAPTER 12

Jesus, the Children's Saviour

*"For God loved the world so much that he gave his only Son.
God gave his Son so that whoever believes in him may not be lost,
but have eternal life."—John 3:16, ICB*

It was a typical potluck-Sabbath scene in an Adventist city church. Choir music resounded through the empty sanctuary as sopranos and basses rehearsed next Sabbath's anthem. Mouth-watering smells filled the air from the kitchen. Adults visited and children scooted around tables and chairs, happily releasing energy accumulated during a morning in church.

Two-year-old Jonathan's mom and dad were rehearsing with the choir and trying to keep an eye on him at the same time. Intent on mastering a difficult passage, mom looked up just in time to see the child climbing the steps to the main platform. Running straight to the microphone used for the pastoral prayer, Jonathan grinned broadly, grabbed the mike, and engagingly announced, "Hi, Jesus!" His parents looked embarrassed, but everyone else grinned at the boy's spontaneous, unaffected communication with the Saviour of the universe.

Growing up with Jesus is what this book is all about—always knowing Him as your best friend so that without Him you feel incomplete. You have been with Him so much you have become a mirror image of His goodness and beauty. His grace dominates your life. I believe that is what God intends for each of us. Isn't that what we want for our children?

Introducing Jesus to Children

What can we do as parents to help our children grow up with Jesus, to delight in their friendship with Him, and ultimately to embrace His saving grace? Introducing our children to Jesus begins in babyhood with our love and care for the little one entrusted to us. Remember the statement about a mother's love and Christ's love? "The mother's [father's] love represents to the child the love of Christ, and the little ones who trust and obey their mother [or father] are learning to trust and obey the Saviour" (*The Desire of Ages*, p. 515).

Here is the secret. Show your children Jesus' love through your own love. Hug your baby while you say, "Mommy loves you and Jesus loves you." Pair your love with Jesus' love as your child grows through babyhood to toddlerhood and on to the active years of childhood. Make Jesus a joyous part of your family.

Paint an attractive picture of Jesus for your children. Emphasize how He loves to share in our happy times. Paint a word picture of a smiling, happy Jesus who approves of what your child does. Some children mostly hear about a sad Jesus who is unhappy with their behavior. Gradually they come to associate Him with unhappy, guilty feelings, and such children turn away from Him. Instead, we want the mention of His name to bring up feelings of love, warmth, happiness, and caring—feelings that will draw children toward Jesus.

Encourage spontaneous conversation with Jesus. Put away your adult inhibitions. When you see a beautiful flower or a gorgeous sunset, smile happily and say, "What a beautiful flower! Thank You, God! I love red roses." "What lovely music! Thank You!" "We can't find Susie's doll. Please help us remember where we put her." "Jesus, Christie feels so sad . . . please help her to feel happy soon." The occasions for talking with Jesus are numberless. They do not require formal prayers—just a sentence or two expressing how we feel. Children soon catch on to the spirit.

Joyfully introduce Jesus through stories and pictures about His life. Before babies are a year old they can enjoy a few pages from the attractive *My Bible Friends* series. You will find other booklets about Jesus especially written for toddlers. Children identify with the baby Jesus and the child Jesus. Decorate your child's room with a beautiful modern picture of Jesus with children. As you read, share Jesus' love for children with your own child. Reflect His compassion and care. Paint a word picture of the loving Jesus who truly cares for children.

As children grow older, tell them more about the life of Jesus, emphasizing His constant concern and protection for people like themselves. Describe to them the great controversy—why Jesus came to earth, died on a cross, and was resurrected just for them! Assure them that Jesus is eagerly waiting for them, making the most beautiful homes, and looking forward to bringing them to live with Him for always. Read them the beautifully illustrated *Forever Stories* series about the conflict between God and Satan.

Remind them that Jesus hurts when they hurt. That He would love to take them in His arms and comfort them. Tell them Jesus can be their best friend, their forever friend, who never moves away, never quarrels or fights or says nasty things, and never rejects them. Jesus is their heavenly friend who never abandons them. Show them how to have a friendship with Jesus. What do friends do? They talk to each other, they tell secrets, they do things together, they love each other, they give each other gifts. Your children can tell Jesus their secrets, talk to Him many times a day, and show their love for Jesus by loving others. Children can listen to what Jesus says to them in His Word, sing praise songs to Him, and learn more about Him every day. Finally they can give Him gifts.

Cultivate joy in Jesus. Happiness is catching. When you excitedly talk about what Jesus has done for you, your children will absorb your own spirit. But if you find your relationship with the Lord a painful burden, your children will shy away from Him. The most important and impressive thing you can do is to show your children openly how much you love Jesus, and they will learn to love Him too.

Those children who have grown up with Jesus, walked hand in hand with Him through childhood, will find accepting His gift of salvation the most natural thing in the world. They will simply put their hand in His and trustingly receive His salvation.

Understanding Salvation

Can children really understand salvation? Of course they can! I love the statement in *Messages to Young People*, page 15: "Christ came to teach the human family the way of salvation, and He made this way so plain that a little child can walk in it." Did you notice the implication of that sentence? Even a child . . . can understand. We are the ones who make things complicated with our insistence on the fine points of justification and sanctification, of perfectionism, of the nature of Christ, and of all the other theological controversies.

Many Bible points are abstract and sometimes difficult to grasp. A full understanding of Bible prophecy and the deeper meaning of many Bible passages does not come until a child matures in thinking processes. But salvation is simple. Children can understand the stories of the Bible. They can have a beautiful friendship with Jesus, can experience the assurance of salvation and the working of God's grace in their lives. Salvation *can* be understood by children. Jesus said so.

Readiness to Accept Salvation

The next question, of course, is When is a child ready to accept Jesus as a personal Saviour? Ellen White makes a suggestion in one of the few statements she has written that mention a specific age: "Children of eight, ten, or twelve years are old enough to be addressed on the subject of personal religion. Do not teach your children with reference to some future period when they shall be old enough to repent and believe the truth. If properly instructed, very young children may have correct views of their state as sinners and of the way of salvation through Christ" (*Child Guidance*, p. 490, 491).

Children naturally possess the qualities of love, trust, and confidence. They are the same qualities needed for a relationship with Jesus the Saviour. There is no specified age when children are ready to receive Jesus as their Saviour. Some might be ready at a younger age, while others might be much older before they accept the gift of salvation. Many things make the difference. Some highly intelligent children are advanced beyond their years and ponder things other children haven't dreamed of yet. They understand what the less mentally mature won't even listen to. And often they are ready to accept Jesus as their personal Saviour during early childhood. Encourage them to answer the call of the Holy Spirit.

Children respond easily to love. In his book *All the Children of the Bible*, Herbert Lockyer stresses the importance of love for the spiritual growth of children: "The language of love is the one a child learns most easily, and it is because its heart is most susceptible to love that it can be won before it is able to give a reason for its hope" (p. 61). Sadly, some children do not know how to love or trust. Not having experienced love in their families, they have great difficulty trusting anyone. As a result they will also have a hard time accepting the Saviour's love and trusting in His saving grace.

Children differ greatly in their knowledge of the Scriptures. The child who has learned to know the Bible, believe the Bible, and love the Bible will also want to respond to the call for salvation and obedience.

Confidence in the Scriptures is the foundation for salvation. A child learns it step by step through the instruction and modeling of adults and the influence of the Holy Spirit.

Religious background makes a great difference. A child reared with regular home and church religious education will understand Christ's mission at a younger age than one not exposed to Christian teaching. If your home is rich in spiritual life, your child will sense a need for the Saviour earlier than one not surrounded with spiritual influences. However, if your child sees many blatant inconsistencies between what you teach and what you live, she will be hard to reach with the gospel. Having lived with hypocrisy, she has, in a sense, "turned off" religion and salvation. She may be more difficult to get through to than the child who comes from a completely non-Christian background, because she has hardened her heart against the Saviour. If religion didn't do the adults in her home any good, she concludes, why should she bother?

When one parent is a Christian and the other parent is not, the child may feel torn between loyalty to each parent. He may put off making a decision, fearing to offend either one. She may be honestly unsure, like a friend's 12-year-old daughter whose father was not a church member. When all of her friends at the local church school were deciding to be baptized, she said to her mother, "How do I know who is right—you or Daddy?" And so she delayed her decision. Sometimes she may see the lifestyle of the non-Christian parent as less restrictive and may turn away from Christ. If you are in a similar situation, pray much for your child and also for yourself that you will show by your life the joy and attractiveness of the Christian walk. Pray for the Holy Spirit to speak to your children.

As I have been giving workshops over the years, I have asked many groups of Adventists when they first recognized that Jesus was their personal Saviour. Generally about a fifth to a fourth of the group will indicate they came to such a realization before they were 8 years old. The overwhelming majority turned to Jesus as their Saviour before they were teenagers. Generally few indicate that they accepted salvation during their early or middle teen years. Usually only one fourth or less turned to Jesus as their personal Saviour after the age of 18. Most such individuals did not grow up in Christian homes and did not become acquainted with Him until adulthood. It appears that the overwhelming majority of children reared in Christian homes find Jesus as their Saviour before the teen years.

Be careful before deciding a child is too young to respond to the Saviour.

Children vary greatly in their spiritual insights and ability to understand salvation. If your child goes through the prime decision years and shows no interest in salvation, try to discover why. But be careful and gentle as you do so. If you encounter barriers between you and your child, pray that God will send someone else into his life who can reach him for the Lord.

Both the head and the heart must respond to the Saviour's invitation. Avoid extreme emotionalism and scare tactics. They are not appropriate for children (probably not for adults, either, but that is not the topic of this book!). Excessive emotionalism or human attempts at motivation may actually work against the promptings of the Holy Spirit that a child experiences through the Scriptures. Young children find themselves easily swayed by feelings. They want to please adults—especially those they admire and like. Thus they may respond to a highly emotional group invitation to accept the Saviour simply because everyone else is, or because they want to please the adults, or because they are afraid. None of these are appropriate reasons for responding to a "call."

Many children respond to the Saviour's invitation during a special Week of Prayer at school or during a campfire at camp. We must be sure that they are not reactions to peer pressure. Because of that danger, I believe we should approach children individually with the call to follow their Lord. As parents and teachers we need to be sensitive to the special moment when the Holy Spirit is summoning a child. We need to pray that the Spirit will speak to the child, and that we will recognize the moment when we can help. If a Sabbath school teacher really knows the children in his class and becomes their friend, he will sense when a particular child is struggling with the decision to follow his Lord. That is the moment to extend the invitation.

Both the Old and the New Testaments assume that the religious instruction of children resides with the family, that it is responsible for guiding the young ones. Parents know their children best. Being with them through all the ups and downs of growing up, you can sense when a child is struggling with a problem. You can then gently point the child to God's forgiveness and to a saving relationship with Jesus.

Is there a difference between adult and child conversion? The answer is both yes and no. Conversion is a conscious turning away from sin and a turning toward God (Acts 9:35) whether the person is young or old. Each must acknowledge his sins and his need of a Saviour. Both must accept the gift of salvation offered by Christ and show evidence of a new life in Christ—a changed life.

On the other hand, the child comes in the relative innocence of childhood with only childish sins to leave behind. Not having been involved in deep sin, he does not carry the scars of sinful living. Thus the child probably does not have many sinful habits to overcome, wrongs to make right, or restitutions to effect. He may not understand in the deepest sense what is happening, but he can accept salvation and love the Lord and become a child of His. The child will grow in Christian understanding and Christian graces as he matures through the passing years. He has before him a lifetime of living and serving Christ.

Be careful about judging the depth of a child's conversion by his emotions. Violent emotion does not necessarily evidence conviction of sin in children. The feelings of childhood are fleeting. Also remember that the child doesn't have the depth of sin from which to repent that the adult may have. It is not easy to tell from the outward responses what the inner conviction might be.

Neither is it necessary to know the exact moment when a child is converted (*The Desire of Ages*, p. 515). Childhood conversion may be gradual. For the youngster brought up in a Christian home, conversion is one step of many toward a goal—godlikeness. You have been preparing your child for this moment from the day he was born.

If your family has only just recently come to know the Saviour, your children will need to make their own individual decisions, too. The younger children, of course, will follow along with what Mom and Dad do. But older ones—10, 12, or more—may resent the changes in the family's lifestyle. They may not be interested in making the same kind of commitment that their parents do. Because they must experience the Lord for themselves, they will need time and much love.

Leading Children to Accept Salvation

What can we do to lead children to accept salvation?

1. Surround the child with sound Christian teaching and love from birth. The Bible provides a foundation for faith and discipleship (2 Tim. 3:15).

2. Help children become accountable to God [Jesus]. When children are young, they are accountable to their parents. As they grow older, however, they need to begin thinking about their accountability to God also. Accepting salvation means becoming responsible to God—a higher authority than parents. Even though parental authority comes from God,

ultimately a child becomes directly accountable to God for the life he lives. Until a child can relate to being responsible to God, he is probably not fully ready to accept Christ's sacrifice. You can help your children move in this direction by encouraging them to be answerable to God [Jesus] and by reminding them that Jesus cares about them and about how they live. Children who have reached this level of understanding may say things like, "I think I need to tell Jennifer I'm sorry. I know that's what Jesus wants me to do" or "I asked Jesus to forgive me, too."

Young children are highly behavior-oriented. They don't generally give much thought to the motives for an action until they near the preteen years. Their accountability to God will first focus on actions, not motives. Consideration of motives will emerge later.

3. Help your child experience the different aspects of coming to Christ as he or she is growing up. These include:

a. Experiencing God's love
b. Feeling guilty over wrongdoing
c. Being sorry for wrongdoing
d. Confessing wrongdoing to Jesus and to the person wronged
e. Yielding the will when appropriate
f. Experiencing forgiveness and forgiving others
g. Making an effort to change wrongdoing
h. Helping others
i. Praying
j. Learning about God through nature and the Scriptures
k. Being joyful in love for Jesus and trusting Him

Other chapters have discussed many of these aspects of Christian living. From the time they are quite small, children can learn about being sorry for doing something wrong, about forgiveness, and about yielding their will to what their parents want them to do. All such experiences make it easier for a child to come to Jesus because he is already acquainted with the needed steps.

Read books about the different steps to salvation to your children. The children's *Steps to Christ* series, published by Pacific Press Publishing Association, is wonderful for 4- to 8-year-olds. An alert 3-year-old might enjoy listening to some of the books, while older children might enjoy reading them for themselves. The series includes books on forgiveness, salvation, God's love, and other aspects of coming to Christ. Recently I read them to my grandchildren. At the end, Jeff, the 5-year-old, took a deep breath and thoughtfully said, "There's something to learn from those books!" On another occasion he commented about the story on forgiveness. "I like that because they *both* had to forgive!"

Ellen White's *Steps to Christ* has recently appeared in a new youth edition with study helps and devotional comments. Your preteens might enjoy it. Child Evangelism Fellowship, in their monthly magazine, *Evangelizing Today's Children*, usually includes a colorfully illustrated story about some aspect of salvation.

4. Help children understand the vocabulary of salvation. Words like sin, Saviour, salvation, grace, Holy Spirit, and forgiveness need explaining. Interpret the meaning of each word using simple language that your child can grasp. Give plenty of opportunity for any questions they might have. Always bring truth to your child's level. Some Bible stories that are helpful in explaining aspects of salvation include Nicodemus (John 3), the woman at the well (John 4), the woman caught in adultery (John 8), Philip and the Ethiopian (Acts 8), and the Philippian jailer (Acts 16).

5. Explain the stages of salvation. Be sure to include each of the following main steps. Use the Bible to show the child what he should do and what Jesus will do, using the following ideas:

a. God loves everyone (1 John 4:8; Jer. 31:3).

b. Everyone does wrong and is a sinner, thus everyone needs salvation because sinners will die forever. Be sure the child recognizes himself as a sinner (Rom. 3:23).

c. God sent Jesus to die so we wouldn't have to die forever (John 3:16). Then He rose again as our Saviour (1 Cor. 15:3, 4). When we receive Jesus, all our sins will be forgiven (Isa. 1:18; Ps. 51:7-11; 1 John 2:1, 2).

d. Each child must receive salvation by personally asking Jesus to be his Saviour (John 1:12). Help the child to pray to receive Him.

e. If you have accepted Jesus, you have become a new person, one who doesn't want to do wrong because you love Jesus and Jesus loves you (John 3:3-7; 2 Cor. 5:17).

f. Be sure your child feels the assurance of salvation (John 3:36; Heb. 13:5). Show her what she must do now if she sins—confess her sins to Jesus, who will forgive her (1 John 1:9). The next chapter gives many more ideas about how to help your child accept grace and live for Jesus on a daily basis.

Make the above ideas as simple as needed for the child to grasp. The most important concept is that he recognize the nature of sin (wrongdoing) and its consequences (eternal death), and then ask Jesus to forgive and be his Saviour.

You can use pictures or drawings to portray the steps. Help the child find the suggested Bible texts and underline them in his or her own Bible. Use stories to explain the concept of new birth. The caterpillar in a cocoon makes a wonderful illustration of becoming a new person in Jesus. John 3 has some excellent illustrations about being "born again." Child Evangelism Fellowship suggests using the "Wordless Book" to explain salvation. Each page is a different color, representing one of the steps in understanding salvation, ending with a gold page symbolizing eternal life.

6. Assist your children from the time they are very small to make little decisions between right and wrong. As they mature they will grow accustomed to choosing positively. Ultimately it will be easier for them to decide to accept salvation and follow Jesus for the rest of their lives.

7. Use everyday, natural situations to teach spiritual lessons about salvation. Be tuned in for indications that the Holy Spirit is convicting your child. It can happen any time—during family worship, while reading a story, riding in the car, working or playing together, or struggling through a difficult situation in your child's life. The possibilities are endless.

8. Sharing a decision for Christ is an important step in your child's life. Help him find an opportunity to tell others about it. You might suggest he announce it to the whole family at worshiptime or at the evening meal. He could let your church pastor know about it. Grandparents would love to hear of his decision, especially if they are Christians too. Telling his best friend might open the way for sharing with other children.

9. While children are usually not great sinners with piles of guilt to give to the Lord, they will feel troubled about past sins. Your child may feel convicted to make restitution but not know how. It gives you a wonderful opportunity to help him, but be very kind and gentle. Assist him in finding Bible promises for forgiveness and instructions about what to do. Talk about how he might make restitution, then pray about it with him. Maybe you will want to go with him to provide support. Saying one is sorry is never easy. Confessing to taking some candy from a store and paying the manager from his allowance or money he has earned takes a lot of courage. Your support will be extremely valuable, but do not do the job for him. Cheating on a test means going to the teacher to confess. It's scary. He has no guarantees about the teacher's response, but Jesus will be with him and give him courage whatever happens. Your child might need

to make a long-distance call or write a letter to the former teacher.

Never, never berate your child or express shock at what he reveals. Always demonstrate forgiveness in how you treat him. And never bring up those things again. If God buries our sins in the depths of the ocean (Micah 7:19), we can do no less. Remember, God accepts all repentant sinners with love. But He shows that love through *you*.

10. Pray daily for the Holy Spirit to draw your child to Jesus. All your efforts will amount to nothing without Him. No human words can perfectly explain salvation. Nor can it be orchestrated on demand. Salvation is the result of the soft voice of the Holy Spirit speaking to your child's heart. He is your most important ally in reaching your children with the Good News of salvation. ''As the Holy Spirit moves upon the hearts of the children, cooperate with His work. Teach them that the Saviour is calling them, that nothing can afford Him greater joy than for them to give themselves to Him in the bloom and freshness of their years'' (*The Ministry of Healing*, p. 44).

KEYS TO ACCEPTING SALVATION

1. Pray for the Holy Spirit to speak to your child's heart.
2. Paint an attractive picture of Jesus for your children.
3. Cultivate joy in Jesus. Show His love through your own.
4. Build a strong foundation of biblical teaching for your children.
5. Help children become accountable to Jesus.
6. Enable children to experience the different aspects of coming to Jesus as they mature.
7. Define the vocabulary of salvation.
8. Explain the steps in salvation.
9. Help children make little decisions involving right and wrong as they grow.
10. Use everyday situations to teach spiritual lessons about salvation.
11. Invite your child to follow Jesus and accept His offer of salvation.
12. Provide opportunities to share his decision to accept salvation.

CHAPTER 13

Growing in Jesus

"Let our sons in their youth grow like strong trees.
Let our daughters be like the decorated stones in the Temple."
—Psalm 144:12, ICB

At my workshops on helping children grow spiritually parents often ask, "How can I keep my child from being such a legalist? I want him to understand righteousness by faith, but he insists on the letter of the law."

Preschool and early elementary children are naturally legalistic—if we mean doing everything exactly according to the rules—because they are at the stage of learning what is right and wrong in the context of rules. So in some quite important ways we do want our young children to be "legalists." They need to understand right and wrong clearly because values are built on a solid knowledge of right and wrong. The preschool years are the most important years for giving children this foundation.

We can do this by making the values we want to teach our children as clear as possible. Figuratively we are building a "value fence" around our children. If the fence is strong, they will have the value base they need for later years. But if we give a mixed message about values, the structure for later values will be weak.

Helping children grow up to be responsible adults—solid citizens who provide the glue that keeps families and society together—is absolutely vital. Millions of people around the world are responsible, moral persons who care for their families and demonstrate their concern for the poor and homeless. Many of them, however, are not Christians or religious in any way. Christ is not the reason for their actions. They know nothing about salvation.

But our goals, as Christian parents, are different. While we desire our children to be responsible and caring adults, we want their motivation to come from a heart filled with Christ and His love. Let's not get behavior and motives confused. As we teach our children good and moral behavior, we also want them to recognize that they are at the same time sinners in need of a Saviour. Their good behavior will never be their ticket to the Holy City. On their own power, they can never be good enough to merit entry to heaven. Jesus Christ, their Saviour, alone provides the only valid ticket to heaven. Yet it is free because Christ paid for it on Calvary.

When we accept Jesus as our Saviour, He also becomes the Lord of our lives. If we begin to cultivate a relationship with Him, that relationship will ultimately bring about drastic changes in the way we live and, incidentally, in our behavior. As we grow more intimate with Jesus, our desires change. As the well-known chorus says, "Things are different now." We like different things, we think differently, we want to do different things—not out of fear that we will be lost, but because Jesus lives in us. Changed, transformed, we no longer want to do those other behaviors.

I like the parable from Ken McFarland's *Gospel Showdown* (also quoted by Morris Venden in *Love God and Do as You Please*). In this parable God is the mother and we are the Mud Puddle Kid.

"Halfway through his nightly recital of the world's hang-ups, the benign anchorman suddenly disappeared, replaced momentarily by that commercial starring the Mud Puddle Kid.

"Draped across various items of living room furniture out there in front of the box were the Three Watchers.

" 'That poor Kid's mother really has a problem,' Number One observed, as, up on the screen, The Kid stomped gleefully through several large mud puddles. 'She probably had him all ready to go to a party, and now look at him with that yucky mud all over his clothes.'

" 'Oh, but there's Good News!' enthused Number Two excitedly. 'Just watch now,' he added, pointing to the screen, 'and you'll see that his mom is going to take all those dirty clothes and wash them in Mud-B-Gone detergent. That will solve everything!'

" 'If you've watched this commercial before, then you ought to know that that doesn't solve everything,' retorted Number One. 'Just keep watching.'

"They did, and sure enough, The Kid, sporting freshly laundered clothes, charged back outside to the nearest puddle. As he splattered himself with muddy goo, his mom shook her head and sighed as she tried to look thankful for her box of Mud-B-Gone.

" 'There, you see,' Number One continued. 'What good does it do for her to clean her Kid up if he goes right back out and jumps in the mud? I'll tell you what the real Good News is. It's when Mom not only can clean The Kid up, but can also take away his desire to play in mud puddles— maybe even make him hate mud.'

"Number Three hadn't said anything so far, but he'd been thinking, and now he was ready with his dime's worth. 'I think both of you may have a point,' he began, 'but even if Mom can clean up The Kid and then make him hate mud puddles, it seems to me that the problem can never be fully solved until someone takes the mud puddles themselves away. To me, that would really be Good News.'

"Well, it pains me to say it, but the Three Watchers became so upset with one another over what constituted the Good News, or the Gospel, that they decided to have a showdown. They stepped out into the street and started slinging mud at one another.

"The last I saw them, they still hadn't figured out that they had all three seen just a part of the Good News—and that it takes all three parts to really solve The Kid's problem.

"But, as Walter Cronkite used to say, 'That's the way it is,' " (pp. 7, 8).

Aren't you glad God washes us clean by His grace and forgives our sins? Wonderful Mud-B-Gone! But wouldn't it be marvelous if we didn't want to wallow in the mud of sin in the first place? But that's our nature—we love the mud! Sometimes we stay away because we have will power and speak sternly to ourselves about romping in the mud. We're afraid we'll be punished if we get dirty. But it's tough to keep out of the mud because we still love to wallow in it.

Can you imagine your children not wanting to play in the mud? Mud and little children seem to go together, just as sin and fallen human beings naturally attract each other. There exists only one way to really change our nature. If Christ lives in us, eventually we don't even want to play in the mud. He has transformed us. "If we consent, He [God] will so identify Himself with our thoughts and aims, so blend our hearts and minds into conformity to His will, that when obeying Him we shall be but carrying out our own impulses" (*The Desire of Ages*, p. 668). Someday God will also get rid of the mud puddles.

Thus it is important to teach our children the difference between right and wrong, to help them grow up to be responsible, moral people who care about their families and their neighbors. But we want more than that as Christian parents. Staying away from the mud of sin is hard work if our children depend only on their own willpower. We want them to dislike the mud puddle of sin, to hate wallowing in it. Only an ongoing, growing relationship with Jesus can change their hearts that way.

While we don't give up teaching them the difference between right and wrong, of helping them develop a solid character, at the same time we introduce them to Jesus. Encouraging them to cultivate the relationship, to become best friends with Him, is the only way to effect a heart change — to enable them to want to stay out of the mud.

Our own attitudes toward God and salvation rub off on our children at an extremely early age. When we act forgiving and caring, our children pick up those same attitudes and attribute them to God. What we say about salvation makes an impact also. "Jesus won't love you if you do that" gives a strong legalistic message — actually an untruth. He and God love us no matter what we do. Another favorite I've heard too often goes like this: "Jesus won't take you to heaven because you . . . (hit your sister, told a lie, etc.)." That encourages them to cling to willpower and to try to stay out of the mud on their own strength.

On the other hand, the message that God is so loving He knows it's really too hard for us to stop wallowing in the mud is equally untrue. What our children need to hear is that God forgives them and wants to live His perfect life *in* them. He can change their desires if they will let Him. If they accept God's love and forgiveness and cultivate an intimate friendship with Him, they will then live eternally in His presence, where there are no mud puddles.

It is not easy to get this message across to children, particularly during early and middle childhood, because they have a hard time separating actions from the person. Bad actions, bad person, they assume automatically, and God doesn't love bad people. We can counter this natural inclination by showing our love even when our children are naughty. Also, we must emphasize God's love rather than His anger. Keep communicating to them that God is just and merciful and the Jesus who always loves us is our Judge and the Saviour (John 5:22; Matt. 1:21). When we combine the qualities of love and firmness for right in our everyday actions with our children, the message of a loving God who accepts us through the righteousness of Jesus will eventually settle into their minds.

Sometimes children surprise us. As the only Adventists in their large family, Carole and her sister were frequently the target of potshots at their beliefs. One time when their extended family had gathered for the funeral of a family member, an uncle, a minister of another denomination, began harassing Stevie, Carole's 5-year-old son. "You don't eat meat, do you?" he asked the child. Stevie agreed that he didn't. "Why don't you eat meat?"

"It's not good for you," the boy replied quickly. But the uncle wasn't satisfied.

"You won't go to heaven if you eat meat, will you?"

His nephew looked a bit puzzled, thought a moment, and then responded positively, "I'll go to heaven if I love Jesus!" Stevie had gotten the message.

Giving the Will to Jesus

How can we help our children get the message of righteousness by grace? First, show your child how to give his life (will) to Jesus. The key to staying out of the mud puddle of sin is asking Jesus to take control of his life. Explain to your child that, because of Satan and sin, we all want to do bad things. That's the way we are. The *only* way we can change is to ask Jesus to give us a new, perfect heart. He can and wants to offer it to us. But it is like a present. We can't go to the store and buy it ourselves. We can only get it from Jesus. When He gives us a new perfect heart, we become His boy or girl.

Use an illustration your child understands. Many children are interested in sports, so you might present the following explanation. In the game called life we find only two teams—Jesus' team and Satan's team. Both captains are trying to get people to play on their side. Satan makes his team look like the most fun. The players don't have to practice hard or get regular sleep or eat the right foods. It seems as if they have fun most of the time. The players on Jesus' team, however, practice a lot, are careful to eat body-building foods, don't use drugs or alcohol, don't smoke, and every day they spend time listening to their Captain and talking to Him. Loving their Captain, they want to be with Him all the time.

When the two teams play, Jesus' team always plays fairly. Sometimes it appears as if Satan's team is going to win because they ignore the rules, don't play fairly, and have a lot larger number of players. Jesus' team plays well, though, and He is always right in there playing with the rest of the members. If a team member gets hurt, Jesus jumps in to help. Satan just stands on the sidelines jeering when any of his players hurt themselves.

Someday Jesus' team will win the last game over Satan's team. Then Satan and his team will be destroyed while everyone on Jesus' team will live with Him forever. Every person in the whole universe must choose whether he wants to join Jesus' team or Satan's team. The captain of the team—Jesus or Satan—calls the shots and tells the player what to do. When your child chooses Jesus' team, Jesus becomes the captain of his life. Jesus knows how to help him be a winner against Satan.

Depending on your child's experiences and understanding, you could use still other illustrations. The Bible talks about creating a "new heart" within a person (Eze. 36:26 and Ps. 51:10); being grafted into the vine plant (John 15:1-8); and having Christ living within (Gal. 2:20). All are ways of depicting the work of the Holy Spirit in a person's life.

Be sure your child understands that she must herself choose to have Jesus as her captain. That means being willing to let Jesus control her life and trusting Him with herself. She made the big choice to be on Jesus' team when she accepted Jesus as her Saviour. However, each day she must decide to do exactly what her Captain [Jesus] wants her to do in order to be a winner against Satan. When she chooses Jesus every day, then she will live happily, knowing that she is safe from Satan.

How can she elect Jesus as her captain every day? By simply saying during her wake-up-in-the-morning talk with Jesus that she wants Him to be her captain for that day. She asks for the new clean heart that He can give her so she won't want to play in the mud puddle of sin. The Holy Spirit loves to respond to such requests.

Cultivating a Friendship With Jesus

Show your child how to get to know Jesus as a friend. The better she knows Jesus, the more she will become like Him. Explain that God's Word is the food that helps our characters to grow more like His. Read stories about Jesus from the Bible or other inspirational books from the time your child is quite small and able to sit on your lap. Even before he can understand the words he will love the sound and comfort of your voice. Add stories about other Bible characters until they too become personal friends. Emphasize how Jesus and God were their friends, too. Reading spiritual stories to your child, studies have found, is one of the most powerful tools you can use to help your child grow spiritually. Keep on reading as a family even after your child can read for himself. Family reading time also gives you an opportunity to discuss what you have read.

Help your children begin to have a private devotional time. They could read a Bible story, listen quietly to see what the Holy Spirit might say to their minds, draw a picture of what they learned from the Bible story or write in a devotional journal, sing a song or listen to a short devotional tape, and finish with talking with Jesus. Encourage them to tell Him just how they feel about every little or big thing in their lives, just like they talk with their human friends. In fact, they can share their secrets with Jesus because He never tells. Gradually Jesus will become their closest friend.

You can encourage your children to have a private devotional time by making it part of the family schedule. For example, everyone in the family should know that the first 20 to 30 minutes after the alarm rings is for each family member to have a private time with Jesus and God. Because it is a special time, no one interrupts the other family members. Such a plan works especially well with school-age children and adolescents, although families who do it have told me their preschool children catch on quickly and enjoy looking at religious books and "talking to Jesus" during this time. If you decide to try this idea, be sure you talk it over as a family before beginning. Help each child gather the materials he or she will need for devotional time (Bible, paper/notebook and pen or crayons/markers, tape of songs, etc.). Give each child a basket or decorated box to keep his or her "Jesus time" materials in.

Becoming More Like Jesus

Jesus is the model for our lives. Begin by telling your child that Scripture shows us how Jesus wants us to live. Help him find a Bible verse or passage to guide him in daily living, such as Philippians 4:8. You might start a notebook of Christian character traits. As you learn about a trait, your child could write a Bible verse that tells about it. Then together you could think of ways to practice that trait in daily living. Write down the suggestions (or draw pictures of the ideas) on the page with the Bible verse. Younger children might find magazine pictures that illustrate different situations in which that particular trait would be helpful. You could find stories about the trait to read to your children. Perhaps start with the Ten Commandments, God's guide for living (Ex. 20:3-17), using the positive traits each commandment suggests. Also you could learn about Peter's ladder of Christian character traits (2 Peter 1:5-8), the fruits of the Spirit (Gal. 5:22), or the Sermon on the Mount (Matt. 5-7). Romans 12:8-13:13 has additional specific suggestions for how to live God's way. Any of these passages would be a wonderful way to get started learning about how Jesus wants us to live and would make an excellent Sabbath-afternoon activity.

Teach your child a special promise for daily living, such as "I can do all things through Christ because he gives me strength" (Phil. 4:13, ICB) or "it is Christ living in me" (Gal. 2:20, ICB). Keep reminding her that she can become like Jesus only when He is her captain. He then gives her a new, clean heart and different desires. Without Jesus she will only get discouraged and become sad and depressed. No one can become more like Jesus without His help. Explain how when she plays on Jesus' team He will walk with her all the time, hold her hand, and help her get up when she stumbles and falls. If she lets go of His hand and runs off by herself, she will soon get into trouble. But when Jesus is holding her hand, even when she stumbles, He immediately lifts her up. Holding Jesus' hand is the key to growing more like Him every day.

Make your instruction in Christian living practical. Include illustrations from your child's life—playground experiences; examples of cheating, obedience, kindness, helpfulness, and jealousy; and incidents of home life. Many times children need ideas for how to deal with the situations in their lives. Role-play a difficult situation to help your child come up with suggestions of how to respond. First, have him play himself and you be the other child. Then reverse roles so he can begin to understand how others feel. Ask him what Jesus would do in this situation. Find a Bible verse or passage that provides a guiding principle.

Claiming God's Promises

Very young children are sure that Jesus will answer their prayers. But as they grow older and learn more about the world, the doubts begin to creep in. You need to remind them often that God's promises are for *them*. Before your child enters adolescence, he needs to have rebuilt his faith in God's promises into something he can cling to during the rest of his life. Show him how to claim God's promises for himself.

The first step in implementing God's promises in his life is to ask with faith—believe in God's Word, believe that He cares and will do what is best for him (James 1:6). The next step is to be willing to do God's will (Prov. 28:9), to obey His Word. If your child is not willing to do what *God* asks, then he can hardly claim God's promises for what *he* wants. Would it be fair? Help him think carefully about his willingness to do what God desires of him. Teach him that he cannot use God's promises for something that is clearly not God's will. When he knows it is wrong to be in a certain place, ask him if it is fair to expect God to give him special protection in a situation he should never have gotten into in the first place. And last, see that your child understands that he must give up his own possibly selfish desires before God can really answer his prayer for guidance. Otherwise he is blocking God's plans. If God knows what is best for us, we must be willing to drop what we want so we can hear what God suggests. If you keep these main ideas in mind, as situations come up in daily life you will be able to help your child learn how to claim God's promises for guidance. Be patient. Teach a little at a time, and step-by-step he will grow in understanding.

Learning to Forgive

Learning to forgive is a tough lesson. When Kristi knocks over the tower Jeff has so carefully built during the previous two days and was intending to show to his teacher, he wants revenge. Forgiveness is not even in his thoughts. In fact, it is not natural to our sinful natures. Rather, forgiveness is a gift from God, who alone has the power to turn us inside out and around 180 degrees.

Children need to experience forgiveness from the time they are little. When your preschooler accidentally breaks something, hug her and say, "I forgive you. It's OK." And then don't mention the incident again. Demonstrate in your relationship with your children how God forgives *and* forgets each of our mistakes. When you say to your 8-year-old, "I don't know if we can trust you after what you did last week," your child recognizes that you have not really forgiven him. Forgiving means not mentioning the indiscretion again.

Teach your children to say "I'm sorry. Please forgive me" when they have hurt someone and are genuinely sorry. Most children need a quiet time by themselves to think about what they have done and for the Holy Spirit to speak to them before they are ready to acknowledge that they are sorry. When you respond to their apology, be sure to say specifically that you forgive them. Hug and make up.

Also teach your children to forgive others. Kristi needs to feel sorry for knocking over Jeff's tower, but Jeff also needs to learn to forgive her for doing it. Pray that the Holy Spirit will speak to each child. Some children have a natural tendency to hold grudges. Inherently proud, they have a hard time forgiving. It is even harder for such children to apologize. Be patient and persistent. In time they will learn the Bible way. Give them quiet time to think about what happened. Insist that your child go to someone she has wronged and apologize and ask for forgiveness. Accompany her to offer support, but don't say the words for her. She needs the experience of asking for and receiving forgiveness.

Along with requesting forgiveness goes restitution, or making things right. What can Kristi do for Jeff? Help her think about how he feels and what she can do so he won't be so angry and sad. Talk about it. And then help her make things right with him.

When two children are really angry with each other, sometimes it helps to have each one sit down in a separate room with paper and pencil. Instruct them to write out what happened and to ask God to help them see the situation as He saw it. Then bring the two children together and let them read from their papers. Occasionally it is easier for children to write out an apology than to voice it. If one apologizes and asks for forgiveness, request the other one to respond. Then the one who has forgiven can demonstrate that forgiveness by tearing up the paper describing the offense. Once it has been torn up, no one can talk about it again.

Demonstrating forgiveness also means doing something nice when the other person doesn't deserve it. Maybe your child rushed off to school and didn't make her bed. If it is a habit, then she needs to experience an appropriate consequence so she can learn a new one. But if it is only a once-in-a-great-while slipup, you might make her bed for her and pin a note to her pillow where she will find it when she goes to sleep. Your note might say, ''I made your bed because I love you. Mom.''

When a child has been especially bad, and you do something unusually nice for him, he experiences God's grace—unmerited favor. Look for opportunities to help your children experience God's grace through you.

A trip to the beach can provide a wonderful illustration of God's forgiveness. As you walk along the beach, point out the footprints in the sand. When the tide comes in, the footprints disappear forever. No one can find them again. Explain that's exactly what Jesus does with our sins.

The wrong things we do and think make a mark on us like the footprints on the beach. But when we ask forgiveness, Jesus washes all the evidence away. It's as if we had never sinned. Your children need to have this assurance deep in their minds. It will carry them through the doubts, discouragement, and guilt of adolescence.

Some children have an extremely hard time forgiving themselves even though they can easily forgive others. It is one of Satan's most subtle traps because eventually such a child will believe that God cannot forgive her either. Her sins are so great that she doesn't merit God's forgiveness. But then actually no one does. It is a free gift given to us because God and Jesus love us.

Often a child who cannot forgive herself holds impossibly high standards for her own behavior. She can never satisfy her demands because she is a perfectionist. As a result she won't try anything new because she is afraid she can't do it perfectly. Sometimes this tendency is an inborn part of an individual's personality. Other times it is an acquired trait because she has lived with impossibly high demands since she was little. The child can never do anything well enough to satisfy her parents. Sometimes such misguided parents, although well intentioned, think it is the way to encourage a child toward excellence. They never compliment, but always point out what could have been done better.

Rudy's parents were that way. As a graduate student in his mid-20s he told me he could never do anything well enough to please them. He remembered that when he was a preschooler he never heard them say anything was well done. Instead, they always pointed out how he could have done it better. By the time Rudy started first grade he was convinced he was the stupidest kid anywhere and was incapable of doing anything right. In reality he was an exceptionally intelligent child with many outstanding abilities.

Once in school he quickly learned to read, and pretty soon he noticed that he could do it better than most of the other children. Gradually he began to think of himself as smarter. But the influence of his parents' attitudes lingered. His girlfriend told me he never complimented her. One time when she made him some cookies, all he said was, "Well, they could have a little more sugar." Even her appearance came in for the same treatment. Naturally, the relationship broke up.

Predictably, Rudy's God was an angry judge who constantly frowned and never forgave. Rudy had an extremely hard time forgiving himself and others for any failure. Perfection alone would appease his God. It would take many experiences with forgiveness and much input from the Holy Spirit for Rudy to believe in a forgiving God and to learn to forgive others for their imperfections.

Coping With Difficulties

Nine-year-old Mike quietly opened and closed the door and scooted to his room, hoping no one would see him. He just didn't feel like talking to anyone just then. At suppertime he seemed dejected, not his usual cheerful self.

"Son, what's wrong? Can we help?" Dad asked.

"Naw," Mike shrugged. But by worshiptime he couldn't contain his fears any longer. The story tumbled out in a rush of feelings. Mike was small for his age and apparently had become the target for a bully in his class. "No one likes Paul because he's so mean, and he doesn't have any friends. But I'm scared. Every day he does something mean to me!"

Mike's family were new Christians so they were just learning how to cope with difficulties. His mother suggested they look in the Bible to see if God had anything to tell them about what to do. Finally they found Romans 12:20. "If your enemy is hungry, feed him; if your enemy is thirsty, give him a drink" (ICB).

"Well, I'd say Paul is definitely your enemy!" Mom commented. "I don't know what good it will do to give him something to eat, but that's what it says here. What does he like?"

After a few moments Mike exclaimed, "I know what he likes! He likes M&Ms. That's his favorite thing."

"Maybe you could buy him a package of M&Ms," Dad suggested.

"What good's that goin' to do?" Mike asked doubtfully.

"I'm not sure myself," Mom replied. "But if God's Word says that's what we should do for our enemies, we should at least try it." They agreed that Mike would give Paul a package of M&Ms at school the next day.

The shocked look on Paul's face was almost enough payment for Mike's trouble. The boy stammered a "thank you" and turned away. The next day Mom made some cookies for Mike to share with the boy at lunchtime, and then some chocolate cake another day. By the end of the week Paul was no longer threatening Mike or doing mean things to him. In another week they had become friends, and Paul considered himself

Mike's protector. God's way out of difficulty had really worked!

Some days are just going to be "bad days." That's the way life comes. Your children need to learn to accept the bad days along with the good ones. The bad days won't last forever, though. In God's scheme of things the sun comes after rain, spring after winter. His promises are sure—He will see us through even the bad times.

On a day when everything seems to go wrong, the first way to cope is to ask God to help. A quick prayer many times puts things in perspective. Teach your children about "instant prayers"—prayers on the run. Younger children often think they cannot pray unless they are kneeling or folding their hands. To them, God's answer depends on the proper position and how they word the prayer. Tell them about "instant prayers" or "trouble prayers." For example, when they hear a little voice in their minds telling them to do something they know is wrong, but they'd like to do it anyway, a "trouble prayer" will bring lots of angels to help. All they have to say is, "Please help me, Jesus," and the angels will be on the way. Children love an imagery of being surrounded with angels to protect and help them. "Trouble prayers" can enable older children to cope with peer pressure, test questions, hurts from other children, temptation—in other words, anything that poses a problem.

Another way to cope with a bad day is to ask, What does God want me to learn from today? You could talk about the day's events during family worship and think about what the child and the whole family can learn from the experience. Sometimes this can help prevent bad days in the future. Maybe the whole day got off to a bad start because Rachelle didn't get up when her alarm clock rang or left her assignment undone until the last minute.

Sometimes no matter what your child does, things will still go wrong. He has no control over other people or events. God's Word has some clear instructions. "Be joyful always; pray continually; give thanks in all circumstances, for this is God's will for you in Christ Jesus" (1 Thess. 5:16-18, NIV). How can children learn to be thankful even for the bad days? They definitely do not feel grateful for losing a class election or being snubbed by their best friend!

The first step in learning to be thankful is for your child to think of what God has done for her. Maybe you or she can write her conclusions in her devotional notebook or discuss them at family worship. Next remember what God did for people in Bible times. Maybe you can come up with a Bible person who experienced something similar. Examine what God did for that person. Then think of God's promises. Find a Bible promise for your child's situation. Read it together. Copy it on a card she can carry with her or post on her bulletin board. Now it's time to imagine what God will do for her in the future. Naturally, she can't know exactly what will happen in the future, but she can pray about it, claim the Bible promises, and believe them. She must be honest with God about her feelings. Encourage her to specifically thank Him for the positive things she has discovered about this situation. As you go through these steps with your child, you will discover that thankfulness has taken the place of discouragement.

God's Plan and Satan's Counterfeits

God has a fool-proof plan for enabling your children to grow spiritually. He wants them to be His friends and to transform them into a mirror-image of His Son. "When one turns away from human imperfections to behold Jesus, a divine transformation takes place in the character. The Spirit of Christ working upon the heart conforms it to His image" (*Christ's Object Lessons*, p. 250). What a wonderful promise for our children! Use it to help them to turn away from looking at their imperfections and instead concentrate on Jesus. His Spirit will do the work of transforming them.

God's plan includes feeling guilty for wrongdoing (Acts 2:37, 38); repenting of sin (Joel 2:13); confessing sins to God and to others hurt by our actions (1 John 1:9); and receiving God's forgiveness, which removes the guilt completely (Jer. 31:34). He also wants us to make restitution to those we have hurt (Luke 19:8) and to turn totally away from sin (John 8:11). Lovingly God restores each person (Phil. 2:13) and focuses on his or her future potential (1 John 3:9). In His sight the past is gone forever.

Satan always comes along with a counterfeit to any of God's plans, especially one that dramatically changes people. His counterfeit parallels every step of the divine one. First he tries to silence the voice of the Holy Spirit speaking to our children's conscience. He attempts to get them to reject the voice of conscience until conscience is "dead" and doesn't speak anymore. If he can't do that, he concentrates on developing a neurotic conscience that suffocates the person (see chapter 6). Another ploy he uses is to make sure that the child doesn't learn any values, leaving his conscience weak.

Not wanting your child to repent, Satan encourages a false repentance. "Just say you're sorry, but you can get even later on when teacher isn't looking!" Rationalizing is another good strategy he might use. "I'm not really guilty. Half the kids in the class are cheating. If I don't I'll get terrible grades." Admitting a mistake is painful. It's always easier to shift the blame to someone else or to circumstances. As your child grows up, don't let him get away with any of these ploys. Instead, help him learn to accept responsibility for his own actions. He will be much more likely to follow God's plan when he has learned to accept the consequences of what he does. Another strategy that Satan employs is that of causing people to give up. "It's too hard to be good." Of course it is too hard to be good on our own, but God has a plan to deal with that fact. Jesus transforms our desires, enabling us to do what we would otherwise not be able to do. Keep reminding your child of God's plan. If you don't, he will have to struggle with strong temptations to give up, especially as he approaches adolescence.

Satan tries to interfere at every step of God's plan. He may whisper, "Confession is too hard. The other person will probably make fun of you!" If he isn't successful with that ploy, he encourages superficial confession. Real confession leads to cleansing and changes in living, while superficial confession only gets rid of the miserable feeling. Forced confession falls in this category too. "Tell your brother you're sorry," you may say, but your child doesn't really feel repentant. He mouths the words but mutters under his breath, "Just wait until I get you outside, you imp!"

Two of Satan's other favorite strategies include encouraging you to be unable to forgive yourself or to refuse to accept God's forgiveness. Something in our human nature demands that we must be punished for the evil we have done. As a result we can hardly believe that God forgives and puts away our sins. You can help counter this tendency by your careful assessment of each situation with your child. If your child is truly repentant, she will probably not need a consequence to remind her to behave differently in the future. Be careful not to fall in the trap of believing that every bad deed must have a punishment. God doesn't work that way, though He may not remove the natural consequences of our actions. We learn from them. But God does not punish us for everything wrong we do. Instead, He accepts our repentance and forgives. Sometimes, for various reasons, your child may know in her mind that God forgives, but she doesn't feel forgiven. Those feelings can really get in the way of moving forward. Remind her that if she persists in believing God's promises, in time her feeling will accept what she already knows in her head.

"Restitution isn't necessary. How can you possibly do that?" Satan argues. And restitution is hard. Your child will need your support. But restitution is an important step in God's plan. Returning the candy bar taken from the corner mini-mart makes a deep impression on your child's developing mind. It also serves as a powerful deterrent in the future. Telling her friends that what she said about Crystal was not true takes courage, but it is also an effective method for change.

We cannot forsake sin through our own efforts. Your child needs to understand this thoroughly. When he tries through his own willpower, he will fail and become more and more discouraged. Therefore keep reminding him of God's way of dealing with sin. Jesus wants to give him a new heart with different desires. Trusting Jesus is the ultimate key to God's plan.

Satan's counterfeits are really traps for the unsuspecting. Discuss them with your children so they can be forewarned of Satan's strategies. Show them God's solution to sin. Help them experience God's loving approach through your own love.

In fully restoring the prodigal son, did not the father open himself to a repeat performance by the son? After all, what was to prevent the young man from taking advantage of his father's spirit of forgiveness? Can we really treat our children this way? Of course we can! It is God's way, even though it does carry risks. Trusting people and allowing them to grow is always risky. God's approach is not natural to the human heart, but He can transform us parents, too. The Lord can show us how to demonstrate His plan to our children. Pray much for His guidance and for the Holy Spirit to speak to your children.

During the past several years my students and I have conducted more than 250 interviews with children and adolescents on the topic of salvation. We have been trying to discover how children develop their ideas and attitudes toward it. One of the questions we have used relates to the assurance of salvation. If Jesus were to come today, we ask them, would He take you to heaven with Him? Children seem to go through different stages in their understanding of salvation. Until about 8 or 9 years of age, they seem to be very confident of salvation. Jesus will take them to heaven—no question about it! However, their ideas about salvation are strongly related to being good, to doing the right things. If you do the right things, they reason, you are good. And they believe that most of the time they do the right things.

Then the doubts begin to creep in. Eventually they aren't so sure Jesus will actually take them to heaven, and they begin to get very critical of their own behavior. "I don't think Jesus would let me into heaven because I forgot to make my bed today." Any little mistake on their part cancels salvation, an idea that seems to persist into early adolescence. But then they gradually begin to understand a little more about what Jesus does for them, how His grace relates to salvation.

I have concluded that it is vital for us as parents to really focus on helping our children understand what Jesus does for us, how He deals with sin, how He gives us a clean heart and changes our desires, and how His perfect life covers our imperfections. It is the most important gift we can give our children—the assurance of salvation.

KEYS TO GROWING IN JESUS

1. Show your child how to give his/her will to Jesus.
2. Help your child cultivate a friendship with Jesus.
3. Show your child how to become more like Jesus.
4. Give practical instruction for Christian living.
5. Show your child how to claim God's promises for his/her life.
6. Help your child experience forgiveness.
7. Teach your child how to cope with difficulties.
8. Show your child God's steps for growing spiritually.
9. Help your child recognize Satan's counterfeits for God's steps for growing spiritually (his traps).
10. Focus strongly on what Jesus does for us, how He deals with sin, how He changes our desires, and how His perfect life covers our imperfections.
11. Share your own experience growing in Jesus.

CHAPTER 14

Family Spirituality

"Tell your children about these things.
And let your children tell their children.
And let your grandchildren tell their children."
—Joel 1:3, ICB

E very family exudes a forceful spiritual atmosphere that surrounds each member and either draws him or her toward God or repels. From observing many families over the years and from reading the research literature about the transmission of values, I have concluded that this spiritual atmosphere is one of the most powerful influences on the growth of mature faith in children of Christian families. Many things contribute to such a spiritual atmosphere.

Joy in the Lord

During a particularly difficult period in my life I fell into the habit of noticing only the disappointments or "bad" things that happened each day—a rather easy thing for me to do. My attitude, of course, soon led to feelings of depression and discouragement.

One day, while reading an article from *Guideposts* magazine, the Lord spoke to me, and I decided to follow the suggestion of the author—begin a Blessings Diary in which I would write about the blessings God sent me each day.

At first it was difficult to find "blessings," and quite a few days I resorted to noting the sunshine (it doesn't shine every day where I live), the summer flowers, or other general blessings. Gradually I was able to begin focusing on personal events, and my Blessings Diary became a real source of encouragement as I reviewed how God was leading and really helping with many small—as well as large—problems in my life.

Helping children grow spiritually may be somewhat like my experience with the Blessings Diary. As parents we feel burdened with correcting all the defects in our children's characters and making sure they grow up to be "good Christians." We talk about the terrible things happening in the church and wonder sometimes if anyone really knows what is "truth" or if it even matters.

In the process we focus more and more on the negative things we see in our children and in our church, and we lose sight of the many wonderful blessings of having a relationship with God. We forget that God is still in charge of the universe—and of the Adventist Church! And our children become confused and embittered adolescents who never knew the *joy* of serving God and the *specialness* of being His child.

If our children don't hear about God's blessings from us, who will tell them? Start a family tradition for the evening meal in which each member of the family, even the preschoolers, tells about something special God did for him or her that day. It might be a special blessing for you personally, an answered prayer, or how God helped someone you know. Prepare a "Thank You, God" scrapbook with your children. It would make a great Sabbath afternoon project, especially during the long summer Sabbaths. You might search for magazine pictures that would represent, or symbolize, the special blessings God has bestowed on your family during the past week. The children could also draw pictures or select pictures on their computer, and you or your older children could write a little story to go with them.

Each week—perhaps for Friday or Sabbath evening worship—the children could select a special story from the scrapbook for retelling. In this way you will build a tradition of the many ways God has led your family. As you tell your children about how God directed your life in times past, include your stories in the scrapbook or record them on tape and collect a cassette library of personal experiences.

Serving God is the most wonderful, joyous experience any child or adult can have. As you begin to focus on God's blessings, joy will enter your family, and your spiritual life will blossom into a beautiful celebration of a relationship with God.

Children are attracted to happiness. I don't know of any better way to lead them to Christ than to help them experience the *joy* of God's blessings. *The Living Bible* says it beautifully: "Our children too shall serve him, for they shall hear from us about the wonders of the Lord; generations yet unborn shall hear of all the miracles he did for us" (Ps. 22:30, 31).

What did God do for you today? Tell your children about it! You will be creating a powerful magnet that will draw them toward Him.

The overall tendency toward joy in the Lord or bitterness generated by an atmosphere charged with criticism and negative statements about the church shapes the spiritual atmosphere of the home. Without your realizing it, comments build up to create either a negative or positive feeling. A passing statement here and another one there and the effect increases. Perhaps a sigh and a "Why can't he say something worthwhile?" reaction to the pastor. "I don't know why she can't control the kids in that school!" about the church school teacher. "I can't believe how the conference spends our money! We should send our tithe somewhere else." "Did you see the youth pastor at McDonald's? I'm sure that was a real 'Mac' he had!" The barrage of tapes and videos from self-proclaimed "purifiers" of the church—whose real message is to tear down—further adds to the effect. And so the pile builds.

It's all too easy to do, but it's extremely hard to undo with our kids. The ultimate results of a steady diet of criticism during the growing-up years almost always lead to a rejection of the church of their parents. After all, what sense does it make to attend a church that seems so terrible?

What kind of spiritual atmosphere does your home have? Joyful or bitter? The answer is crucial to your child's spiritual development.

Family Worship Experiences

I believe that daily family worship (or lack of it) makes such a powerful statement about the family's priorities that it cannot be ignored. Family worship is a key component of the family's spiritual atmosphere.

Recent scientific surveys of SDA youth (including Valuegenesis and surveys from the Institute for Alcoholism and Drug Dependency) have pointed out the importance of family worship. Youth who have grown up with regular family worship have stronger religious values and are less likely to smoke or use drugs. In fact, family worship has a stronger relationship to smoking and drug use than any other factor studied. In the Valuegenesis study, positive feelings about family worship in their homes was the best predictor of a teenager's desirable attitudes and behavior. Such studies only affirm what we have always heard—family worship is important.

However, the results of several surveys suggest that only about one fourth of SDA families have daily family worship. Another fourth have worship at least once a week, but not daily. Approximately one half of SDA families do not have family worship at all, or very infrequently. Yet we know that family worship is an important influence in aiding children to develop Christian values. How can it be that we don't take advantage of such a powerful means of helping our children?

Maybe you grew up in a home without family worship so you don't know what to do, or you have terrible memories of the long, boring sessions you endured as a child. You'd rather not inflict that memory on your children. Maybe you know in your heart it is important, but your spouse doesn't see it that way. Or maybe it's just the hectic life we all live—we can barely get the kids and ourselves out the door in the morning, let alone have worship! And in the evening . . . well, we're so tired we can hardly get a meal on the table and the kids in bed before we collapse.

I have good news for you! Worship need not be long, boring, or a lot of work. Family worship should really be short, simple, sweet, and, of course, spiritual. If you follow these four guidelines, your children will have pleasant memories of family worship and you will give them a tremendous advantage in values and spiritual development.

First, make family worship **short**. Five to 10 minutes is long enough for preschoolers, while 15 to 20 minutes is about right for children from 6 to 12 years old. Leave them wanting more. Then they will eagerly anticipate tomorrow's worshiptime.

Second, keep family worship **simple**. Buy a plastic storage box (or prepare your own from a cardboard box covered with attractive paper or cloth), in which you will put worship materials. In your box put a Bible, the Sabbath school quarterlies, the current copy of your children's church papers, and a book (or audiotape) of children's religious songs. This will get you started.

Later you can add the Family Worship felts, the Kindergarten Worship Set, additional tapes of religious songs, a Scripture passage illustrated book (Psalm 23, Psalm 91, 1 Corinthians 13, or others), tapes of Bible and character-building stories, and other resources available at your Adventist Book Center or through NAD Church Ministries (5040 Prescott Ave., Lincoln, NE 68506). You can also add homemade materials, such as a scrapbook or tapes you record yourself. The "Activity Time" and "Worship Time" sections in the cradle roll Sabbath school quarterly have many suggestions for inexpensive, easy-to-do family activities. The quarterlies for the other divisions also have ideas for family activities.

Once you have stocked your box with the needed supplies, decide on a convenient storage place. That way your worship box will always be ready. No more frantic looking for the quarterly, *Little Friend*, or *Guide*.

Now you're ready to start. Remember, keep it simple: a song, a Bible story, a family activity, and a short prayer. Keep it short: five to 10 minutes for the youngest children.

The third guideline, keep it **sweet**, assures that your children will look forward to worshiptime. It is not an occasion for scolding, handing out chores, or reminding children of their homework. Worship is the time to come to God with our joys and our concerns, to listen to and to learn from Him, and to draw family members closer together.

How can we keep worship sweet? Children love to be close to Mom and Dad. Cuddling while you read or tell the Bible story and holding hands for prayer create a special feeling of love and togetherness. Your own "theme song" that calls everyone to worship will build fond memories.

Fun-to-do activities add to the joy of worship. Preschoolers love to sing action songs, act out the Bible story, make a scrapbook of pictures about Bible stories, or find nature objects during the day that they can use as "surprises" for worshiptime. Older children love to be "in charge" of worship sometimes.

Worship can be the most joyous time of the day. Make each family member feel happy and loved by creating a "Family Memory" tape or book. Add to it each day by telling something extra nice or special about each family member. Everyone can contribute. Pretty soon you will all be looking for special things to put in your "Family Memory." If you record the experiences on an audio or video cassette, children can then replay it during the day. You may be surprised how often they want to replay the parts telling about something they did!

Family worship can also be especially pleasant if it is the time to right wrongs with each other and ask forgiveness. Kiss and make up. The warmth exuded by such a worship experience remains as a glowing memory. On the other hand, memories of authoritarian worships in which Dad reads long portions of Scripture and loudly proclaims the faults of everyone present while "preaching" prayers that last for 10 minutes will only repel children. Keep it a sweet family togetherness time.

The last guideline, keep it **spiritual**, differentiates worship from other daily activities. The family has many other times to sing secular songs and play games, but worship is reserved for spiritual activities. It is our time to bring God into our homes in a focused way, to let our children know that His Word is our guide for life, and that we love Him and want to live forever with Him. Worship is the special occasion for the Holy Spirit to influence our family. It is a spiritual time more than anything else, so all our worship activities must center on God, His written Word, and His Word in nature. This is when we teach our children God's values.

Make the Bible an important part of worship. Find the Sabbath school memory verse in the Bible and read the lesson from the Bible at least once during the week, using a modern version that children can more easily understand. Share what God is doing in your life, pray for friends, and keep a prayer journal in which the children write or draw pictures of prayer requests. Talk about the special joys of heaven and how much Jesus loves us. Pray for each family member as you separate for the day. Also pray for the Holy Spirit to be an important part of your family worship experience, and He will be there to speak to your children's hearts and draw them to Jesus.

Family worship doesn't need to be a drag. If you keep it short, simple, sweet, and spiritual, you will create memories that will still draw your children to God long after they have left home. The spiritual atmosphere of your home will continue to influence them for years afterward.

Family Choices

Each day we are making an enduring statement about what is most important in our lives by the choices we make for our family. Such choices contribute powerfully to the family's spiritual atmosphere. They are religion in action, a message our children read easily.

If Bible study merits five minutes and the football game three hours, the implication is clear. If the family has money for a luxury car or the latest in video and stereo equipment but only complains that "all the church wants is money," again the point is unmistakable. If your family chooses to go on a Maranatha trip for your vacation, the values come through loud and clear. And if your family joyfully entertains guests from church and volunteers to spend a Sunday fixing your elderly neighbor's retaining wall, your children will know what is most important in your life. Every choice your family makes strengthens the value message. Your children are not stupid. In fact, they are extremely smart when it comes to understanding value messages.

Several years ago a young woman asked me a hard question—one to which I had no ready answer. We were talking about raising "missionary kids"—children who grow up overseas because their parents are missionaries for their church—when she said, "What did you do differently?" Her query took me by surprise, and for a moment I couldn't think of any appropriate response. "You know," she went on, "the Browns (all names, of course, have been changed) are such wonderful people. They are so missionary-minded and everyone loves them, yet their children have left the church." And she went on to mention the names of several other families whose children no longer profess to be Seventh-day Adventists.

"What did you do differently?" she persisted. "I want to know. My children are only babies, but I want to know what to do now so they will love God when they are grown."

I didn't know what to say. What *had* made the difference? Sometimes it's very hard—almost impossible—to unscramble all the influences on a child's life to find the answer to a "why" question. I had known the families she mentioned quite well. All of us resided in that community because we were all dedicated to furthering the Lord's mission on earth. Our children went to the same school, and I had been their Sabbath school leader and music teacher for years. Sadly, many of those children who were in my junior-earliteen division 25 years ago are no longer looking for Christ's second coming. Why?

In search of the answer, I decided to ask our son what he thought made the difference. His carefully thought-out response was enlightening. "I think," he said, "that you gave us a different message about what was important in life. The things we did as a family were different. We went to the beach (the usual recreation where we lived) the least of any of the families—not that we didn't go at all—but we went far less. Instead, we would go to the mountains to conduct medical and dental clinics for poor people. We accompanied you on Sabbath school workshops. For two or three years I went with Daddy every Monday evening to conduct open-air meetings in the plaza at a town near the beach. There's a church in that town now. I think you gave us a different message about what is important in life by the things we did."

I also asked the same question, "What did your family do differently?'' of several of our children's friends from that same community who as adults are dedicated to their Lord and active in their churches. Their responses were similar. They spoke of being involved in their parents' missionary work, of having a sense of doing something for the Lord, of being involved as a family in helping other people. Also, they mentioned knowing their parents were sincere and honest, transparently the same at home and outside. The adults made no pretense. What they did was not for show—they did it from the heart. The parents were what they appeared to be. I remember that all of those families also gave many of their ''free'' days to helping in extra missionary activities, always taking their children with them and involving them. It was a family affair, and the value message was clear.

Think about what your family does during a week and ask yourself: What value messages are my children learning from the choices our family makes? The answer is vitally important for your children's spiritual growth.

Seing and Hearing

What children see and hear in their homes will powerfully influence them. The pictures on the wall, the magazines and books, the music, and the television programs all help to create the family's spiritual atmosphere.

My father, a traveling church executive, was rarely at home. When he was gone we daily checked the mail for letters from him and impatiently waited for his return—days that we had marked with red on our calendar. Almost always he brought little gifts for my brother and me—nothing expensive, we knew, because his minister's salary wouldn't allow that. Nevertheless, those mementos of his travels captured our imaginations as treasured reminders of Daddy.

One memorable day he arrived home carrying an enormous package. ''What is it, Daddy? What is it?'' we teased, but he only replied ''Something very special!'' as he carefully unpacked his suitcases. All our entreaties failed to persuade him to open the package immediately. Soon we were savoring Mother's special homecoming meal, and then gathered in the living room for worship. After the singing and Bible reading, Daddy reached for the package, carefully unwrapping the brown paper to reveal beautifully framed copies of Sallman's *Head of Christ* and *Christ Knocking at the Door*.

We sat in awed silence as Daddy told the story of Christ knocking at the heart's door. The invisible latch, only openable from the inside, especially impressed me. Christ would not enter my life uninvited. He would only gently knock, awaiting my response.

I cherished this very special gift from my father. Throughout childhood and adolescence my treasure accompanied me on each move, even to my academy dorm room. Later, it went to my first married home, a never-failing reminder of my father and his God.

Desiring to continue the same tradition with my own children, my husband and I hung Harry Anderson's *What Happened to Your Hand?* in their room when they were young. As they grew, we added *Christ at the Helm*, a wonderful action picture for adolescents. Because childhood memories are a permanent part of life, I wanted our children to grow up with a picture of Christ to remind them of His great love.

Also, I desired for our children to experience the beauty and guidance of favorite Bible and Ellen G. White statements. As I came across meaningful Bible verses or key sentences I copied them on small cards and placed the cards where we could frequently see them. The wall above the kitchen sink always had several, while mirrors in the bathrooms and the refrigerator door also caught their share. When our son left to be a student missionary, his farewell letter included several favorite quotations and Bible verses, and frequently during graduate school our daughter received a special "thought for the week" slipped into a letter.

Reading to your children is a powerful way to increase the spiritual messages in your home. In a home where television and videos monopolize everyone's time, adults and children get their information and values from television gurus. Many adults rarely or never read a book for pleasure. As a result the Bible seems difficult and archaic. Even the modern versions are beyond their reading skills. Ellen White's books never get opened. Their nineteenth-century language doesn't fit with today's hurried visual pace of life. Yet reading is one of the important keys to helping our children grow spiritually. The value messages of television and videos are overwhelmingly antireligious. We must take forceful action to instill spiritual values in our children. Reading communicates a strong message of family values.

Reading to children provides close family togetherness, a sense of warmth and caring, and time with the most important people in their lives—their parents. Babies 6 to 9 months old enjoy a few minutes of reading a colorful book of Bible stories and other character building ideas. Toddlers and preschoolers who have been read to since they were little become eager listeners. They will beg for "one more" story and want many books read over and over again. They also love rhythm and rhyme and the up and down cadence of the human voice. Reading provides a natural time to talk about spiritual values. You will be preparing your child for school, also. Children who have been read to during the preschool years usually have an easier time learning to read and find reading itself fascinating. They want to read for themselves because they already know the pleasure books can bring.

As children get older, their understanding expands. During early elementary school they will begin to enjoy more complicated plots and stories with more characters. Their own reading skills are not good enough yet to read such books for themselves, but they love the closeness of Mom or Dad reading to them. A bedtime story tradition builds memories of happy times together. Choose stories that will help your children grow in character. The selection is vast. Be sure the stories you read represent the values you want your children to learn.

Children need to gradually learn to appreciate the language of the Bible and the books written by Ellen White. They will not suddenly like these books when they become teenagers or adults. Instead, they must learn earlier how to understand the vocabulary and sentence structure of these books. Begin by reading the Sabbath school lesson passages to your children from the *International Children's Bible*. This translation has a third-grade reading vocabulary. Four- to 6-year-olds can understand the Bible story read directly from a version such as the ICB. The *New International Version* (NIV) has a seventh-grade reading vocabulary.

As your child grows in understanding, introduce portions of the Bible story as told in the Conflict of the Ages Series of books by Ellen White. At the beginning of each week's Bible lesson in the quarterly your child receives at Sabbath school you will find suggested sources of enrichment from other books, including those by Ellen White. If you introduce these stories, your child will grow mentally and spiritually as he grapples with a new way of expression. When your child gets to be a teenager, Ellen White will be a familiar and comforting source of help. *Steps to Christ* will be a cherished book pointing the way to Christ.

Don't give up reading together because your child has learned to read proficiently for himself. Family reading always provides shared values and shared companionship. You can enhance the spiritual influence of your home immensely through reading.

As we evaluate the religious atmosphere of our homes, we must ask ourselves an important question. What do our children see and hear in our home? Their effect on spiritual development is powerful. Check the books, the magazines, the music, the videos, the TV programs, the pictures and posters. Do they teach the same values we preach? Children are acutely aware of discrepancies between what we proclaim and what we live. They are more likely to follow what we live.

We teach our children to respect the laws of our city and our country—but then we expose them to TV dramas and movies in which "getting away with it" is often the essence of a hero.

We tell our children that alcohol and drugs are bad for them—but then let them see commercial after commercial proclaiming the joy and happiness that "real men and women" get from drinking.

We want our children to be kind, generous, and loving to other people—but then let them watch cartoons in which hitting, pushing, beating, and other violent actions are "funny" and, by implication, OK.

We explain to our children about the power of God and the great controversy between God and Satan—but then fill their minds with ET and *Star Wars* and other cosmic struggles that downplay the divine role in the future of the universe.

We hold for our children the ideal of service, of seeking God's kingdom first—but then expose them to 350,000 commercials by age 18 whose main message is to seek greater pleasure for self.

Our efforts to help our children grow spiritually would be much more fruitful if we always remembered that "It is a law of the . . . spiritual nature that *by beholding we become changed*. The mind gradually adapts itself to the subjects upon which it is allowed to dwell" (*The Great Controversy*, page 555; italics supplied).

Parents' Religiousness

As parents we create the spiritual atmosphere in our homes by our own religiousness and the way we share it with our children. The Valuegenesis study found that teenagers with higher levels of faith maturity and commitment to the SDA Church had parents who attended church frequently and were highly religious themselves. Such parents were open to talking about faith and often shared their faith with their children. Parents and children frequently discussed religion. Mom and Dad were also in basic agreement on religious issues.

Children need to see how religion works in our own lives. If we keep our faith a well-kept secret, they have no model for how the grace of Christ really impacts on a person. In fact, they may think that we are all "talk" and no action.

They need to see how to deal with sin, how to confess and accept forgiveness, how to cling to God's promises for the future. Remember, they know we aren't perfect—they see our imperfections every day. If we never say we are sorry and ask forgiveness for our hasty words and actions, their hearts close toward us and God. When we humbly ask pardon and demonstrate what God can really do with sinful human beings, they feel surprisingly warm toward us. We have just removed ourselves from the "hypocrite" category. Children respect and love transparency, honesty, and sincerity.

Infants and toddlers naturally don't have questions about religion, but as children grow older the questions burst forth. According to research studies, 4- and 5-year-olds ask more questions about God, death, and the hereafter than at any other age. Answering their questions is important. The questions continue throughout childhood. As children approach the teen years, the pace accelerates.

Ten- to 13-year-olds begin to grapple with some of the hard questions about God and their personal faith. No longer are they willing just to accept a parent's dictum as the right way to live. They want to know why. Talking about your faith with your children is critical at this point. It helps them find the answers to the why questions. If you don't have a ready answer, it's OK to say, "I really don't know. Let's see if we can find out." Searching together for the explanation strengthens your relationship with each other and with God. It gives your children the message that they and their questions are important.

As I was beginning to write this book, I asked Liza, our 7-year-old granddaughter, what questions she had about God and the Bible. Many of them showed a growing interest in the reasons behind God's actions. Some aren't that easy to answer in 7-year-old terms. For example, Why did God take Moses to heaven when he killed a man? How come Jesus wanted to die on a cross? How did God lead the animals into the ark? How is Jesus going to come again? Why did Adam and Eve have to leave the garden? Why did God destroy the Tower of Babel?

Sharing insights gained from your personal devotions and Bible study is a helpful way to let your children know you are searching and growing spiritually, too. Develop a family atmosphere that eagerly welcomes everyone's contribution. Be open to considering any question from "why can't I wear jewelry?" to "why did Grandpa have to die?" or "will my dog be in heaven?" Turn to God's Word and share your own personal struggles with different issues. You may be surprised at how your children will respond to a personal sharing approach. Dan was. As he shared his story with me one day, I was astounded at how the Holy Spirit can use an open spirit of sharing to really reach a child.

Dan had been studying child development and had come to the conclusion that he wanted to get to know his 6-year-old son, Tony, more intimately. The young father had already made steps in that direction the previous year by changing from a traveling job to one where he saw his family every day. Every evening he tried to play with his son just after mealtime and then they had worship together before he tucked Tony into bed. But Dan felt a strong desire to get to know his son more in depth.

So one evening, after worship and bedtime routines, he lay down beside Tony and quietly started talking man-to-man. Pretty soon Dan began describing some of the temptations he faced as he was growing up. Tony listened intently for a while, then began to cry. Dan hugged him but had no idea why the boy was crying. Although he knew Tony was a sensitive child who felt deeply, he could only guess whether Tony sympathized with his father or whether he himself had some deep concern. Dan didn't push for a response—he just continued to hug his son. After a while Tony's sobs quieted down. The father lay beside him for a while longer, and the boy finally fell asleep.

The next day, when Dan arrived home for lunch, his wife quickly signaled she wanted to talk with him alone. As she shared what had happened, Dan became more and more concerned. That morning Tony had told his mother that, when he was 4 years old, a teenage boy from their church had "done things" to him sexually. Apparently it had happened more than once. Tony was too frightened to mention it to his father because he was sure Dan would punish him severely. But his mother encouraged him to tell Dan about what happened, reassuring him that his father would not reprimand him.

Dan, of course, was deeply concerned and aghast that something like that could have happened to his son. He and his wife talked about the situation, went over every angle, cried tears of frustration and anguish, and prayed for wisdom.

That evening, after playing with Tony and having family worship, Dan again lay down beside his son when he tucked him into bed. Again they talked quietly and intimately. This time, with his heart in his mouth and desperate prayers for wisdom racing through his mind, Dan shared with his son some of his own youthful sexual temptations, although they were not exactly like what had happened to Tony.

Soon the child started crying as if his heart would break. Between sobs he told his father about his experience. Dan hugged his son reassuringly and gently spoke about forgiveness, both God's and his own. After a while he asked Tony if he wanted to pray about it. The child nodded. They both prayed, and with the prayers a burden seemed to roll away from the child. Pretty soon he fell asleep, secure in his father's embrace. When Dan shared the experience with me the next day, he commented with awe in his voice, ''When I decided I wanted to get to know my son more intimately, I had no idea the results would be so immediate!'' Clearly the Holy Spirit works in surprising ways when we open ourselves to His leading. Because of Dan's willingness to share his own stumbling walk with the Lord, his son gained the courage to confess a burden he had carried deep in his heart for more than two years.

God will work for you, too, in powerful ways as you begin to create a spiritual atmosphere in your home that will draw your children toward heaven.

KEYS TO FAMILY SPIRITUALITY

1. Share your joy in the Lord.
2. Focus on the blessings God gives your family.
3. Never criticize the church and its members.
4. Make daily family worship a priority.
5. Keep family worship short, simple, sweet, and spiritual.
6. Choose family activities that teach the values you want your children to learn.
7. Provide many opportunities for your children to see and hear spiritual ideas in your home.
8. Share your personal religious experience with your children.
9. Demonstrate in your own life the power of God's grace.
10. Show yourself open to talking about religion with your children and discussing their questions.

CHAPTER 15

Service—Love in Action

"I give you these powers freely.
So help other people freely."
—Matthew 10:8, ICB

Timmie was only 19 months old when he showed me clearly that even toddlers can have generous, loving impulses.

Before he taught me that lesson I had really wondered about that statement in *The Desire of Ages* that states, "If we wish our children to possess the tender spirit of Jesus, and the sympathy that angels manifest for us, we must encourage the generous, loving impulses of childhood" (p. 516). Most children I knew, my own included, seemed to be "me first" kids. And most parents, like myself, struggled to teach their children to share and to be helpful.

The occasion for my lesson in toddler generosity was unusual. I had invited three toddlers and their parents for a videotaping session in the audiovisual studio on the campus where I teach. I was trying to produce a demonstration videotape of a toddler Sabbath school class to show my students how to present a Bible story to young children.

The bright lights and cameras were on while I taught the story of Zacchaeus. The babies did wonderfully well ignoring the camera paraphernalia and the unfamiliar surroundings as they participated in the familiar Bible story.

We had finished the Bible story itself and were practicing different ways of obeying Mommy and Daddy like Zacchaeus had obeyed Jesus when it happened. I was explaining about obeying when Mommy or Daddy says, "Please sit still so I can put on your shoes."

I had only one pair of shoes for the three children to hold, so I gave one shoe to Timmie and one to Susie. That left Eric, the oldest of the group, without a shoe. I was going to suggest later that someone share with Eric, but Timmie didn't give me a chance. As soon as he got his shoe he looked over at Susie, then at Eric, glanced back at the shoe in his hand, and rushed over to give it to Eric. With a satisfied expression, he returned to his chair and grinned while pointing to Eric, who was happily playing with the shoe.

His show of generosity stunned me because it was so contrary to what I usually saw in toddlers. Since then I have looked for evidences of the "generous, loving impulses of childhood" and have seen many. Of course, I've also seen strong demonstrations of Satan's "me first" way. Which impulse are we encouraging in our children? We are strengthening either one or the other by the experiences our children have.

Soon after babies are 12 months old they begin to show signs of sympathy and caring. But they assume that others have the same feelings they do. Have you seen a toddler holding out her bottle to a crying or sad older child? She is offering sympathy and consolation but doesn't yet understand that others are consoled in different ways. By the time children are 2 or 3 years old, they grasp that other people don't have the same feelings and they can empathize with more complex emotions. If Mommy is crying, Mr. Two may pat her arm gently to show his sympathy. When Mommy says "Thank you" and looks appreciative, it encourages Mr. Two to be sympathetic on another occasion. But if Mommy gives no response or shoves him away, he may not try the next time. His budding feelings of sympathy will have been dampened a little.

Such feelings and actions are the beginning of empathy, a vital aspect of moral development. Before children and teenagers can respond with love and caring to another person's distress, they must be able to empathize with what that person is feeling. They must be able to put themselves in that person's shoes and look at life through his eyes and feelings. Children develop this ability gradually as they mature.

Sharing, helping, comforting, and cooperating are all part of the response to feelings of empathy. Such responses are easier to learn when the family must work together to survive or when the entire village has a sense of unity and cooperation in their daily work. Some cultures are more cooperative and group-oriented. They place the interests of the group—the family, in particular—above personal desires. Individualistic, competitive societies work against cooperation, helpfulness, and sharing. If we raise our children to triumph over others at school and at play, we effectively snuff out their inclination to help others. Children acquire competitiveness at an extremely young age. After all, it surrounds them. We foster this attitude when we encourage children to win at all costs, to be the first and the best, and to have the most and the best things.

The Valuegenesis study found that one of the most important predictors of faith maturity and commitment to the SDA Church was the value the young people placed on service. Teenagers who valued service highly also showed a high level of faith maturity and commitment to the SDA Church. These same teenagers also came from families who worked together on helping projects. This shouldn't be surprising. After all, the Bible says: "Serve each other with love. . . . 'Love your neighbor as you love yourself' " (Gal. 5:13, 14, ICB. "I was hungry, and you gave me food. I was thirsty, and you gave me something to drink. . . . I was without clothes, and you gave me something to wear" (Matt. 25:34-36, ICB). The last three steps on Peter's ladder of Christian growth are service for God, kindness, and love. Sharing, helping, comforting, and serving others are the central core of the Christian life. They proclaim to the world that God lives in us (1 John 4:12). Service to others is an expression of the love of God and a main purpose for our existence on earth. It also provides the perfect antidote for selfishness and self-centeredness, the natural inclination of our sinful beings.

How can we encourage an attitude of caring and service to others in our children? First, **communicate deep disapproval of hurting people or animals**. Don't be amused by your child's aggressive behavior. Place clear limits on hurting others. To do so emphasizes to your child that other people have feelings that they must respect. It places a high value on how other people feel and teaches your child to respect others. You are laying the foundation for empathy and caring when you indicate your disapproval of hurting anyone. The child allowed to injure others will miss the first step in learning to be empathetic.

Next, **help children understand how other people feel**. While even very young children seem to have some innate feelings of sympathy, the potential must be developed so they will be able to empathize, to walk in someone else's shoes and grasp what that person feels. Tell young children how the other person feels. "You made Jon cry—it's not nice to bite." Combine how the other child feels with explaining to your child what you think of his behavior. In order to develop empathy, children need to hear feeling reasons and rational explanations of what to do or what not to do. Always give your reasons for expecting your child to act unselfishly or kindly. As children grow older, try to get them to think about the effects of their actions on others. Ask how they believe the other child feels. "You made Maria cry. How do you think she felt when you smashed her playhouse?" Don't let your child off the hook—expect an answer and wait for it. Follow up with another question: "What can you do to help Maria feel better?" Persist in teaching your child how other people feel. Over the years you will notice that your child will become more tuned in to how her actions affect others.

Third, **set an example of how to be caring toward others**. One of the most effective ways of teaching children to be loving and caring is to give them a living example in your own life. Warm and friendly adults who model altruistic behavior and who teach children how to be unselfish and helpful are the most effective in helping children grow up to be altruistic themselves. Be thoughtful to other members of the family. When the neighbors have an emergency, rally your family to help. Baby-sit, provide transportation, cook, shop—whatever needs to be done. Respond to your children's distress. Show empathy and help them solve their problem. Your own caring spirit will surround your children with a model they cannot ignore. By demonstrating such behavior, eventually you will notice that your children will aid both family members and others.

Fourth, **promote a positive view of people**. Assume the best of others. Avoid criticisms and negative statements. Children are more likely to develop empathy and caring when they view people positively. But it will not happen when they hear a continual barrage of criticisms and negative comments about everyone they know. Research studies about altruism have noted that those most likely to help others have a positive view of people in general. Help your children develop friendships with children of various cultures and races. Invite individuals to your home from different backgrounds. Enlarge the boundaries of your comfort to include people of other ethnic groups. Children who grow up in multicultural environments are much more likely to be helpful and friendly to everyone.

Fifth, **give children many opportunities to help**. Let your toddler carry the bottle for the new baby. Show your 3-year-old how to find the two socks that match and put them away in the right drawer. Allow your 4-year-old to vacuum part of a room. Children who grow up helping, naturally choose to be more helpful later on. Five-year-olds can set the table and clear the table after the meal. They can also assist in putting away their toys and clothes. Make helping a game. Work with your children. Plan a surprise at the end of a work session. Don't be too particular—overlook their childish mistakes. Learning to enjoy being helpful is the main idea. In time they will become more careful. Unless children learn to help when they are quite young, by the time they are old enough to do things unsupervised, they won't want to. The habit of being helpful must be acquired at a young age. Older children can be responsible for many different household and yard chores. You might have a list of jobs and rotate who does them. Compliment helpfulness. You might crown a helpfulness "king" or "queen" for the day—a family member who was especially cooperative the day before. The main idea is to enable children to grow up feeling responsible for others.

Sixth, **encourage children to think of themselves as helpful, caring people**. Make it a part of their self-concept. When children are learning to describe themselves psychologically, usually between the ages of 6 and 9, they are especially sensitive to what you say about them. During those years you have a special opportunity to build into their self-concept the idea that they are caring people. "Thank you, Christie, for setting the table. That was a big help to me. You are such a helpful girl!" "Joe, Grandma really appreciated your going to the drugstore for her. You are such a caring, helpful guy!"

Research on altruism has discovered that adults inclined to be helpful are usually people who feel in control of what happens in their lives, who have little need for approval from others, and who are generally in a positive state of mind—characteristics that often go along with self-respect and a positive self-concept. The child who feels confident and good about himself is much more likely to be able to ignore the taunts of his classmates and help the "scapegoat" of the group. Emotionally strong enough to do what he knows is right, he sees himself as in control of the situation. Helping your children develop a positive sense of self-respect pays big dividends in many areas of their lives.

Seventh, **counteract children's natural inclinations to selfishness**. All of us have an inherent bent toward wanting more and more. Selfishness and jealousy sent Satan hurling from heaven. They are the opposite of love and service. Have you noticed that the more things we have, the more we want? It's the natural way of the sinful human heart. God tells us something completely different—"be content with what you have'' (Heb. 13:5, NIV). "It is more blessed to give than to receive'' (Acts 20:35, NIV). God's way is one of satisfaction, not dissatisfaction—thankfulness, not demanding self-indulgence. How can we turn things around in our children's lives? Dissatisfaction is, after all, Satan's way, and he is going to make it look extremely attractive!

A number of reasons cause us to sometimes buy too many things for our children. We might do it to make up for what we didn't have when we were young or to impress other people. Perhaps we feel guilty about the little amount of time we spend with our children. Maybe we're impulsive or unconscious puppets of the advertisers, or we simply get tired of hearing our kids' begging. God can help us change our own attitude. With a new attitude we can then take a tour around our home.

Do our children have too many things? Toy boxes running over? Closets stuffed? Do they have a bad case of "give-me-itis"? Time for a change. Take inventory with your children. Sort their toys and clothes. Help them set aside things they don't use to give to a needy family or the Community Services Center. A drastic suggestion might be to encourage your children to give away a toy every time they get a new one—or at least pass it on to a younger brother or sister. Maybe that's also not a bad idea for our own overstuffed wardrobes! An even more dramatic approach might be for your children to donate their very *best* toy to someone else. After all, God gave His best, didn't He?

Provide young children consistent lessons in sharing. Make your point clearly and often. They will eventually get the message. At Christmastime have a special family sharing project. Decide how much money your family can spend on Christmas and then discuss how much of that amount you will set aside to help someone else. Or your children could earn some money to aid another family who might otherwise not have any Christmas at all. Help your children make or buy gifts for others rather than spending all their time talking about what they want. Surprising someone else is great fun! Investment birthday parties are another way of counteracting the tendency toward selfishness. Invite your child's friends to bring money for Sabbath school Investment instead of a regular gift. They could come dressed as a child from another country, and you could play games from other countries or show a video about children from other places. I have seen children just as excited adding up their total for Investment as they ever were with the toys at previous parties. Your child could ask party guests to bring a child's garment or a toy for a certain age. At the party you could pack the gifts in a large basket and go together to deliver them to a needy family. Then you could invite the children from the family as special guests to the rest of the party.

Eighth, **get your family involved in helping projects on a regular basis**. In order for such projects to be successful and to enable your children to grow spiritually, your children need to participate in a way that touches them personally. Just earning money to send overseas won't do it. Choose a family project and get everyone involved.

FAMILY HELPING PROJECTS

Join a Maranatha project for a family vacation.
Make good-cheer visits to an elderly person; take flowers, books, tapes.
Make scrapbooks for children's hospital wards. Deliver, if possible.
Make or buy toys for hospital wards. Deliver, if possible.
Make or buy toys for a needy family. Deliver. Get to know the family.
Share toys with other families in need. Deliver. Get to know family.
Sort and give away outgrown clothes. Help pack boxes for ADRA.
Invite a needy family for Thanksgiving or New Year's dinner.
Take a loaf of homemade bread or jam to the people on your block.
Collect canned goods at Halloween and give to a needy family. Visit.
Help elderly person or single parent in your neighborhood or church.
    Paint, rake leaves, shovel snow, mow grass, get mail, get groceries,
    fix roof, fix fence, mend clothes. Accept no pay. This is a love gift.
Correspond with a missionary. Send things they need.
Sacrifice candy for a month and save money for one of the above projects.
Help an "isolated" child at school.
Stand up for a classmate being ridiculed or teased. Make this child your family's special project.
Help with a local soup kitchen.
Collect food and clothes for the homeless. Help distribute the items.

Family helping projects are limited only by your imagination. The world's needs are unending. Your family's involvement will create for your children a sense of caring, of helpfulness, and of generosity that will be your lifelong gift to them. "The spirit of unselfish labor for others gives depth, stability, and Christlike loveliness to the character, and bring peace and happiness to its possessor" *(Steps to Christ*, p. 80). What a gift!

KEYS TO SERVICE

1. Communicate strong disapproval of your child hurting animals or other people.
2. Help your child understand how other people feel.
3. Model how to be a caring person.
4. Always show a positive view of people.
5. Provide many opportunities to help others.
6. Encourage your child to think of herself as a helpful and caring person.
7. Avoid "give-me-itis." Limit wardrobes and toys to reasonable amounts. Encourage sharing with others.
8. Get your family regularly involved in helping projects.

♥

CHAPTER 16

Sabbath—a Day for Families

"If you call the Sabbath a delight . . . , then
you will find your joy in the Lord."
—Isaiah 58:13, 14, NIV

In a world of frantic rushing, in which fathers, and sometimes mothers, hardly see their children during the week, God has given us a special gift—the gift of time to be with our families. In the 24 hours of the Sabbath He has provided opportunity for families to be together and to worship Him. "In His own day He preserves for the family opportunity for communion with Him, with nature, and with one another" (*Education*, p. 251). God apparently intended the Sabbath to be a special day for families. If we use the Sabbath to build God-centered family memories, I think we will go a long way toward keeping our families together and helping our children grow spiritually.

Three P's will help make Sabbath a special day for your family: **Preparation**, **Preservation**, and **Presence**. For very important reasons, God reminds us to "remember the Sabbath day." As we keep it in mind during the week through **preparation**, it reminds us of a loving God who cares for us each day of the week.

As we remember it on the Sabbath day itself through our **preservation** of its sacredness, we come to know God better and draw our children closer to us.

In future years our children will treasure those childhood Sabbaths largely because of our **presence** as we create for them a storehouse of happy "Sabbath memories" that will continually draw them back to the Sabbath and its Creator.

In our frantic schedules, **preparation** for Sabbath must begin at least by Thursday, maybe even Wednesday. Friday is the day to finish getting ready for Sabbath—not to begin it!

When planning for Sabbath with children and teenagers, *be one jump ahead!* When our children were preteens and teenagers, I would generally bring up on Wednesdays the topic of what we might do on Sabbath, suggesting several options. Sometimes we had no choice over the matter—the children had a choir trip or a school-planned Sabbath activity they wanted to do. If not, then they had a day to think about what they might like to do on Sabbath before we made our decision on Thursday. After deciding on our Sabbath activity, they still had a day to ask friends to join us for Sabbath. I never made any plans of my own for Sabbath until I was sure we had everything settled for the children's Sabbath.

Preparation isn't quite so elaborate or long range for younger children. However, your 4- to-6-year-old would enjoy a special calendar with large squares for each day where he can count the days until Sabbath. Preschoolers can help get ready for Sabbath by picking up their toys, finding their Sabbath clothes, putting away secular papers, helping make a special favorite food, polishing shoes, running errands, emptying the wastebaskets, and maybe vacuuming one room or sweeping the sidewalk. School-age children can do all of these things, too, but instead of vacuuming one room, they could do several. They can be responsible for cleaning their rooms and getting their clothes ready. Also, they can help make a favorite dish. Remember, work is really play for children when they do it with Mom or Dad.

Children can also assist in planning special Sabbath activities— something to look forward to. Six- to 8-year-olds could make a drawing on each paper napkin to be used for Sabbath dinner—something special for each person. Sing while you're working together, songs like "We Get Ready for the Sabbath," or make up tunes and words as you go along. When the whole family prepares for Sabbath together, it becomes a special family time.

If the sun goes down early during certain times of the year where you live, you will have to arrange all of the preparations for Thursday, since the family will arrive home from work and school only a short time before the Sabbath begins. Locations where sundown times vary several hours during the course of the year make it more difficult to maintain the Sabbath traditions. Friday evening church services can begin before sundown and supper gets eaten in a hurry as we rush around with last-minute preparations for Sabbath. I think we have to work especially hard in such situations to preserve the specialness of the early Sabbath hours.

It's important to begin Sabbath with a little energy left for celebration! How can a busy mother or father of preschoolers and older children do that? By simplifying life as much as possible. Potluck with another family to share a Sabbath meal instead of doing it all yourself. How about soup, hearty bread, and a salad for Sabbath dinner? Such a meal takes real courage because most of us feel we must put on a feast for Sabbath, especially for company. Maybe you can start a new trend in your church. Picking up things lying around the house makes it look "clean," even though every corner isn't immaculate! Using permanent-press clothes and colors that don't show soiling readily will reduce the effort of getting clothes ready for Sabbath. Crates or baskets you can carry from room to room will simplify picking up household clutter.

Put on religious tapes or CDs a half hour before sundown to create a Sabbath atmosphere. While you finish preparing for Sabbath, children could be listening to stories and songs. As you read to the children during the week, you could also be recording tapes for future use. Put your infant or toddler in a playpen to keep him safe from harm and mischief while the older children listen to tapes.

Welcome the Sabbath with a joyful family celebration! Select a Sabbath sundown theme song as your family's "Sabbath song." Sing it every week to begin the Sabbath. Follow with the family saying the fourth commandment in unison. Illustrate the commandment with pictures pasted on cards or in a small scrapbook, with simple silhouettes, or with felts (available from the ABC or Sabbath School Evangelism Center). Next you might have a children's Sabbath song, such as "The Seventh Is for Jesus" or "Sabbath Is a Happy Day." Receiving the Sabbath could be concluded with a prayer by Mom or Dad, or a family prayer with everyone contributing a sentence or two.

If you have older children, each member of the family could repeat a favorite Bible verse and tell why it is special to him or her. Or a family member could relate an experience during the week that was especially meaningful spiritually. You could have a "Praise" time to greet the Sabbath with each family member telling something for which he or she wants to thank the Lord for this week.

Adventists in the Spanish Caribbean countries have a delightful custom of wishing everyone in the family a ''Happy Sabbath'' just after the prayer. Each member of the family hugs or kisses other members while wishing them a *Feliz Sabado* (Happy Sabbath). They also conclude the Sabbath the same way by saying to each other *Feliz Semana* (Happy Week). You might like to start the custom in your own family. Such family traditions build never-to-be-forgotten Sabbath memories.

Some families have a special menu served every Friday evening. Others use a Sabbath candle that they light to begin the Sabbath day. Your older children might like to research how the Jews greet the beginning of the Sabbath and adapt such Jewish customs for your own family.

Our goal is to make ''Sabbath memories'' of a very special day, one different from other days, in which our family is together, more relaxed, with time for each other and for getting acquainted with God in ways not possible during the rest of the week.

Planning a Friday evening meal with candles and a special table setting or location—something to look forward to—begins the celebration. Going to bed on time is important so everyone can get up early enough not to have to rush on Sabbath morning. I'm afraid many of us have Sabbath memories of rush, rush, rush—the kind we'd like to forget, not the kind that will draw us to God's day.

Plan ahead who will be responsible for each chore on Sabbath morning. Each parent could dress a child, or older children could help younger ones. Your 7- or 8-year-old could clean up after breakfast and possibly set the table for dinner while you care for younger children. A playpen is a big help with infants and toddlers. It keeps them out of mischief while other members of the family get ready for church. A religious coloring or sticker book or some records and tapes can occupy preschoolers while they wait for you. Allow more time than you think will be needed—children have a way of creating last-minute emergencies!

A beautifully set table creates delightful Sabbath memories. Use your best dishes and tablecloth (put a clear plastic sheet on top if you have little ones) with napkins or name cards one of your children made or pretty colored leaves your 3- or 4-year-old gathered while you prepared the meal (a good opportunity for exercise after church). The meal doesn't have to be fancy—just special and different from every other day. Background religious music helps create a Sabbath feeling.

Share your simple meal with someone in need—a visitor at church, an elderly individual, a single person, or someone who just looks lonely. They will love participating in a bit of family life, and you will be enabling your children to experience the joy of helping others. Plan uplifting conversation, maybe reading a short article or story to start a discussion.

For preschoolers, a box of "Sabbath toys" helps create a special day. Put away other toys and get out the box of "Sabbath toys" that you reserve for the Sabbath only. The box could include a special doll, a Noah's ark, a small church, stuffed animals, books, cassette tapes, a farm set, plastic fruit and flowers, religious or nature coloring and sticker books, felt sets, etc.

Sabbath *with* our children—not the adults napping while they amuse themselves—is the key to delightful Sabbath memories. Our **presence** is essential! I firmly believe our children are our most important missionary activity on Sabbath afternoons. However, many outreach activities provide opportunities to be together as a family on the Sabbath, even with young children.

Helping others can provide a special sense of closeness to God that even young children pick up. Make short visits to elderly or confined persons. Have your child take a small bunch of flowers or carry a book to lend or maybe sing a song. Keep the visit short. They will love seeing the children.

Conduct a Neighborhood Bible Club in your home with your children as members of the group. Plan to contact one home in your neighborhood each Sabbath afternoon. Take a special gift—a loaf of homemade bread, a book or cassette, flowers—and just get acquainted. Visit a needy family and let your children share toys or outgrown clothes.

Sabbath afternoon provides a special opportunity for your family to meet God through nature. When the great God of creation speaks to His children through His created works, it is more like a treasure hunt than an entertainment movie. We have to search for God's message in nature. But it can be an exciting search—even for families who don't consider themselves "outdoorsy types."

Nature study on the Sabbath should draw each member of the family closer to God and to each other. It is not just a biology lesson—it is learning about God. To get started, you will need five things: (1) a place to observe nature, (2) a nature guidebook, (3) a Bible with a concordance,

(4) a bit of the adventurer's spirit and, of course, (5) a desire to discover God through nature.

Where can you go to observe nature? First of all, your own yard, if you have one, or the park in your neighborhood. You could also visit the beach, a nature preserve, a bird sanctuary, a county or state park, or a woods, field, or river near your home. An aspect of planning for Sabbath memories could include purchasing memberships for the best nature areas near you so you can visit freely on Sabbath.

What about a guidebook? If you grew up with nature, you might not need one at first. But if nature activities are new to you, a guidebook will be essential. Check at your local ABC for a family nature guide that not only describes various activities but also gives ideas for spiritual lessons one can learn from the nature activity. Most bookstores have sections on nature. Such books, however, will not provide ideas for spiritual lessons, although they will help with identification of various birds, shells, or flowers. The *Pathfinder Manual* and the *Adventurer Club Manual* have many ideas for nature study. Your children would have fun working on one of the nature Honors outlined in them.

A Bible with a concordance will assist you in finding texts that speak about different parts of nature. For example, you might try to find the things Jesus talked about in His nature parables or stories. Or, while observing some ants diligently carrying a large piece of food to their nest, you could look up a Bible verse about ants (Prov. 6:6) and discuss what God teaches us through them (to work hard on a tough job).

The adventurer's spirit will be most helpful when a sudden downpour interrupts your walk or when trying to follow the elusive tracks of a deer through the woods. In fact, without the adventurer's spirit, you probably won't get farther than your front door! The desire to learn about God through nature will give you ideas for spiritual lessons as the Holy Spirit helps you lead your family in their new adventure.

Now for some activity ideas. Make up an observation sheet for a Sabbath afternoon walk, using pictures for younger children and words for older ones. Put stars beside each one the child finds. Do a creation walk, looking for objects God made on different days of the week. Collect nature items to make 3-D pictures or displays (sand, dirt, stones, sticks, moss, bits of plants, seeds, bird feathers, shells, etc.). Put the pictures together on a Sabbath afternoon with inclement weather. Do a nature treasure hunt. Make nature prints of spider webs, footprints, or leaves. Prepare a nature calendar with large squares for each day of the month. In each square illustrate a nature happening for that day. Visit a farm with animals. Feed the ducks at the local park. The list of things your family could do is limited only by your imagination.

Nature activities are one of the most important spiritual links between you and your children. Ellen White places nature in its rightful place for Sabbath memories in the following statement: "In the minds of the children the very thought of the Sabbath should be bound up with the beauty of natural things. . . . By such associations parents may bind their children to their hearts, and thus to God, by ties that can never be broken" (*Education,* p. 251).

Bible and instructional activities are another important part of Sabbath memories. They are especially needed for Sabbath when the weather doesn't permit nature activities, or for the long summer Sabbath afternoons. Reading stories, pantomiming Bible stories, dramatizing a Bible story in a small sandbox, drawing dot-to-dot pictures, playing Bible games, or conducting Sabbath school with dolls or younger brothers or sisters are only a few of the possibilities.

At the end of this chapter you will find some ideas for Sabbath activities with children. I have divided them up by type of activity, and each one tells what age of children would probably like it the best. The suggestions should be enough to get you started. As you practice making Sabbath memories, you will think of many more ideas.

The Sabbath plays a vital role in the spiritual life of each person— child or adult. Memorializing creation, it is a sign of God's creative power and a strong argument against evolution. The Sabbath acknowledges God's sovereignty in the world and in my personal life. God is the source of existence and knowledge. The Sabbath recalls man's primeval glory and witnesses to God's purpose to re-create us in His own image through redemption. Also, the Sabbath identifies God's people through a special test of allegiance at the end of time.

Preparation, Preservation, and Presence—might they be one of God's most important ways to teach our children about Him and to keep our families together? It is our privilege to tie cords of love between our children and ourselves through a special day, a day to remember forever.

KEYS TO SABBATH MEMORIES

1. Prepare for Sabbath throughout the week.
2. Simplify housework. Get the whole family to help.
3. Develop a family tradition for beginning the Sabbath.
4. Simplify Sabbath morning routines.
5. Plan special Sabbath activities with your children.
6. Connect the Sabbath with nature in your children's minds.
7. Create Sabbath memories that will link your children's hearts to you and to God.

Sabbath Activities for Children

	Age of Child			
	Pre-school 1-5	Younger Elementary 6-9	Older Elementary 10-13	Teens 14-

Nature Activities

Activity	Pre-school 1-5	Younger Elementary 6-9	Older Elementary 10-13	Teens 14-
Go on a nature walk (woods, field, beach).	♥	♥	♥	♥
Visit the zoo (depending on atmosphere and admission requirements).	♥	♥	♥	♥
Feed wild animals (ducks, birds, squirrels, etc.).	♥	♥	♥	♥
Observe wild animals (birds building nest, ants carrying food, bees, etc.).	♥	♥	♥	♥
Make collections of nature objects (leaves, rocks, seeds, insects, shells, sand, etc.).	?	♥	♥ ♥	♥
Read nature stories (parents or older children read to younger children).	♥	♥	♥	♥
Identify nature objects found (without collecting them), using books on species identification.	?	?	♥	♥ ♥
Keep a bird list (or wildflower list).		?	♥	♥
Study interesting facts about nature (use fact books, flannel board illustrations, real nature objects as available).	♥	♥	♥	♥
Observe a particular aspect of nature through the changing seasons (collecting pictures of the different seasons, drawing pictures of seasons).	?	♥	♥	♥
Find "sermons" in nature.		♥	♥	♥
Find nature objects which help us imagine what heaven will be like.		♥	♥	♥
Find nature objects mentioned in different Bible verses.		?	♥	♥
Make up an observation sheet for a Sabbath afternoon walk. (Use pictures of objects for younger children, words for older. Put stars beside each thing a child finds. Could be adapted to younger and older children on the outing. Older children could make one for younger children.)	?	♥	♥	♥

Sabbath Activities for Children

	Pre-School 1-5	Younger Elementary 6-9	Older Elementary 10-13	Teens 14-
NATURE ACTIVITIES				
Creation walk. (Find objects created on different days of Creation week.)	?	♥	♥	
Make pictures. (Build up nature pictures from sand, dirt, stones, sticks, moss, bits of plants, seeds, bird feathers, etc. Could be made permanent by gluing to a small board or heavy card. Teens could make artwork using nature objects.)	?	♥	♥	♥
Nature treasure hunt. (Each child has a list and a paper bag in which he will keep the specimens he finds from those listed.)		♥	♥	♥
Star study. (Lay out constellations on paper with silver stars, or in sand with pebbles, or on the rug with marbles or other small objects, study star books, purchase or make a small telescope.)		?	♥	♥
Animal scrapbook. (Make up a scrapbook using the characteristics of animals—flying animals, desert animals, etc.)	?	♥	♥	♥
Nature object lessons. (Adult prepares to present to children or older children prepare for younger siblings. See books in ABC.)		♥	♥ ♥	♥
Youth nature honors. (Work on requirements in *Pathfinder Manual* or *Youth Manual*.)	?	♥	♥	♥
Nature prints. (See a good book on nature activities for descriptions and how-to information for casting animal footprints, preserving spider's webs, waxing leaves, etc.)	?	♥	♥	♥
Nature calendar. (Draw large squares for each day of the month—and in each square illustrate a nature happening of that day—such as the first Robin, etc.)	?	♥	♥	♥
Visit a wildlife reserve. (Check on entrance fee, maybe purchase a season pass.)	♥	♥	♥	♥
Visit a farm.	♥	♥	♥	♥

SABBATH ACTIVITIES FOR CHILDREN

	AGE OF CHILD			
	PRE-SCHOOL 1-5	YOUNGER ELEMENTARY 6-9	OLDER ELEMENTARY 10-13	TEENS 14-
NATURE ACTIVITIES				
Nature games. (See selection at ABC.)		♥	♥	♥
Nature coloring books.	?	♥		♥
Quizzes on nature subjects. (See books in ABC.)		♥	♥ ♥	♥
Nature acrostics and other words games. (See books in ABC.)			♥	♥
Learn to identify different birds, fish, animals, etc. (Use cards with picture and description. See ABC or educational supply store.)	♥	♥	♥	♥
OUTREACH AND FELLOWSHIP ACTIVITIES				
Visit elderly or confined. (Very small child can take a bunch of flowers or carry a book. Keep visit short if accomanied by children. Adults enjoy hearing children sing. Teens can go as a group.)	♥	♥	♥	♥
Help in literature distribution. (Younger children can accompany parents or older children.)	?	♥	♥	♥
Make a scrapbook of nature pictures to take to a sick friend or for use in hospital wards. (Parents or older children can help younger children do this.)	?	♥	♥	♥
Invite friends to a branch Sabbath school or a story hour.	♥	♥	♥	♥
Participate in conducting a story hour program. (Younger children can be members of audience.)		♥	♥	♥
Read to younger brothers or sisters.		?	♥	♥
Participate in church-sponsored outreach activities.		?	♥	♥
Sunshine bands.	♥	♥	♥	♥
Visit a new family in the neighborhood (of course, with parents).	♥	♥	♥	♥
Visit a needy family.	♥	♥	♥	♥

Sabbath Activities for Children

	Pre-School 1-5	Younger Elementary 6-9	Older Elementary 10-13	Teens 14-
Age of Child				
OUTREACH AND FELLOWSHIP ACTIVITIES				
Sing-and-share time. (Use illustrated songs for younger children; mix types and age levels for a mixed group. Sing-along with records or tapes. Have teens bring their instruments. Several families could get together, each family planning part of activities.)	♥	♥	♥	♥
Visit every home in your neighborhood— just to get acquainted. Take a loaf of homemade bread. The whole family could participate.	♥	♥	♥	♥
Conduct Bible study groups using videos (available through ABC).			♥	♥
BIBLE/INSTRUCTIONAL ACTIVITIES				
Bible pantomine. (Act out Bible stories. Help younger children.)	♥	♥	♥	♥
Character-building stories. (Read to younger children, family read together, older children sometimes read to themselves. Visit ABC for ideas, also use bound copies of old religious magazines.)	♥	♥	♥	♥
Books with especially attractive nature pictures, Bible, or character-building pictures	♥	♥		
Paper objects. (Make objects from Bible stories out of paper or cardboard; tell story as you go along. Older chidlren can make their own.)	♥	♥	♥	
Sandbox Bible stories. (Children love to act out Bible stories using a sandbox.)	♥	♥ ♥	♥	
Tapes, records, or videos of Bible or character-building stories. (See chapter 8 for selection guidelines.)	♥	♥	♥	
Dot-to-dot pictures about Bible or nature stories.		♥ ♥		
Bible story coloring books.	?	♥	?	
Bible games. (Family plays together. See excellent selection at ABC.)	?	♥	♥	♥

Sabbath Activities for Children

	Pre-school 1-5	Younger Elementary 6-9	Older Elementary 10-13	Teens 14-
Age of Child				
Bible/Instructional Activities				
Flannel board illustrations of Bible stories. (Children tell story or parents tell story.)	?	♥	♥	
Box Bible stories. (Make a 3-D Bible scene in a shoe box or diorama.)	?	♥	♥	
Play Sabbath school with dolls or younger brothers and sisters.	♥	♥	♥	
Make Bible scenes using colored construction paper, scrap cloth, string, etc.	?	♥	♥	
Bible puzzles.	?	♥	♥	♥
Bible crossword puzzles.			♥ ♥	♥
Bible quizzes.		♥	♥ ♥	♥
Make models of Bible objects (lamp for ten virgins, Palestine home, fishing boat, etc.).	?	♥	♥	
Study Bible doctrines. (Find locations in Bible for key texts, simple explanations; make a notebook with texts and simple wording.)		♥	♥	♥
Make a "prophecy scrapbook." (Assemble newspaper clippings during the week that depict the fulfillment of Bible prophecy; on Sabbath find key texts and paste in scrapbook.)			♥	♥
Read Junior or Senior Bible Year.			♥	♥
Make a Sabbath scrapbook (one page for each Sabbath: sermon topic, special place visited, nature object found, memory verse for that day, something interesting learned from the Bible, etc.).	?	?	♥	
Make maps of Bible journeys, studying lives of Bible characters.			♥	?
Study a topic of mutual interest through the Bible and the Spirit of Prophecy (especially good for older children and teens).			♥	♥

SABBATH ACTIVITIES FOR CHILDREN

	AGE OF CHILD			
	PRE-SCHOOL 1-5	YOUNGER ELEMENTARY 6-9	OLDER ELEMENTARY 10-13	TEENS 14-

BIBLE/INSTRUCTIONAL ACTIVITIES

	PRE-SCHOOL 1-5	YOUNGER ELEMENTARY 6-9	OLDER ELEMENTARY 10-13	TEENS 14-
Make mobiles of nature or Bible objects.	?	♥	♥	♥
Make a list of all the Sabbaths in the year and plan what you and your family can study together on each of them.	?	♥	♥	♥
Box of "Sabbath toys" (only used on Sabbath, such as a special doll, Noah's ark, plastic fruit and flowers, small church, stuffed animals, etc.).	♥ ♥	♥		
Talk about the Sabbath sermon. Discuss main points, how it applies to your family. Younger children might draw a picture of something they heard in the sermon.	?	♥	♥	♥
Talk about Sabbath school. Each member tell about one thing that happened in it that day.	♥	♥	♥	♥
Learn about the countries benefiting from the Thirteenth Sabbath Offering. Look in the *SDA Yearbook* for information about Adventist work in those countries. Find pictures of those countries. Note how particular characteristics might affect God's work in those countries. Find countries on the map or globe.	?	♥	♥	♥
Correspond with a missionary or national church employee in the countries benefiting from the Thirteenth Sabbath Offering. Learn about their needs firsthand. Send a box of needed supplies.	?	♥	♥	♥
Bible computer games.		♥	♥ ♥	♥
Review memory verses for quarter. Use memory verse cards or picture in quarterly.	♥	♥	♥	♥
Read about Bible times and culture.			♥	♥
Learn to use Bible study helps (dictionary, commentary, source book, etc.).			♥	♥

Note: ? = Depends on maturity of individual child.

♥

CHAPTER 17

The Church and the Child

"Enter his gates with thanksgiving
and his courts with praise;
give thanks to him and praise his name."
—Psalm 100:4, NIV

Today was 3-week-old Celeste's first visit to church. Karen and Marty proudly unwrapped the tiny pink bundle. Moms, dads, and kids oohed and aahed over the infant. Toddlers excitedly rocked the cradle during the "welcome to cradle roll" song. Grandmas cooed over the tiny features and declared she looked exactly like Karen.

Church will become a major part of Celeste's life. She will join the cradle roll, be dedicated by the pastor, be promoted to kindergarten, say the memory verses for Thirteenth Sabbath, proudly tell everyone how she earned money for Investment, act out Sabbath school and church with her dolls, play the piano for the juniors, carry the flag on Pathfinder Day, walk down the aisle accepting Jesus as her Saviour, slip beneath the baptistry waters committing herself to a lifelong walk with her Lord, march down the aisle for eighth-grade graduation, and say, "I do" as she looks into the eyes of the man she loves. Church is for all of her life.

It all begins with the cradle roll, and for Mom and Dad the novelty may disappear quickly. "Another week of cradle roll! I wonder when Joey will be old enough to go by himself. I'd love to hear something besides 'Jesus Loves the Little Ones' for a change!" you mutter to yourself as you grab Joey, wriggle him into the jump chair, drop the diaper bag in the too-small space beside his chair, and let yourself plop down behind him.

Wait! Don't give up yet! Cradle roll is the start of religious education for your child. Going to Sabbath school with your infant or toddler *can* provide a special time for teaching spiritual lessons. If you are an active parent-teacher, your child will learn much more in Sabbath school than if you are merely a blob sitting in the chair behind him keeping order when required and passively handing out toys as directed. Take charge of your child's learning.

First, **begin to teach your child reverence by showing her that Sabbath school is a special place.** Help her fold her hands and kneel for prayer and participate in activities. Don't let her run around the room playing with anything she wants to either before or after Sabbath school. Be a good example of reverence yourself—visit with your friends only during intermission. If she gets too noisy, take her out briefly. Usually it is better to feed her somewhere else, as it may distract other children.

When baby is small your presence provides constant security. As he gets older you can train him to sit independently in the small chair in front of you and encourage him to do what the leader suggests. As he becomes more independent and wants to crawl or run around the room, don't hesitate to bring him back to his chair so he will learn to pay attention and follow the activities. When you do this, you are helping him to adjust to social situations and participate in group activities.

One of the ways little children learn is by associating an object or picture with a particular song or activity. **Be sure your toddler is holding the object that corresponds to what the group is singing or doing.** If you let her play with a different object from the one that goes with the group activity, she will not absorb the planned association.

Little children love singing. You can help your baby's learning by **singing clearly and softly** near his ear so he understands all the words. Babies and toddlers rarely sing in Sabbath school, but they are listening and will sometimes recognize the songs with pleasure when they are only a few months old. As they get older, they will try to sing what they have heard. Singing the Sabbath school songs at home will help reinforce learning. The songbooks are available at the ABC. Many of the songs also appear on cassettes for sing-along at home.

Babies and toddlers are learning to recognize and name pictures. **Show your child the important parts of the picture** the Sabbath school leader is using. Talk softly in your daughter's ear to name the object in the picture. If your child does not understand a word the teacher used, whisper one she does know. Tying the known and unknown words together will help increase her vocabulary.

Help your child do the motions for the different songs and other activities. Go through them at home, too. You'll be surprised at how

HTHYCRLJ-7

quickly baby will learn. Since babies and toddlers are just discovering how to use their bodies, your little one will need help with all the physical activities. *Cradle Roll Lessons for Sabbath School and Home* has many ideas for motion activities you will enjoy performing at home.

In the hubbub of a cradle roll division, sometimes toddlers need help with focusing their attention. If your little one's attention lags, **point to something interesting** that is happening. **Name the object you are pointing to.** Remind her of something she already knows about that object. It will help her learn to focus her attention on the most important thing occurring in her class.

When it is time to shift to another activity, **help your child learn to give up the object he is holding.** It may be hard if he really hasn't had enough time to thoroughly examine it. However, no matter how long your child has had the object, the time will come when he must go on to another activity. Some children do it easily, but others find transitions especially upsetting. At first you may need to substitute the object to be released with the next one to be used. If there isn't an immediate substitute object, point to something interesting that is happening or bring out a small quiet object you brought from home. Some children respond to "It's almost time to do something else" to get them ready for the next activity. The leader might assist you by coming back to your child, thus giving him a little more time to make the transition. If you consistently try to keep him on course, your toddler will gradually learn the routines of Sabbath school and will anticipate the next activity. It is good practice for sharing and changing activities at home and for learning "please" and "thank you."

If your 2-year-old feels shy and doesn't want to go up front, don't force the issue. Another Sabbath she may feel more confident. Toddlers really still need Mom or Dad as home base. They're ready to explore the world but like to look back to see if their parents are still there. If your little one is especially shy—and some children are naturally this way—don't push her. To do so can be very traumatic. She needs to feel confident before she will move out. Don't label her as "shy," either. The label can be hard to overcome. Go up front with her to build confidence. Let her choose the activities with which she feels most comfortable.

Even though you can hardly wait to get back to the adult Sabbath school, don't pressure your little one to stay by himself until he is ready. On the other hand, gradually encourage more and more independence. In a small group he will probably be ready sooner than if you attend a large division. As he learns to sit by himself and go through the routines of Sabbath school, move to a place at the back of the room rather than remain right beside him. It will act as a transition toward independence. When he seems quite secure with that arrangement, start talking about how "big" he is and how "big boys" go to Sabbath school all by themselves. If he gets a look of absolute horror, he still isn't ready for total independence. Wait a few weeks before bringing up the subject again. But if he seems rather intrigued by the idea of going by himself, the time may be right for this transition. You might start by stepping outside for a few minutes. Leave your coat or something personal so he will know you are returning. Some children are naturally independent and confident, while others need more reassurance and a slower transition to independence. By the time they are 3, most children will be going to Sabbath school by themselves.

It is your privilege to provide that individual teaching during Sabbath school and its repetition at home that will make church a vital part of your child's life. Don't be too quick to give up the opportunities of a parent-teacher! (By the way, when parent-teachers are busy teaching their child during Sabbath school, the leaders usually hate to see them leave, too.) After your child is going on his own, however, keep in touch with the leader so your home instruction can fit in with Sabbath school.

Many people in the church help with your child's religious education—Sabbath school teachers and leaders, Pathfinder leaders, the pastor, church school teachers—but **you** are the director. You are the person who plans for your child's religious education and who really knows your child's spiritual needs. Don't just drop your child off for Sabbath school each week assuming the teachers will present her all she needs to know. Your child's religious education will be much more effective if you work with the church.

After your child can go to Sabbath school by herself, ask the leaders what they are teaching so you can reinforce the learning at home. Sing the new songs for worship. Do an activity that repeats what your child is doing in Sabbath school. Always teach your child the Bible lesson and the memory verse. Bible learning needs daily repetition to stick.

After Sabbath school, Karen and Marty gently laid Celeste in her infant carrier and followed the crowd to the sanctuary for the worship service. They weren't used to sitting in the back row but decided it might be a good idea in case the infant started crying. But their first church service went well. After nursing between Sabbath school and church, the baby slept peacefully until the last song. Karen breathed a sigh of relief. They had made it!

Taking young children to church isn't easy. It requires preparation as well as patience and persistence. During the first few months baby may sleep peacefully—if church coincides with naptime—and appear to generally ignore the activities. But by the time an infant can sit up, church will become a real challenge.

Many parents prefer an early church service, if one is available. Children are not so tired and can then go to Sabbath school afterward, which is more active and geared toward children's interests. Take toddlers out to exercise between Sabbath school and church service and attend to their toileting needs.

Babies and toddlers are naturally exuberant and uninhibited. Learning to be quiet in church is quite an achievement! You can make it easier if you try to get the wiggles out ahead of time. If you are sitting on a wooden bench, remove your baby's shoes to avoid noise. Practice at home being quiet for a short time while you read the child a story or the Sabbath school lesson. Teach your baby what "Sh-sh-sh!" means.

Come prepared with a change of clothes and bottles so baby can be comfortable. An uncomfortable infant will soon let everyone know how he feels! Bring some "church toys" that do not make any noise: a "quiet book" with different activities to keep your toddler occupied; pipe cleaners to bend into novel shapes; a clean cloth or handkerchief to make a bunny or a baby in a cradle, or just to play with and feel; small stuffed animals; a small cloth doll with a blanket; or a small cloth picture book for babies. If baby is at the throwing stage, tie the object to a long ribbon so you can retrieve it easily. Save the toys for church so they will be novel and interesting to your child.

As your child gets older, add a small felt board with simple objects; a Sabbath coloring book with crayons; paper and pencil; a more advanced "quiet book"; and other books.

Children soon learn exactly what to expect in church. Entertainment is really only a stopgap until the child can sit still for longer periods of time. It is only a means to an end! Any activities you bring for your child should be appropriate for the Sabbath and used only for church. That way they will retain their novelty and interest.

However, don't allow children to have an activity as soon as you walk into the sanctuary. Remember, the goal is to help children learn to sit still for longer periods of time and begin to listen to what is going on. It is unreasonable to expect toddlers and 2- or 3-year-olds to sit quietly in church with nothing to do when they do not understand anything around them. Two-year-olds may sit and give rapt attention to a TV program, but church is not a TV program. Children need something to do during part of the service. But activities need to be judiciously used.

Try to postpone providing activities until as late as possible during the service, maybe about the time the sermon begins. Before then your child will find more to watch and do. I have seen many children come into church, grab a coloring book or a *Guide*, and proceed to ignore everything else until the benediction. That is not training them for participation in church.

Help your child stand up for songs, listen to the organ and the special music, kneel for prayer, and give an offering. The stained glass windows, the hushed tones, and the organ music create a sense of awe that children pick up. If members make spoken prayer requests, explain to your 4-year-old what is happening and what the people are saying. He may want to make a prayer request also. Get your children as involved as possible in the worship service.

On Thanksgiving Sabbath, when the pastor at 4-year-old Jonathan's church asked for public expressions of thankfulness, several people responded. Jonathan waved his hand, but the pastor didn't see him and proceeded on to another part of the service, to the child's great disappointment. At the close of the service Jonathan insisted that he wanted to tell the pastor something. So his grandma took him to greet the pastor. Promptly the boy announced to the minister that he had wanted to tell about what he was thankful for. The pastor graciously apologized for overlooking his hand, and Jonathan eagerly told him what he was thankful for. It was a delightful exchange between a small boy and his pastor.

Children will test the limits of behavior in church, as they do in other places. The child who will not behave needs to know the boundaries and that punishment will always follow misbehavior. Good behavior might be rewarded with a special treat after dinner, but willful misbehavior should be punished immediately. Be sure to come back into church afterward, otherwise you will be teaching the child he can go out and have "fun" if he misbehaves. Also be consistent in establishing the limits for behavior during church, and in time you will be rewarded with a child who listens.

If properly trained when young, by late preschool years children know how to behave in church. They may need an occasional reminder, however. You will avoid many problems if you insist on sitting together as a family during worship service until your children have finished academy. Children can sit with friends during Sabbath school and youth meetings, but church is family worshiptime. Naturally, occasionally your child might invite a friend to sit with your family or accept an invitation from another family to join them. But you should be sure your child is with responsible adults during the service. You will have many occasions to bless the day you decided to worship together as a family!

Training for participation in church service goes on through the elementary years. If your child is old enough to read *Primary Treasure* or *Guide*, she is old enough to listen. Do not allow reading in church. Children who read the magazines during church will have nothing left for Sabbath afternoon. Again, help children be part of the worship service. Sitting near the front enables them to see what is happening and to feel a part of the service.

By 5 or 6 years, children can make a list of key words used during the sermon. Begin by writing one or two words at the top of the page and have the child make a mark every time the preacher uses them. The topic of the sermon should give you a clue for selecting words that might appear frequently. Children love to do this and find it fun to tell the preacher he used the word ''Joseph'' 25 times during the sermon. Older children can make an outline of the sermon and find the Bible texts. You can help younger children find the verses. If your pastor becomes aware that children are trying to follow his sermon, he may introduce more items of interest to them.

All churches have special services and rituals with particular significance for members. Our denomination is no exception. Baptism, Communion, and ordination fall in this category. How do children relate to the ordinances?

We live in a fast-paced, impatient world where everyone wants instant gratification of every desire. Children long to experience everything before they are 16—sex, credit cards, babies, their own apartment, Medicaid, and food stamps. As David Elkind, world-renowned authority on child development from Yale University, puts it so well in his two books *The Hurried Child* and *All Grown Up and No Place to Go*, we push children to become little adults long before their time. Childhood has disappeared as children go from toddlerhood to adulthood. Do you think

I am exaggerating? Not in the least. If our kids haven't heard it from us, they've seen it on the evening news, the late night show, or HBO while we were at work. I'll concede that some kids don't watch HBO or the late night shows, but most see the evening news. It's all there.

In most single parent families, children—especially the oldest one—are their parent's confidants. They act as consultants for every major decision—even though they're only 8—hearing about every date and all the financial problems. In effect, they have no childhood. As Elkind points out, kids feel flattered to be included in the world of adults and eagerly listen to tales of love and offer their "advice" about Mom's date life. But they pay a price down the line for their pseudo adulthood. By mid to late teens many of these kids realize that they had no childhood and they become angry. Instinctively, although they don't express it this way, they know they have been deprived of something important and essential—childhood. Their anger shows itself in rebellion against everything their parents stand for, including religion.

To ensure a solid developmental foundation on which to build adult life, children need the innocence of childhood. They don't need adult cares and knowledge thrust on them before they are mentally capable of coping with such a burden. Adulthood will come soon enough. Children need to look forward to what child development specialists call "rites of passage," significant accomplishments that mean they are growing up. More primitive cultures initiate children into the adult world through a well-planned and acknowledged ceremony—the rite of passage. In simpler times Western-ized cultures also had rites of passage too. Girls looked forward to their first bra and their first pair of hose, their first shoes with heels. Now I see 7-year-olds wearing hose and heels and bras, even though they have a child's figure. Little girls barely out of kindergarten use face powder and lipstick. What happened to the idea that such things indicated you were growing up? Few children are grown up in that way at 7 and 8!

Society used to reserve dating and "boyfriends" and "girlfriends" for when you were at least a teenager, perhaps much later. Now parents ask their first graders about their "girlfriend." One of the few rites of passage left is the driver's license. Most localities impose an age limit—16, usually—for driving a car. But I see families that not only allow but encourage their boys to drive long before that. On back roads, you understand, when the policeman is not looking. Never mind the rules!

Why have I gone into a discussion of lost childhood in a chapter on the church? Because I am afraid the church has become part of the "grow up early" syndrome, too. Not too long ago I visited a church that had child elders. One was an 8-year-old girl! I applaud trying to get children more involved in the church, but as an elder? Children can be spiritual leaders among their peers, but surely we are creative enough to find a different name and make a different job description for what they do.

I have seen 6-year-olds baptized into church fellowship. And I have watched 3- and 4-year-olds participating in the Communion service. Now, I know enough about child development to tell you, beyond any reasonable doubt, that 6-year-olds do not understand what baptism is all about and 3- and 4-year-olds have no conception of what the Communion service means. Both rites are highly symbolic. Their spiritual significance resides in understanding their symbolic meaning.

Seated beside us at the foot washing at our church recently were a father and a boy who looked about 4 years old. The father truly wanted his son to understand the significance of what they were doing together. Carefully and patiently he explained to the little fellow what the foot washing meant. The little boy looked puzzled and bored and kept making comments like, "But I washed my feet in the shower. They aren't dirty." The symbolic meaning was simply beyond him.

One Sabbath morning when Liza was 3 and the family was getting ready for church, her mother noticed the child had put some crackers in her little black purse. "What are those for?" Mom asked. "You're going to have something to eat in church, so I brought some crackers for me," little Miss Prepared replied. It was an appropriate response for a child. The bread and wine are simply "something to eat" at this age.

When we allow extremely young children to participate in such church ceremonies, we are denying them a rite of passage that would have great significance for them when they are older. But when they are old enough to grasp the meaning, the ceremony has already lost its significance. It is "old hat," childish. The freshness, delight, and deep spiritual meaning of a first Communion service following baptism can never be recovered. We have sacrificed it on the altar of "hurry-up."

Children do not need to do everything adults do. In fact, they **shouldn't**. They can be meaningfully involved in church life at the level of their ability to contribute and understand. Anticipation is one of the great delights of childhood—looking forward to the next step in growing up. When they have no anticipation, spiritual and psychological boredom and paralysis set in. The boredom of today's children is in part owing to having experienced too much too soon. One of the powerful drives of healthy childhood is curiosity and a desire to explore and learn about the world. Too much too soon satisfies that drive too young, and boredom is the natural result. Don't deny your children the delights of anticipation. They are an important and vital part of growing up not only spiritually but also in other ways.

Most children do not understand the meaning of symbolic ideas until they have acquired a mental age of 11 or 12 years. For the average child that occurs at about the same chronological age. But some children do not reach this level of understanding until later, while others get to it earlier. Intellectually gifted children often think abstractly by the time they are 8 or 9 years old.

Let me give you a quick and easy way to find out if your child is thinking abstractly. Ask him or her to tell you the meaning of three of the following words: love, faith, patience, salvation, freedom, justice, or obedience. You will notice that none of them is a concrete word you can draw a picture of—like chair, house, garden, boy, or baby—although they are all nouns. If you get responses at the abstract level, you can be pretty sure your child can understand symbolic ideas. Abstract definitions will sound a bit like dictionary definitions or will employ a synonym at the same theoretical level. If your child still thinks at the concrete level, the responses will seem more like illustrations of what the word means than definitions. For example, an abstract definition of faith might be "confidence or trust in a person," or "belief when you don't have any proof," or "believing when you can't see the person or you don't know everything." A concrete-level description might be, "faith is like when my mom says she'll pick me up after the party, and I'm sure she'll do it. I have faith she'll do it." Children who have advanced to abstract-level thinking may give both kinds of meanings.

If your child can respond abstractly, you can be pretty sure she can understand—at least at a beginning level—the symbolic-based ideas of the Bible. But if he offers only concrete level meanings, you will need to explain the symbolic ideas of the Scriptures in a way he can understand— usually with an illustration of the meaning. Sometimes children cannot understand even a concrete-level illustration. The idea is simply beyond them at their present level of mental development. Don't worry. They'll eventually get there.

Again, what does all this have to do with the church? Plenty. A question that never fails to generate a certain amount of discussion is When is a child ready for baptism? Baptism, of course, includes church membership. So we might ask the question another way: When is a child ready for church membership? The second question might help clarify what we really have in mind. Today baptism has the added dimension of church membership that was not present in the same way in New Testament times. What I said in an earlier book describes well the complexity of the answer:

"Many children will accept Christ as their Saviour when they are quite young. The church may want to delay baptism until the child is a bit older. On the other hand, when the child is continually told he should delay baptism, he may lose interest and feel the church does not need or want him. This has happened. Church membership can steady a child through the turbulent adolescent years; it can give him a purpose and goal in life" (*How to Teach Children in Sabbath School*, p. 156).

The answer is still complex. We can set no definite age for baptism because children differ so much in their level of maturity. As I mentioned in an earlier chapter, most SDA children get baptized sometime between 10 and 14 years, with 12 years being the peak time. During these years their thinking matures enough to understand what baptism means and to grasp the fundamentals of church doctrines. An exceptional 8- or 9-year-old may understand, but most do not have the mental maturity to know what baptism or church membership means.

The December 1972 issue of *Ministry* offered the following guidelines for baptism:

The person should:

1. Know the significance of baptism.
2. Be surrendered to Christ, accepting His sacrifice for him.
3. Understand the principles of our faith.
4. Understand the significance of church membership.

Ellen White makes it very clear that even children will show clearly by the way they live that they have surrendered their life to God (see *Child Guidance*, p. 490). So we might add a fifth guideline,

5. Give evidence in the life of a commitment to God.

Probably numbers 3 and 4 of the *Ministry* guidelines embrace the fifth guideline. Certainly the significance of church membership implies that Christ has become Lord of the person's life, and that he shows evidence of his new commitment in the way he lives.

Naturally, a child of 10, 12, or even 14 will not have the same understanding of the meaning of baptism and the other church doctrines as an adult candidate. But the youngster reared in an Adventist home will have more of a practical knowledge of what the doctrines mean in everyday life than the adult just coming into the church.

Baptism is a serious step and needs adequate preparation. The Adventist church has excellent children's materials to help in their preparation. Your child can study the meaning of baptism and learn about the main doctrines of the Adventist Church through a baptismal class conducted at church or school. Get in touch with your pastor. Ideally, your child should feel comfortable enough with your pastor to approach him on her own.

We were stunned when our 11-year-old son announced after church one week that he was going to be baptized the next Sabbath, since it was the first we had heard about his desire. "I've already talked to Pastor Fred and everything's OK," he explained. The pastor was a personal friend of the family. On reflection we were thrilled that our son had such a comfortable relationship with his pastor. During the following week the pastor came to talk with us about our son's baptism. We agreed that he was ready, and we committed ourselves to continue to nurture him in the Christian life.

If your family cannot attend church regularly because you are too far away from a congregation, the Adventist Book Center can get you a copy of the children's baptismal manual that pastors use for the baptismal class. You can study it with your child, making sure she has a basic understanding of what the church she wants to join believes.

As your child is studying church doctrines, make sure she has plenty of opportunities to ask questions. Some children are shy and will not ask questions in a large group. Show yourself to be open to explaining what she is learning in the class. Many times children will not acknowledge that they don't understand something because to do so makes them feel inferior. You can get past this reticence by commenting on one of the more difficult parts of a particular topic: "When I was learning about the 2300 days, I always wondered . . ." Your whole family might use the opportunity to go over the doctrines during worship once a week. It is a splendid chance for your child to review what she learned in the previous class period by explaining it to the family.

Few children 10 to 14 years of age who participated in our research interviews about salvation understood the complete meaning of baptism. Frequently they responded that it means being born again. The idea that baptism washes away your sins and that you are forgiven was also strong during those years. Very few connected the symbolism of Christ's death and resurrection with baptism. Many gave responses that showed little understanding of the significance of baptism. Check with your child. Ask him to tell you what baptism means. You may be surprised. Romans 6:3, 4 in the *International Children's Bible* or the New International Version clarifies the meaning considerably.

Baptism also means the child is joining the Seventh-day Adventist Church. Only a few children and adolescents mentioned this aspect of baptism. What does it mean to be a member? Children can usually understand a comparison of the church as a family. What does it mean to be a family member? Family members care about each other, help each other, pitch in to do the work of the family, assist the family financially, are loyal to the family, live by the family's rules, and carry the family name (usually!). Baptism is a public statement about joining the family, a little like a wedding. God calls the church His bride.

Ask your child how church members show they care about each other and help each other. What kind of work is there to do for the church family? What can your child do to help with the church work? How can he assist the church financially? What does it mean to be loyal to the church family? What are the church family's rules? As you go through each part of what it means to be a church member, your child will begin to understand what she is committing herself to do when she becomes a church family member.

From 5 to 7 years children have only vague ideas about church membership or what belonging to a denomination means. They easily confuse being Protestant with being Irish or Russian and have little or no idea about how to recognize an Adventist. Most likely they will not be able to tell you the difference between a Catholic and an Adventist. Many children this age do not even know what church they belong to.

By the time children are between 7 and 9 years old, however, they have sorted things out a little better. They can tell you that a dog or a cat cannot be a church member because they cannot participate in church services. Also, they know that all children do not belong to the same denomination. But they generally use external signs to tell that a person belongs to a certain church. For instance, "I know he's a Catholic because he goes into the Catholic church.'' If asked how a person becomes an Adventist, they will probably say, ''By being baptized.''

Not until children are 10 to 12 years old does the word ''religion'' appear spontaneously in response to questions about churches. They now grasp that religious identity is an inner commitment and will describe it by using words such as repent, pray to God, etc. In addition, they recognize that religious membership means the person thinks, studies, and observes a certain code. Their understanding of church membership has matured considerably from their preschool notions. For this reason, many denominations have special services that confirm the child as a church member around the age of 12, even though the child was baptized by sprinkling as an infant. The Adventist Church combines both baptism and study of church doctrines and confirmation as a church member into one rite—baptism by immersion—which provides a way for a child to make a real choice to follow his Lord.

Even 12- and 14-year-olds do not understand the teachings of their church completely, and they are only beginning their walk with the Lord. Parents make a commitment, too, when their children are baptized—to nurture the new Christians. Ellen White says it beautifully in *Child Guidance*, pages 499-501:

''In consenting to the baptism of their children, parents sacredly pledge themselves to be faithful stewards over these children, to guide them in their character building. They pledge themselves to guard with special interest these lambs of the flock, that they may not dishonor the faith they profess. . . .

''Cooperate with God by working diligently for their salvation. If they err, do not scold them. Never taunt them with being baptized and yet doing wrong. Remember that they have much to learn in regard to the duties of a child of God.''

Baptism is the beginning—not the accomplished end—of learning more about God and drawing closer to our Saviour and Redeemer. Nurturing the new member is vital.

As our children grow up in the church, we cannot leave their relationship to it to chance. We must be involved in making the church a place they love to go and where they feel they belong. Children need interesting religious education programs suited to their stage of development. Sabbath school, Adventurer Club, and Pathfinders are a start. But they don't happen by themselves. Many parents have discovered that if they want interesting activities for their children, they must be involved in running them. Interesting and challenging Sabbath school programs need thought and planning. They don't result when the leader tries to pull things together 10 minutes before starting time! Great Pathfinder Clubs require a lot of work. But it is work that pays off in keeping children interested in the church. Insist that the nominating committee in your church fill the positions relating to children *first* with the best people available. Campaign in your church for adequate physical facilities for children's activities. Lack of a suitable place to meet will seriously hamper religious education of children. The message from a church that provides only inferior facilities is clear: Kids don't count for much in this congregation!

All the adults in the church should take an interest in the children—not just the parents. The congregation's children must feel warmth and caring from all the members. Needing to feel they belong, they must be loved into the congregation. The congregation must notice their concerns and care for them. Many adults attribute their relationship with the Lord to a caring Sabbath school teacher, Pathfinder leader, or church adult friend. "I'm a Seventh-day Adventist minister today because of one man in our church who cared about me," John told me one day when we were talking about churches. "I was a lonely and discouraged kid. Noticing that my father didn't have any time for me, he stepped in to fill the gap. He invited me to go camping with their family and always had a kind word for me. I knew he cared. To him I owe my religious commitment. Without him I would have slipped out the back door of the church."

Congregations have an emotional atmosphere just like families. Many things contribute to the emotional tone of a church family—the spirit of acceptance or rejection, criticism or approval, caring and concern for each member, the attitude of forgiveness, the tone of the sermons (grace and love or legalism), cooperation, and openness to new ideas. If the emotional atmosphere of the church you attend is poisonous, what can you do to change it? If no change is possible, can you transfer to a church where the atmosphere is more conducive to spiritual health for your family, even if it means driving a longer distance? The religious education programs of the church, the attitude of individual members toward the children, and the emotional atmosphere of the congregation matter a great deal in the formation of your child's attitudes toward the church, especially as he or she approaches adolescence. The church you attend is an important component of your child's spiritual development.

KEYS TO CHURCH

1. Be an active parent-teacher. Take charge of your child's religious education.
2. Work closely with church leaders to be sure your child gets the best religious education possible.
3. Study the Sabbath school lesson with your child every day.
4. When training your child how to behave in church, plan ahead, be patient, and be persistent.
5. Help your child participate in the church service.
6. Sit together in church as a family during childhood and adolescence.
7. Be involved in church activities for children.
8. Encourage an attitude of caring and openness to new ideas and thinking in your church.
9. Work to help church leaders and members realize the importance of nurturing the children in the congregation.

CHAPTER 18

Confronting the World

"I am not asking you to take them out of the world.
But I am asking you keep them safe from the Evil One."
—John 17:15, ICB

All morning 3-year-old Mark eagerly watched the activity next door as the men shoveled and carted away loads of dirt, hammered the forms for the new cement driveway and entryway, and leveled the foundation. Later in the day, when he came into the house he had a small stick dangling from his mouth.

"What's that in your mouth?" his mother asked.

"My mouth candle," Mark replied. "You know, like the men who are making the driveway."

Suddenly Mommy understood. "You mean a cigarette, don't you?"

"My mouth candle," the child insisted.

With a quick prayer heavenward, Mommy decided it was time for a lesson on the dangers of smoking. Carefully she explained about how cigarettes make people sick, emphasizing that Jesus wants us to keep our bodies healthy and strong. Mark, as usual, was full of questions about how "mouth candles" could cause people to be sick and why it wasn't good to smoke.

The next morning Mark was up early, eager to watch the men pouring cement. But this time he had something important on his mind. At the first opportunity, during a work break, he spoke to one of the men.

"Mister, why don't you stop smoking? It's not good for you! You'll get sick!"

"Well, Mark, I don't know why I don't stop. I should. My wife wants me to stop and my daughters want me to stop."

"Then, why don't you?" the child insisted.

"I really don't know. Guess I'll have to think about it."

The next week when Grandma came to visit, Mark wanted to ride his tricycle to the nearby park. On the way back he noticed a squashed cigarette carton lying beside the road and quickly ran to pick it up.

"Gra'ma, that's cigarettes, and they're bad for you! Very bad!"

Grandma agreed, and Mark enthusiastically expounded about the evils of smoking. He had learned his lesson well and was quick to volunteer his new knowledge to anyone.

Like Mark, our children are surrounded with the world—a world becoming more secular every day. Its polluted values assault their senses and their thoughts. Don't you yearn some days to grab your children in your arms and "shrink wrap" them in protective plastic so no evil can touch them? Christ recognized the problem when He told His disciples, "My prayer is not that you take them out of the world but that you protect them from the evil one" (John 17:15, NIV). Maybe He *will* help us "shrink wrap" our children to "protect them from the evil one"!

Mark is fortunate. His parents are patiently and carefully teaching him about God's way of living. They are doing their best to help God "shrink wrap" him protectively. He doesn't have to live with secondhand smoke and all its health dangers. His baby-sitter, grandparents, and friends don't smoke, either. All the most important people in his life are giving him the same message: Smoking isn't good for you!

The child will have many more lessons to learn about God's way of living, but he has made an important start. If all the significant people in his life continue to teach him in a united voice, as opportunities arise each day, he will discover God's way naturally as he matures and will grow up with a clear sense of right and wrong.

Unless we are extremely careful, the communications media will shape our children's values. Maybe right now you're shrugging your shoulders and rolling your eyes and saying, "Leave me alone! TV doesn't hurt me. I can control what I watch." Maybe you can and maybe you do. But Satan is a master change agent. He introduces his ideas subtly, carefully, little by little, until he has transformed us and we never even realize it! Then he sits back with a smirk, rolling his eyes in glee. "Got 'em!" he whispers. Kids are pretty easy to get.

Clinical psychologists use a well-known, highly effective technique known as systematic desensitization. It is especially effective for helping people get rid of phobias that interfere with their daily living. Carole, a biology major in college, intends to take premed. Let's suppose she has a terrible fear of rats of any kind and can't get near the white rats used in the biology lab. She'll never be able to go on with her plans for becoming a doctor unless she can get over her crippling phobia. So she goes to the campus counseling center to obtain some help. Her counselor first teaches her to relax. She practices relaxation techniques until she can do so easily. Then her counselor shows her a card with the word ''Rat'' written on it. Immediately she begins to feel tense. The counselor encourages her to employ the relaxation techniques she has learned. Carole practices relaxing while looking at the word ''rat'' until she no longer feels tense. Then the counselor introduces a picture of a white rat. Again Carole employs the techniques until she can relax while looking at the rat picture. The procedure continues, over time, until the counselor actually brings a white rat into their session. When Carole can hold the white rat while still feeling relaxed she has conquered her phobia. What was previously distasteful to her has now become pleasurable, or at least tolerable.

Simply stated, the technique is effective because an individual cannot be both tense and relaxed at the same time. Relaxation replaces the tenseness. Also, while in a relaxed state Carole is gradually introduced to more and more distasteful stimuli. But she is able to conquer her fear because she is more open to new experiences while in a relaxed state. This technique also involves modeling that occurs when Carole is in a relaxed state.

What does desensitization have to do with values and your kids? Plenty! Satan, astute student of the human mind that he is, uses desensitization cleverly. The human brain has three kinds of electrical waves important to this discussion: alpha, beta, and delta. Beta waves come from the alert, thinking brain, delta from the sleeping brain. Alpha waves result from an awake, but relaxed, nonthinking state of the brain. Because of the nature of television, rapid linear movements occur hundreds of times per minute. The linear movements overwhelm the brain, which seeks relief by going into alpha state—the relaxed, nonthinking mode that takes in stimuli uncritically. During studies of brain waves while watching television, few children could go more than 30 seconds in beta (thinking) state before dropping to alpha state. Some adults could control their brain state for 10 minutes, but rarely for more than that.

Because of the nature of the television picture, most of our watching occurs in a relaxed, uncritical state in which we can easily be desensitized. What at first we abhorred, we later embrace. Our values have changed, and we weren't even aware of the shift! Children are especially vulnerable to television messages.

From television our children learn that happiness comes through "things," food is for fun and instant power, and that violence, sex, magic, or individuals who can do things normal people cannot will solve all our problems. They also discover that marital commitment and sex don't mix and that religion, at best, has nothing to say to our lives and, at worst, is a detriment to really living. In one of their studies, Action for Children's Television found that 96 percent of the sex shown is fornication, rape, homosexuality, adultery, or prostitution. Only 4 percent occurs between husband and wife, and that usually has a negative connotation. Television also encourages children to be bystanders in life, passively uninvolved. Instant gratification is the norm. Alcohol ads extensively use systematic desensitization. Drugs get glorified. As someone has said, All TV is educational TV. The question is: What are your children learning? Are they the values you want them to absorb?

Kate Moody, in her book *Growing Up on Television*, suggests some questions to ask when evaluating a particular program:

1. What kind of distinction does it make between the real and the make-believe?
2. How are problems solved?
3. What role models does it offer?
4. What special effects, music, noise, or confusion level does it use?
5. How does it employ humor?
6. How does it portray the world? Is it a dangerous place to fear, or a wonder to explore?
7. What kind of commercials accompany the program?
8. What is the child's response to the program? What kinds of play follow it? What kinds of behavior has the program encouraged? What body movements? Eye movements? Hand use?

To her questions we might add some specifically related to our Christian viewpoint:

9. Does the program ridicule, deride, or cast doubt on the Deity or the Word of God?
10. Does it inspire Christian living in accordance with God's Holy Word? Or does it make sin appear attractive? Does it enhance the development of the fruit of the Spirit?
11. Does the program increase our desire to be with Christ? What motives for living does it appeal to?

12. Is the program good enough to be worth our time?
13. What does the program add to my child's life that is indispensable for character growth? Or by watching it, what will get removed from my child's life that would be beneficial for character growth?

At least once or twice a year I spend a couple hours wandering up and down the aisles of a major toy store to see what manufacturers are selling to families. While I have not done a precise count, my general impression is that close to half, maybe more, of the toys I see incorporate values contrary to God's Word. Aisles stacked almost to the ceiling contain toys focusing on violence, the occult, monsters, and extraterrestrial beings. Other aisles are heaped with toys that promote a self-centered, pleasure-filled lifestyle in which a person's appearance is the most important aspect of life. Are they the values we want our children to acquire?

Children do not miss the values messages of toys. Researcher Diana Foutz of the University of Southern California studied their reactions to three different adult "personality dolls." The dolls—Mrs. Heart, She-Ra, and Barbie—have had heavy marketing and include clothing, furniture, and other props. Mrs. Heart is a housewife with a husband and family of children, She-Ra a daredevil adventurer, and Barbie the beauty queen type. Foutz had boys and girls ages 4 to 6 play with the dolls, then asked them to decide who they would want for a friend and for a mother and mentor. Their choices were similar to the dolls' marketed personalities. One girl said she wanted to be like Barbie "because she has a better body." Others chose She-Ra because "she can help me get my way." Dr. Foutz concluded, "Parents should realize that the media images of dolls often become the ideals of children."

In an article appearing in *Women Alive!* Fran Sandin told about a creative way she used to handle the gift of a Barbie doll that her daughter received at her tenth birthday party. After the party, Fran and her daughter read Proverbs 31:10-31. When they finished, Mrs. Sandin asked, "Does this doll, as she is dressed right now, represent a godly woman?" Her daughter thoughtfully responded, "No. I see what you mean. She looks like a nightclub dancer."

Fran went on to tell her daughter that there is nothing wrong with having a beautiful face and body. They are gifts from God, and we honor Him when we take care of ourselves. But the thoughts inside our hearts make the difference in our choices. Then Fran suggested that she would teach her daughter how to sew, and they would pretend that, since the

Barbie doll was in their family, her heart's desire was to honor Jesus. Mother and daughter had a lot of fun making clothes for the toy. They even bought her some props that fit in with their Christian lifestyle.

You might think of a different solution to the doll dilemma, but I believe God will give you one that will help you teach your children Christian values. Many families have found creative solutions to the television dilemma. Some families have chosen to get rid of their television set, while others have decided on a program of carefully planned viewing. The family chooses the programs ahead of time and limits viewing time. Some families rate programs and assign numbers for each category. Children can select from the approved programs to make up the total number of points allowed for the week. Other families give out coupons worth 30 minutes of viewing of preselected programs. If the children do not use the coupons, at the end of the week they can redeem them for cash.

Today the media poses a real challenge for Christian families. Pray for guidance and creativity. God will show you what to do in your family to lessen the influence of the secular media. The first major step in helping children confront the world is to **protect their minds while they are young**. Shelter them from the world's values. **Nurture them with Christian values**. It will take constant vigilance and creativity, but in the end you will be glad you did. Children nurtured with Christian values have a totally different base from which to make decisions as they confront the world. When a child's mind has been protected during the most impressionable years, he more easily recognizes evil for what it is. Children exposed to much evil, however, become desensitized, and the difference between good and evil becomes hazy at best.

The next major step in helping children confront the world is to **make the difference between good and evil clear**. Children are not born knowing what is good or evil. They learn it from their families, their church, and their teachers (if they attend a religious school). During the preschool years, as children explore their world parents must clearly indicate what is good and what is bad. This is right, that is wrong. Parents are the main source of such information for their children. Mark understood well that "mouth candles" are wrong because of what his mother told him.

Even young children need reasons for why something is good and something else is bad. Mark's mother carefully explained to him why cigarettes are "bad" for people. Fran talked with her daughter about the ideals of Christian womanhood and led her to understand what was wrong with the way Barbie was dressed. Naturally the reasons you give preschoolers will be simple ones they can understand. As children grow older, your explanations can be more complex. And as you provide them, you also build principles that will guide behavior throughout life. The preschool years are the time for establishing clear right and wrong boundaries. The elementary school years enlarge the concepts of right and wrong and construct principles that will serve as a launching pad for the adolescent to try his decision-making skills. The teenager who does not have a strong base of principles learned during earlier years confronts the world without spiritual and ethical armor.

The third step in equipping children to confront the world is to **help your child develop a solid sense of self-respect and confidence**. The child who respects herself is much less likely to be swayed by peer pressure. She will have the confidence to say no and the assurance to stop and think about the issues involved before she makes a decision. Also, she will have the courage to suggest an alternative or to stand up for what she believes is right. A sense of self-respect and confidence is one of the best gifts you can give your child.

We hear a lot these days about self-concept and how we all need a "good" one. It gets promoted in a lot of gimmicky ways—workbooks, exercises, games. But self-concept is not a gimmick. As a fundamental part of the personality, it is much harder to change than the sellers of the self-help books would have you believe. Self-concept, self-esteem, and self-respect are all closely related terms having something to do with what we think of ourselves. I think the term *self-respect* comes closest to what our children really need to help them confront the world. The *Random House Dictionary* defines *self-respect* as "proper esteem or regard for the dignity of one's own character." Notice that it involves both dignity and character. It is the term Ellen White uses when describing how we should feel about ourselves. Self-respect implies that you regard yourself too highly to do anything degrading to yourself. This part of the personality develops gradually during childhood and adolescence.

A put-down here, an angry scolding there, a disappointed look or a sigh—little by little the impressions build until by the time your child goes to kindergarten she carries with her a picture of herself, autographed by Mom and Dad with some help from the baby-sitter and other important people. A child isn't born with a self-concept or self-respect. Rather, it is a reflection of how his parents feel about themselves and about him and their family. Since children do not have any way of judging the accuracy of what adults do, they accept what their parents or other important people say about them as the truth. And thus the self-concept picture gets painted brush stroke by brush stroke.

Helping your child develop positive self-respect doesn't really depend on specific activities focusing on self-respect. Rather, it is the result of fundamental experiences as children grow up. First, a Christian's self-respect is based on God's love. Norman Wright, well-known family educator and counselor, has suggested that the proper formula for a Christian's self-concept is God + Me = A Whole Person. Teach your children that God loves them and made each individual special with unique characteristics. He loves them even when they do wrong, He died to save them, and He plans for them to live in heaven with Him for eternity. Few of us have really grasped the significance of what one person means to God. How can I look down on myself if Jesus would have died just for me! God is definitely the Christian's foundation for self-respect. To the God foundation we can add the other components of self-esteem identified by experts in this field.

Stanley Coopersmith, well-known for his research on self-esteem and self-respect, suggests four essential components to building self-esteem: competence, significance, power, and virtue. If you can help your child develop in these four areas, the chances are good that he will emerge from childhood with a proper self-respect and confidence.

Significance, to a child, means: **I need to feel loved and approved by people vital to me.** Parents are the most important people to children. Does your child feel loved and approved by you? Or does it seem he can't do anything well enough to please you? Does she feel important to you, or is she playing second or third place to other things in your life? Is she getting the crumbs of your attention? Feeling loved and approved by one's parents is the most fundamental building block of self-respect.

We could translate competence into: **I need to perform well on tasks that are important to me.** Mr. Three learning to put on his own socks and shoes is acquiring competence. It takes patience to watch while Miss Four awkwardly fumbles with the serving spoon, but competence suffers when we take over. Time invested in helping Mr. Eight improve his baseball serve builds self-respect. Encouraging little steps toward mastery develops competence. Don't take over for your children. Let them struggle through to mastery and competence.

Power is: **I need to influence my own life and that of others.**

Children need to make meaningful choices about their everyday activities. They must know that their voice counts in family affairs too. When their opinion is respected, even though not always followed, self-respect receives a boost. Does your child have opportunity to make choices every day about things vital and significant to him? Is her opinion respected—or is she belittled for honest thoughts about her preferences? When children feel powerless to control their lives, it seriously impairs their ability to confront the world. Since they feel they have no control over what happens, they will blindly follow along with whatever the crowd wants. The adolescent girl who lacks a sense of power, or control over her own life, will find it almost impossible to turn down the physical advances of her boyfriend even when she has doubts about getting involved.

Virtue simply means: **I need to do what is right in order to respect myself.** Children must have a clear picture of what is right and wrong. Many don't really know because family and society have garbled the messages to them. When children do what they know is right, they feel good about themselves. Teaching them consideration for other people along with fairness and honesty, and helping them nurture a relationship with God, are important components of the self-respect picture.

We must aid children in setting realistic goals for themselves. Unrealistic ones tear down self-esteem. Instead of saying to a child who gets only a quarter of the spelling words right, ''I know you can get them all right this week!'' say, ''I know you can get two more words right than you did last week.'' It is a realistic, achievable goal that will build confidence.

Assist children in dealing with mistakes and setbacks. Demonstrate in your own life how to laugh at yourself, how to pick yourself up and go on. Children terribly afraid of making a mistake seldom try anything new, an attitude that reinforces a negative self-esteem.

Help children develop their natural talents and abilities, including their personal appearance. Teach them how to look attractive and use their bodies confidently. Enable them to recognize their talents and to strengthen and expand them. Enable children to compensate for their weaknesses. Teach them specific strategies for dealing with weak areas. Encourage your children to work on a life plan for character development, identifying both their strengths and weaknesses.

You don't need a workbook of exercises to help your child paint a beautiful picture of self-respect. The fundamental paintbrushes are God's love, significance, competence, power, and virtue. Concentrate on them, and self-respect and confidence will be much more likely to emerge. While it is easiest to develop a secure sense of self-respect during childhood, remember, it is never too late to change the picture you see in the mirror.

The next step in helping children confront the world is to **teach them how to make decisions**. Daddy was going to the hardware store for a quick purchase, and 3-year-old Shelley wanted to accompany him. Rushing out the door, however, she noticed Mommy and her brother Michael cuddled on the sofa reading her favorite storybook. Suddenly the trip to the hardware store didn't seem so attractive . . . she loved to ride with Daddy . . . but she also loved to cuddle with Mommy and read books . . . Daddy was almost out to the car. "Why can't I do both?" she wailed miserably.

Sometimes making choices is easy, but more often it is difficult for preschoolers. This time Mommy easily resolved Shelley's dilemma when she offered to reread the girl's favorite story when she got back from the store. But many times it isn't possible to have it both ways. Helping our children learn to make choices is an important part of spiritual growth as each day we are guiding them toward life's ultimate choice—loving and serving God in a world where most people have chosen the opposite side.

When 10-month-old Denny refuses to eat any more, he is letting you know about his choice—he's full. It is important to respect Denny's decisions as often as possible. It gives him confidence that he can influence his world. Of course, at times his choice isn't the best for him and Mom or Dad must insist on their decision. So Denny has to learn that important balance between his choices and obeying Mom or Dad. Obeying is easier for Denny, however, if his parents frequently respect his personal preferences.

Two-year-old Melissa is in that "no" stage. Then it's better to simply say, "Let's put on your coat" and proceed with the task. Asking Melissa if she wants to put on her coat is not helping her learn to make decisions anyway because you know she really has to put on her coat.

Teaching your youngster how to make decisions means offering him a choice between two alternatives (the "fence") equally acceptable to you but that are mutually exclusive. In other words, either way is OK with you, but he can't have it both ways. Let's see how that might work with 3-year-old Tommy.

It's time to get dressed on a weekday morning. If you said "Tommy, what do you want to wear today?" and Tommy chose his Sabbath clothes, he would simply be making a choice within the alternatives (the fence) you set up for him. You don't want him to wear his Sabbath clothes for play, so you say, "Oh, no, you can't wear your Sabbath clothes today!" The child then selects something else that you don't want him to wear, either. And so it goes until, in frustration, he protests, "But you said I could choose!" What went wrong?

First, you need to make a "fence," or boundary, within which any choice is OK with you. Then, within the security of that fence, Tommy can make a true decision of his own. You might say, "Tommy, which play shirt would you like to wear with your jeans today? The red one or the blue one?" You have set up a simple "fence" within which Tommy can make a real choice. Obviously, the boy isn't going to wear both shirts just now—although he may before the day is over!

Tommy needs lots of practice at this simple level of choices before moving on to more difficult ones (larger fences). Here is the first key to helping children learn to make choices: Make it a real decision between real alternatives, but within a small enough "fence" so the child can cope with it. Then accept the choice and allow the child to follow through on the decision. As your child gains experience you will see real growth in choice-making skills.

The chart on the following page has 10 basic suggestions for helping your child develop skill in decision making. Being able to make a good choice and following through on it are crucial skills.

The fourth step in helping children confront the world is to **provide an alternative to peer pressure**. Peer pressure begins in preschool and the pace accelerates on through childhood, adolescence, and youth. While adults feel peer pressure sometimes, the intensity does lessen after youth. Peer pressure is not an invention of the twentieth century. It has been around since Cain and Abel, but many experts feel it has escalated during the past two decades. Sharon Scott, a nationally recognized expert on peer pressure and author of *Peer Pressure Reversal*, has suggested that the following societal changes have decreased the influence of the family on the developing child and increased peer pressure. The new trends have lessened the quality and quantity of adult-child interaction. In other words, kids don't spend as much time with adults as they used to!

Families are more mobile, so neighborhoods lack unity. In former times, neighbors watched out for everyone's kids. Fewer families live near their extended families. Grandparents, aunts, uncles, and cousins once all took care of each other. It was harder for kids to get away with something when so many people might know about it. The increase in single parent families and dual parent working families has sharply decreased the amount of time children spend with their parents. Moms and

TEACHING CHILDREN TO MAKE DECISIONS

1. Begin early with simple choices between two alternatives equally accept- able, but mutually exclusive.
2. Give lots of practice at this simple level before moving on to more difficult choices.
3. Accept the child's choice. Don't berate it.
4. Help the child follow through on the decision.
5. Gradually enlarge the "fence" within which the child may make the deci- sion. Be sure the boundaries are clear.
6. Allow natural consequences to take place in case of a wrong decision. Be supportive, but do not remove the consequences.
7. As children get older, help them weigh alternatives and long-range conse- quences:
   a. Pray for God's guidance in the decision.
   b. Study God's Word for principles that may guide the decision.
   c. Write out the pros and cons.
   d. Try to anticipate the consequences.
   e. Ask if there is a clear right or wrong in the situation.
   f. Is it only a matter of preference, with no right or wrong?
   g. Will it affect other people? How?
   h. What are the limits (the "fence") within which the child must decide?
8. If the decision is within the child's capabilities (within the "fence"), allow complete freedom of decision. Do not make the decision for the child!
9. Express confidence in the child's ability to make the decision and follow through.
10. Help the child realize, mentally and emotionally, that God is deeply inter- ested in every aspect of his/her life and will guide in every decision.

dads are simply too busy to be with their kids very much. Consequently kids find themselves on their own with their peers. The average work week in the United States has increased several hours during the past two decades. The number one item on a recent survey of family life concerns at a large SDA church was how to deal with time pressures. Hectic schedules simply do not allow as much time for families to interact. The media also create more negative peer pressure. Teens—and younger—on TV provide predominantly negative models. Real teens— and younger—feel pressured to be like the kids on TV! Rock stars, movie stars, and sports stars in general do not provide positive role models for kids today. Greed and unrestrained and irresponsible sex are the norm. Electrical devices—dishwashers, computers, video games, TVs, and Walkmans separate families. Each person lives in his own world, not interacting with other members of the family. The easy availability of alcohol and other drugs increases the pressure to be part of the gang.

Decreasing such societal influences is an important part of helping our children cope with peer pressure. What can Christian families do to decrease their impact? What can your family do? Go through the previous paragraph once more and think about each area. What can you do to lessen the impact of such changes on your family? What can you do to increase the amount of time your children spend with adults and lessen that spent with their peers? Sharon Scott feels this is an important key to reducing the power of peer pressure.

When your child goes out to confront the world, how quickly he or she caves in to peer pressure will often be the bottom line. You need a planned program to immunize your kids against peer pressure. **Begin early with the idea that sometimes we cannot do what everyone else is doing.** That we choose to do something different because God wants us to. Explain that following the crowd is not always God's way. We are individually accountable to Him.

Make your propaganda early! Talk about teenage activities before your child is a teenager. Establish what you expect for her behavior before the turmoil arrives. Discuss peer pressure and its effects. Talk over boyfriends and girlfriends, clothes, cars, and dates long before your child reaches the age he or she finds himself or herself caught up in them. Explore principles to guide entertainment selection. Consider how to choose friends. Get ready for plunging into the stream before your child arrives at the water's edge. Prepare, prepare, prepare!

Encourage family, rather than peer, orientation. Research on substance abuse has pointed out that young people who have a stronger family orientation are less likely to abuse alcohol and drugs or to succumb to peer pressure in other areas. The stronger the child's ties to the family, the more influence the family has in establishing values. If your family structure is weak—and you know it—run, don't walk, to the nearest Christian counselor and begin to change today! For the sake of your children's future you need a strong family now.

If your basic family structure is sound, but you've bought into the idea that kids need to be with their peers most of the time, try some of the following ideas:

STRENGHTENING FAMILY TIES

1. Be interested in what your child is doing.
2. Cultivate family hobbies and interests.
3. Be one jump ahead. Plan many interesting family activities.
4. Limit time with peers in favor of family activities.
5. Invite other children to do things with your family. Welcome your children's friends.
6. Let children help plan family activities.
7. Cultivate your children's friendship. At least once every two weeks have a "date" with each of your children.
8. Be creative in finding time to be with your children.
9. Respect your child's growing maturity.
10. Make home the most attractive place in the world. Keep things picked up and the cookie jar full. Send out a message of warmth and welcome.

Encourage active involvement in worthwhile activities. The child who participates in extracurricular activities at school, plays in the band, serves on the staff of the school paper, and is active with an outreach program at church will acquire friends also involved in those same activities. They will usually be the kids who have a positive influence on others. While your child is still in grade school, help him learn some skills that will open doors for worthwhile activities in the academy or high school. Such skills will give status, satisfaction, and involvement in worthwhile activities, and provide opportunities for friendships with the "good" kids. The person respected for his/her ability in some area is more often respected in other decisions also. After-school jobs—mowing lawns, baby-sitting, or a paper route—teach responsibility and give kids confidence.

Help your child learn to dress attractively and know what to do in social situations. The child who feels confident in social situations will much less likely find herself overwhelmed with peer pressure. She knows how to handle things. Respected by the other kids, she "belongs" even though she doesn't always agree with what the crowd wants to do.

Establish clear guidelines for your child's behavior. "My dad said I can't" is a good backup for a child's decision. The family is the guardian of standards, as the Valuegenesis study so clearly pointed out. Teenagers with mature faith and positive attitudes toward the SDA Church came from families that had clear standards for behavior and enforced them. Teenagers accepted standards from their family much better than from either the church or the school. Moms and dads, it's up to us! It takes a lot of time on our knees and with His Book to be able to tell the difference between moral issues on which we should take a clear position and passing cultural fads with no real moral implications, even though they're different from the way we did things. And it demands a lot more time on our knees to acquire the patience and stamina to stay by our convictions and make the consequences stick!

Teach your child how to recognize and respond to peer pressure. Sharon Scott, in *Peer Pressure Reversal,* suggests that a child, after recognizing that he is in a peer pressure situation, needs to have the tools to get out of the situation in 30 seconds. Otherwise he will succumb to the pressure. Escaping a bad situation in 30 seconds means your child requires some automatic responses that he can use almost without thinking. He must practice them ahead of time in order to make them automatic. Kids feel the most pressure from their close friends or boyfriend/girlfriend. Such situations are the hardest to refuse because your child fears losing the friendship.

Starting when your child is around 7 or 8 years old, teach him the signs to look for that suggest the other kids are trying to get him do something he shouldn't. Have your child listen on the playground or when with friends to see if he can figure out when someone is pressuring other kids. What does he himself say when he wants to persuade a friend to do something? Then teach your child how to respond to such pressure tactics. Practice the techniques until they become automatic. Your child's response to pressure needs to fit her personality. Some kids can defuse a bad situation with a joke, but others would fall flat on their face if they tried a humorous approach. Know your child and what might be most comfortable for him or her. Be sure she has at least four or five options from which to choose. Repeatedly go over the steps of how to escape a bad situation—make your statement, then turn around and depart without any further comments or arguments. Leave with dignity and go on to another activity. To pull it off acceptably a child will have to rehearse it. Emphasize the 30-second rule—in and out of the bad situation in 30 seconds!

The research on how we influence others to think the way we do suggests that it is easier to sway a group if you state your conviction at the beginning. If you present your ideas positively, others will probably follow along. Teach your child this technique. Give your child a repertoire of positive ideas for activities that she can suggest instead of the negative ones. Practicing the ideas at home until they have become almost automatic will prepare your child to successfully confront negative peer pressure. And be sure she knows how to reach you and always has coins to make a phone call. "Come get me!" should send you on a rescue mission with no questions asked.

Last, **inspire your children with high ideals from God's Word**. They need a clear "thus saith the Lord" to back up the principles you have taught them. Search together in God's Word for guidelines for the situations your child must confront. Challenge him to live in relationship with God every day. It is the best insurance against peer pressure.

Choosing God's way *is* a choice that each of our children must make for himself or herself alone. We can do nothing to force a loving, saving relationship with our Lord. All we can do is to make it an attractive choice and gently lead in that direction. "Children cannot be brought to the Lord by force. They can be led, but not driven" *(The Adventist Home,* p. 307).

KEYS TO CONFRONTING THE WORLD

1. Protect your child's mind from evil.
2. Nuture your child with Christian values.
3. Take control of the media in your home.
4. Provide toys that communicate the values you want your children to learn.
5. Make the difference between good and evil clear. Have clear consequences for ignoring the standards of the home.
6. Help your child develop a solid sense of self-respect and confidence.
7. Show your child how to deal positively with mistakes and setbacks.
8. Teach your child to make decisions.
9. Provide an alternative to peer pressure.
10. Inspire your child with high ideals from God's Word.

Appendix

THE CHILD AND THE FATHER

First Parable. I took a little child's hand in mine. He and I were to walk together for a while. I was to lead him to the Father. It was a task that overcame me, so awful was the responsibility. I talked to the little child of the Father. I painted the sternness of the Father's face were the child to displease Him. We walked under tall trees. I said the Father had power to send them crashing down, struck by His thunderbolts. We walked in the sunshine. I told him the greatness of the Father who made the burning, blazing sun.

And one twilight we met the Father. The child hid behind me, he was afraid; he would not look up at the face so loving. He remembered my picture; he would not put his hand in the Father's hand. I was between the child and the Father. I wondered. I had been so conscientious, so serious.

Second Parable: I took a little child's hand in mine. I was to lead him to the Father. I felt burdened by the multitude of things I was to teach him. We did not ramble; we hastened on from spot to spot. At one moment we compared the leaves of the different trees, in the next we were examining a bird's nest. While the child was questioning me about it, I hurried him away to chase a butterfly. Did he chance to fall asleep, I wakened him, lest he should miss something I wanted him to see. We spoke of the Father often and rapidly. I poured into his ears all the stories he ought to know. But we were interrupted often by the coming of the stars, which we must needs study; by the gurgling brook, which we must trace to its source.

And then in the twilight we met the Father. The child merely glanced at Him. The Father stretched out His hand, but the child was not interested enough to take it. Feverish spots burned on his cheeks. He dropped to the ground exhausted and fell asleep. Again I was between the child and the Father. I wondered. I had taught so many, many things.

Third Parable. I took a little child's hand in mind to lead him to the Father. My heart was full of gratitude for the glad privilege. We walked slowly. I suited my steps to the short steps of the child. We spoke of the things the child noticed. Sometimes it was one of the Father's birds; we watched it build a nest, we saw the eggs that were laid. We wondered, later, at the care it gave its young. Sometimes we picked the Father's flowers, and stroked their soft petals and loved their bright colors. Often we told stories of the Father. I told them to the child and the child told them to me. We told them, the child and I, over and over again. Sometimes we stopped to rest, leaning against the Father's trees, and letting His air cool our brows, and never speaking.

And then in the twilight we met the Father. The child's eyes shone. He looked up lovingly, trustingly, eagerly, into the Father's face; he put his hand into the Father's hand. I was for the moment forgotten. I was content.